IMAGINING CARE

Responsibility, Dependency, and Canadian Literature

Imagining Care brings literature and philosophy into dialogue by examining representations of caregiving in contemporary Canadian literature alongside the ethics of care philosophy. Through close readings of fiction and memoirs by Margaret Atwood, Alice Munro, Michael Ignatieff, Ian Brown, and David Chariandy, Amelia DeFalco argues that these narratives expose the tangled particularities of relations of care, dependency, and responsibility, as well as issues of marginalization on the basis of gender, race, and class.

DeFalco complicates the myth of Canada as an unwaveringly caring nation that is characterized by equality and compassion. Caregiving is unpredictable: one person's altruism can be another's narcissism; one's compassion, another's condescension or even cruelty. In a country that conceives of itself as a caring society, these texts depict in stark terms the ethical dilemmas that arise from our attempts to respond to the needs of others.

AMELIA DeFALCO is an adjunct faculty member in the Department of English and Cultural Studies at McMaster University and the author of *Uncanny Subjects: Aging in Contemporary Narrative*. In 2009 she received the Polanyi Prize for literature from the Government of Ontario.

AMELIA DEFALCO

Imagining Care

Responsibility, Dependency, and Canadian Literature

UNIVERSITY OF TORONTO PRESS
Toronto Buffalo London

© University of Toronto Press 2016
Toronto Buffalo London
utorontopress.com

Reprinted in paperback 2022

ISBN 978-1-4426-3703-0 (cloth)
ISBN 978-1-4875-5381-4 (paper)

Publication cataloguing information is available from Library and Archives Canada.

This book has been published with the help of a grant from the Federation for the Humanities and Social Sciences, through the Awards to Scholarly Publications Program, using funds provided by the Social Sciences and Humanities Research Council of Canada.

We wish to acknowledge the land on which the University of Toronto Press operates. This land is the traditional territory of the Wendat, the Anishnaabeg, the Haudenosaunee, the Métis, and the Mississaugas of the Credit First Nation.

University of Toronto Press acknowledges the financial support of the Government of Canada, the Canada Council for the Arts, and the Ontario Arts Council, an agency of the Government of Ontario, for its publishing activities.

For Robert and Morris, my fellow adventurers.

Contents

Acknowledgments

In a book focused on experiences and theories of interdependence I would be remiss not to acknowledge the network of assistance and care that made this work possible.

First, I'd like to thank Lorraine York for being an early (and enduring) supporter and reader of this project. Discussing care over cocktails with Lorraine was one of the many joys of this work. As well, I'm grateful to Marlene Goldman at the University of Toronto for inviting me to participate in the Jackman Humanities Institute working groups on aging that she organized from 2010 to 2015. Our monthly conversations were energizing and illuminating. And, as always, thanks to Linda Hutcheon for being such a willing and thoughtful reader whose enthusiasm and brilliance are always inspiring.

In addition, I'm indebted to the institutions and publications that have supported me along the way. *Imagining Care* was supported by several fellowships, including a Banting postdoctoral fellowship funded by the Social Science and Humanities Research Council of Canada. McMaster University's Department of English and Cultural Studies hosted me throughout my various fellowships, providing me with the opportunity to create and teach graduate courses devoted to topics related to literature and care. The students who enrolled in those courses helped me to think about the subjects of dependency, responsibility, and care in new and exciting ways. Parts of this work have appeared in shorter and earlier versions in various journals (*Journal of Medical Humanities*, *Twentieth-Century Literature*, and *Contemporary Literature*). My thanks go to their reviewers and editors for their interest and suggestions. As well, I'm grateful to editor Siobhan McMenemy at University of Toronto Press for being such a capable guide throughout the revisions process.

Finally, and most importantly, I'm grateful to the family and friends who have taught me so much about the everyday practice of care, both its pleasures and perils. To Robert and, most recently, to little Morris, I extend my love and gratitude for showing me what it is to give and receive care day after day.

IMAGINING CARE

Responsibility, Dependency, and Canadian Literature

Introduction: Literature, Care, and Canada

In Alice Munro's short story, "The Bear Came over the Mountain," the onset of a woman's dementia transforms her husband into a quasi-procurer who finds himself negotiating the restitution of his wife's new relationship in an effort to restore her failing health. The story offers an apt introduction to care and ethics in Canadian literature in its depiction of an ethical dilemma that positions the needs of the husband, Grant, in opposition to the needs of the wife. Fiona has developed a passionate attachment to a temporary resident, Aubrey, whose own wife has placed him in the facility for respite care. When Aubrey leaves Meadowlake, Fiona is bereft, her health deteriorating so precipitously that facility employees suggest she may need to move to the dreaded second floor, reserved for those who have "really lost it" (Munro 298). Because residents rarely return from their second-floor internment, Grant is desperate to avoid Fiona's relocation. As a result, Grant attempts to retrieve the usurper of his wife's affections, in effect, "proving his own fidelity to Fiona by facilitating her 'infidelity' to him" (McGill, "No Nation" 100), an altruistic gesture that requires him to suppress his own longing for Fiona's recognition and affection.

In this brief sketch of the story, Grant appears as an ethical hero, his noble prioritization of Fiona's needs over his own evidence of his devotion and care. Indeed, the 2006 film adaptation of the story directed by Canadian Sarah Polley, *Away from Her*, endorses such an interpretation, casting Grant as a suffering husband who trades his own happiness for his wife's survival.[1] However, closer attention to the story, to its narrative voice, its diction, tone, and imagery, belies this relatively straightforward account of the story's ethical implications. "The Bear Came over the Mountain" incorporates a degree of ambiguity that inspires numerous interpretative questions: How does Grant's history of unfaithfulness affect his motivation? To what degree is the return of Aubrey the result of Grant's self-satisfied seduction of Aubrey's wife Marian? And what of Fiona? Readers get little sense of her perspective. How complete is her delusion? Is her ignorance of Grant's adultery feigned? Might this be a revenge story? The story's ethical irreducibility contributes to its powerful effect. Denying readers complete knowledge, it denies us the comfort of assuming a self-assured moralizing position, condoning certain characters and actions while castigating others as "wrong."

Munro's story rehearses one of the central concerns of ethics, namely, what is one to do with, or about, another person's suffering? What is one's obligation to other people, friends, family, strangers? And what is one's obligation to oneself? Ethical commitment can prove to be a high-wire act, a struggle to balance distance and presence, evaluation and interaction, abstraction and action, the needs of others and of the self. Practical ethics, what Derek Attridge categorizes as "morality" (28), requires that the self be, as philosopher James Mensch explains, "able to distance itself from itself, but not to the point that it uncouples from the world in which it acts" (Mensch 12). Responding to the other is an ethical act at the heart of ethics of care philosophy. Questions regarding who should give and receive care, and even more fundamentally, what exactly the giving and receiving of care means, are enquiries with both ethical and ontological implications. The larger issues of ethics and moral philosophy are brought into focus by ethics of care philosophy, which draws theoretical principles and abstractions into the everyday world of dependency, responsibility, and work. *Imagining Care* takes Canadian narrative literature like "The Bear Came over the Mountain" seriously as a discourse with the potential to both complement and complicate ethics of care philosophy. Its goal is to bring philosophical and literary discourses into dialogue by exploring care in fiction and memoirs by a selection of contemporary Canadian writers.

What Is Care?

The *Oxford English Dictionary* tells us that the English word "care" has been around for a long time, possibly as long as a thousand years. As one might expect, its meaning has evolved over the years. In its original Old English incarnation, "*caru*," or "*cearu*," the term denoted "suffering" and "sorrow," "mourning" and "lamentation" ("care, *n*.1" def. 1 a–b), as well as other affective burdens: anxiety, concern, and "mental perturbation" (def. 2). Evidence suggests that the connection between "care" and responsibility, as in the construction "to care for: to take thought for, provide for, look after, take care of," emerged in the thirteenth century ("care, v." def. 3). Around this time, "care" became associated with "oversight" over and "preservation" of objects or people (def. 4a). Since its emergence around the turn of the first millennium, "care" has functioned as both verb and noun – one both cares and has cares – a dual function that continues to this day. We give care, take care, care for, care about, have cares, and don't care. In its broadest sense, care is affection, devotion, responsibility, even obligation; it is action, behaviour, motivation, and practice: care feels and care does. Often the noun and verb usages are linked: having cares routinely coincides with doing care, although not always. As many of the examples studied throughout *Imagining Care* suggest, the frequent incompatibility of feeling care and doing care complicate the broader theorization of care.

"Care" continues to denote "serious or grave mental attention; the charging of the mind with anything; concern; heed, heedfulness, attention, regard; caution, pains" (*n.*1 def. 3a), an association between care and burdens and pains that harkens back to the original "*caru.*" As much as care is valuable, nay, essential for human survival and identity, it remains connected to its etymological roots: to pain and lamentation. *Imagining Care* considers the so-called burdens of care involving responsibility for one in need, a need often precipitated by illness or impairment that creates an imbalance of ability or means between the two parties involved. In such uneven relationships the decisions and activities associated with care accentuate the complexities of ethics of care philosophy, which considers and evaluates how subjects might, and often should, respond to another's needs or vulnerabilities. As ethics of care philosophers make clear, not all care is ethical care, and these philosophers have done valuable work theorizing what care *should* be. For example, Patricia Benner, Suzanne Gordon, and Nel Noddings insist that care depends on receptivity between subjects: "Caring demands that one *dwell* – as Martin Heiddegger would have described it – with another ... The product of care is embedded in the person who is cared for and cannot be segregated from that human life. Caring is not dependent on what I do *to* you, but on what I do and how *you receive or respond to it*" (Benner et al., emphasis in original xiii). As I discuss below, many of the definitions and parameters offered by ethics of care philosophers are necessarily abstract in their privileging of reciprocity and responsivity. *Imagining Care* considers the unique insights offered by short stories, novels, and memoirs that depict devoted, yet reluctant or thwarted, moving, sometimes frustrating narratives of care in practice. This inquiry follows Peta Bowden's claim that "caring expresses ethically significant ways in which we matter to each other, transforming interpersonal relatedness into something beyond ontological necessity or brute survival" (1). The depictions of care in the literary texts of *Imagining Care* bring to light how and why this "mattering" is so complicated and difficult, and yet inescapable and important.

This inquiry into the cultural meanings of caregiving was inspired by the research into aging and narrative undertaken for my previous book, *Uncanny Subjects: Aging in Contemporary Narrative* (2010). While completing a chapter on narratives of dementia I became aware of the complexity of the caregiver/care-receiver relationship, which deserved more detailed attention than I could provide in a project focused on aging. In *Imagining Care* I attend fully to the ethical questions raised by literary narratives of caregiving. In so doing, this project proposes that literary explorations of caregiving have much to offer the larger understanding of the ethics of care, as well as illuminating how we imagine and construct the meaning of care in contemporary Canadian culture. The ambiguity and complexity of caregiving scenarios depicted in literature, scenarios complicated by the human desire for power, for attention, for affection, provide compelling territory for investigating both the satisfaction and connection, along with the ambivalence and unease produced by caregiving relations.

Who Cares?

It's a common question: who cares? Everyone cares. As ethics of care philosophers make clear, human survival depends on care. Infants are entirely helpless and would perish without some degree of care. As a result, we can say that all of us who have survived infancy have been involved in a caring relationship. Of course, as ethics of care philosophers are quick to point out, survival is not a marker of good, or ethical care, but merely a sign of care's presence. Survival is possible with poor care. Ethics of care philosophy is preoccupied with understanding and conveying what good care is or might be, and how Western society might function if care were highly valued and human dependence (and the caring relationships it necessitates), replaced independence as the privileged human state. I share these ideals. However, my focus on representation forces an engagement with the limitations and failures of care. As fiction and memoirs make clear, the circumstances of particular vulnerabilities and relationships mean that many give and receive inadequate care, and are overwhelmed by its demands. In the literary texts that follow one finds the ideals of reciprocity and responsivity set against human limitations.

Though caregiving takes many forms, in *Imagining Care* I am concerned with depictions of non-professional caregiving provided by untrained caregivers, most often family members or friends. The project is focused on what I term "para-ordinary" care. Though care may be universal and ordinary, there are experiences of care that often catch participants off guard: the demands made by a loved one's sudden illness or impairment; the birth of a medically fragile child; a parent's development of dementia. These situations are analogous to, yet distinct from everyday, ordinary experiences of care. Hence the designation "para-ordinary care": care adjacent to the ordinary. Such situations are by no means extraordinary – they are common, even ordinary – yet, their demands are high and often unpredictable, drawing attention to the ethical difficulty of responding to another's needs. In other words, I use "para-ordinary" to refer to caregiving that is not taken for granted and habitually represented within popular culture in the same way as "ordinary" care relations, particularly caregiving relations between parents and their healthy children or health care providers and their patients. Instead, my focus is on care necessitated by illness and impairment, but occurring outside the health care system, caregiving provided by parents of disabled children (chapter 1), or children of disabled parents (chapters 1, 3, 4, and 6), or friends, acquaintances, and even strangers (chapters 2 and 5). Despite its ubiquity in society, such para-ordinary care remains underrepresented in the popular imagination, and even in ethics of care philosophy itself, which tends to theorize relations between equivalently abled participants in which reciprocity and mutuality are straightforward, or at least achievable.[2] Indeed, for many ethics of care philosophers, parenting is a quintessential manifestation of many of the demands of care. Ethics of care philosophers Virginia Held and Maurice Hamington both reference childhood and child rearing as evidence of the unavoidability of care relations for human survival. Held's attention to the needs of children is representative of the field: "All persons need care for at least their early years. Prospects for human progress and flourishing hinge fundamentally on the care that those needing it receive, and the ethics of care stresses the moral force of the responsibility to respond to the needs of the dependent" (10). This is care at its most ordinary, normative core. My own inquiry involves care relationships beyond the ordinary – "para-ordinary" – and the distinct challenges such circumstances pose for ethical commitment and the maintenance of subjectivity.

My primary aim is to explore how literature has the capacity to enrich our understanding of the complexities and vicissitudes of care. Because my attention is devoted to the habitual experiences and practices of non-professional care between individuals, the realm of professional caregivers, including nurses, doctors, physiotherapists, midwives, pharmacists, and other health care professionals who are directed by professional standards and ethics, is beyond the scope of this inquiry.[3] The original germ for this project, an interest in analysing narratives of dementia care, remained a pivotal guide as I selected primary texts for interpretation, texts that explore private, as opposed to public, worlds of care. I sought out representations of caregiving experiences that are often unexpected and unprescribed, including caring for parents with dementia or disabled children, caring for sick friends or family members, caring for vulnerable acquaintances, even strangers. Whether entirely fictionalized or based on personal experience, narrative representation shows its readers care in action. While fiction is assumed to be the product of a writer's imagination, and life writing uses actual people and events as its material, both genres are fundamentally narrative forms that depict particular lives, either fabricated or actual. Despite their differences, which I discuss further in chapter 1, they have in common a reliance upon narrative, which Brian Richardson calls "the fundamental mode of human knowledge" (3). In other words, the narratives we choose to reproduce, circulate, and consume offer important insights into individual and cultural identities and knowledges. The Canadian narratives of caregiving I examine furnish readers with particular characters struggling in particular Canadian caregiving situations, depicting in stark terms the ethical quandaries arising from attempts to respond to the needs of others. In *Imagining Care* I argue that these narratives can convey ethical dilemmas that are meaningfully infused with the subjectivity and particularity that complicate straightforward "right" or "superior" moral reasoning. Canadian literary narratives of care expose the burdens and risks of caregiving, the many ways that ethical responsibility can draw attention to gendered, racial, and class-based marginalization. Throughout, I seek to demonstrate how Canadian literature imagines and, in a sense, theorizes relations of care, and how these literary representations interact with the claims made by ethics of care philosophers and feminist theorists.

Moral Dilemmas and the Gender of Ethics

Over the last several decades, care has become a pivotal idea for feminist philosophers seeking an alternative to traditional moral philosophy, which they regard as problematically gendered in its frequent emphasis on autonomy and individualism. The roots of ethics of care philosophy can be traced to the implicitly gendered work on moral development done by Harvard psychologist Lawrence Kohlberg. In 1958 Kohlberg completed a doctoral thesis that provided the groundwork for his conception of the six psychological stages of moral development, which would be the focus of his research for the next twenty years (Kohlberg, *Philosophy* x). His work focused on moral development in adolescents, which he quantified and qualified based on responses to narratives depicting ethical dilemmas. In other words, Kohlberg gauged moral development according to a subject's interpretations of narrative. The most famous of Kohlberg's narratives of moral difficulty is "the Heinz Dilemma":

> In Europe, a woman was near death from a very bad disease, a special form of cancer. There was a drug that the doctors thought might save her. It was a form of radium that a druggist in the same town had recently discovered. The drug was expensive to make, but the druggist was charging ten times what the drug cost him to make. He paid $200 for the radium and charged $2,000 for a small dose of the drug. The sick woman's husband, Heinz, went to everyone he knew to borrow the money, but he could get together only about $1,000, which was half of what it cost. He told the druggist that his wife was dying and asked him to sell it cheaper or let him pay later. But the druggist said, "No, I discovered the drug and I'm going to make money from it." The husband got desperate and broke into the man's store to steal the drug for his wife. (Kohlberg, *Philosophy* 12)

The dilemma was followed by a series of questions, such as, "Should the husband have done that? Was it right or wrong? Is your decision that it is right (or wrong) objectively right, is it morally universal, or is it your personal opinion?" (12). According to Kohlberg, children with advanced moral development would explain the necessity of theft using abstract, principled reasoning to defend their affirmative answer to the dilemma's concluding query. Although his interview subjects were primarily white and exclusively male (Detlef 39; Gilligan 18), Kohlberg used his findings to develop a universal hierarchy of moral development. His model, comprised of three levels, the pre-conventional, conventional, and post-conventional, charted the individual's progress from ego-centric preoccupation with the needs of the self, towards an emerging awareness of interpersonal and societal conventions, and a more mature understanding of individual rights and abstract ethical principles.[4]

However, in what has become an influential, even revolutionary counter-interpretation, Kohlberg's research assistant, Carol Gilligan, argued that Kohlberg's moral development theory relies too heavily on abstraction, universalism, and a limited conception of rationality. In her groundbreaking book on gendered morality, *A Different Voice* (1982), Gilligan outlined the results of her own study of both male and female subjects responding to the Heinz dilemma and other moral problems, results that cast doubt on the simple legibility of the Heinz narrative itself. As Gilligan explains in *A Different Voice*, the dilemma relies on a conflict between values of property and life (26), and assumes a straightforward moral conclusion: life is more important than property; therefore, the man ought to steal the drug. However, this kind of absolutism comes under scrutiny in Gilligan's analysis, which draws attention to what the Heinz dilemma lacks: human particularity, context, the details of life. Female respondents, Gilligan notes, were more likely to question the parameters of the dilemma, to request further information, and point out problems with the "right" answer (i.e., the husband ought to steal the drug). As one test subject insisted, there must be another solution to the problem besides theft, pointing out that the husband will be of no use to his gravely ill wife if he is incarcerated (Gilligan 28). According to Gilligan's interpretation, this test subject, "Amy," regards the dilemma as "a narrative of relationships that extends over time" (28), and her reaction suggests the "problem in the dilemma … arise[s] not from the druggist's assertion of rights but from his failure of response" (28). Gilligan uses these "unconventional" female responses, which would have been classified as less mature than those provided by their "rational" male counterparts within Kohlberg's androcentric model, to develop an alternative moral framework, in which

the moral problem arises from conflicting responsibilities rather than from competing rights and requires for its resolution a mode of thinking that is contextual and narrative rather than formal and abstract. This conception of morality as concerned with the activity of care centers moral development around the understanding of responsibility and relationships, just as the conception of morality as fairness ties moral development to the understanding of rights and rules. (19)

Whereas Kohlberg associates "morality with justice … with recognition of the rights of others as these are defined naturally or intrinsically," Gilligan's work suggests that women have "a different voice" when its comes to moral reasoning, a voice based on their socialization, their determination by cultural forces that associate femininity with care, comfort, and concern (Gilligan 20).[5] Gilligan's work draws attention to a particular trend in her subjects' answers, a recurring, gendered "contrast between a self defined through separation and a self delineated through connection, between a self measured against an abstract ideal of perfection and a self assessed through particular activities of care" (35). Although this connected, contextual self does not represent advanced, "post-conventional" morality according to Kohlberg's scheme, Gilligan recognized its potential for an ethic based on responsibility and care as opposed to rules and justice, for a "different" kind of morality. Following Gilligan's model, my own study tends towards this more open-ended vision of ethical relations. Consequently, despite Gilligan's example, I employ the term "ethics" rather than "morality," since the latter implies a belief system shaped by culturally specific categories of right and wrong. As philosopher Bernard Williams explains, "morality" "should be understood as a particular development of the ethical, one that has a special significance in modern Western culture. It peculiarly emphasizes certain ethical notions rather than others, developing in particular a special notion of obligation, and it has some peculiar presuppositions" (6).

In the years since Gilligan's provocative research, ethics of care philosophy has developed into a vital feminist discourse that challenges philosophical traditions based on independence and autonomy, rights, and justice.[6] A second look at Kohlberg's Heinz dilemma helps outline the contrasting perspectives of justice- and care-based ethical philosophies. As Grace Clement explains, "those who approach [the Heinz] dilemma from the justice perspective reach differing conclusions about whether Heinz is justified in stealing the drug, but they are likely to accept the dilemma as presented and to resolve it by fitting the situation under a general rule. In contrast, those who approach the Heinz dilemma using an ethic of care are generally frustrated by its lack of detail" (12). For many philosophers, ethics of care has represented a welcome alternative to prescriptive, justice-oriented patriarchal ethics, which tend to involve abstract principles and rules that have little relevance to the day-to-day lives of individual subjects.[7] In broader terms, the ethics of care is largely a rebuttal to "the liberal tradition of Locke, Kant, and most recently Rawls," which "posits an autonomous moral agent who discovers and applies a set of fundamental rules through the use of universal and abstract reason" (Kittay and Meyers 3). Gilligan's work responded to the masculine bias in ethical theory by presenting an alternative discourse of care and responsibility that acknowledges human dependence as fundamental and inevitable. As legal scholar Martha Fineman explains, "[Western] society mythologizes concepts such as 'independence' and 'autonomy' despite the concrete indications surrounding us that these ideals are, in fact, unrealizable and unrealistic. Those members of society who openly manifest the reality of dependency – either as dependents or caretakers in need of economic subsidy – are rendered deviants" ("Masking Dependency" 215–16). In opposition to such marginalizing inclinations, ethics of care philosophers typically regard dependency as inevitable and universal, pointing out that all of us begin our lives entirely helpless, making caring essential for both survival and identity, an inevitability that leads Held to propose care as "probably the most deeply fundamental [human] value" (17).[8] Vulnerability and the dependency that results, insist philosophers Eva Kittay and Ellen Feder, "must function in our very conception of ourselves as subjects and moral agents" (3). In other words, autonomy is but an illusion that obscures care as a central concern for all human beings.

However, the primacy of care is complicated by the instability of the concept itself; "care" is an idea with definitions and parameters that are apt to vary: "Caring is thus experienced as an unspecific and unspecifiable kind of labour, the contours of which shift constantly … [I]t is only visible when it is not done" (Graham 26). In discarding rigid rules and principles, the ethics of care remains perpetually vague, open to interpretation: "In broad terms, caring is a concept encompassing that range of human experiences that has to do with feeling concern for and taking care of the well-being of others. This definition tells us that caring is both about activities and feelings" (Waerness 234). There is some agreement on this final point, that care involves both action and emotion – though some theorists, like Bubeck, emphasize action, while others, like Noddings, emphasize emotion – but the precise parameters of caring, both its activities and feelings, are hard to distinguish. For feminist theorists Berenice Fisher and Joan Tronto, caring *"includes everything that we do to maintain, continue, and repair our 'world' so that we can live in it as well as possible"* (emphasis in original 40). But whether ethics of care philosophers attend to "the world" or to two people interacting, most theorists express care as positive, as a "morally appropriate reaction to another's needs" (S. Miller 142), as "a set of relational practices that foster mutual recognition and realization, growth, development, protection, empowerment, and human community, culture, and possibility … [nurturing] relationships that are devoted … [to] assisting others to cope with their weaknesses while affirming their strengths" (Benner et al. xiii). As prominent ethics of care philosophers Benhabib, Gilligan, Held, Kittay, and others insist, identity is unavoidably relational, making care integral to being and subjectivity.

In summary, according to ethics of care philosophers, whereas the "morality of justice" stresses rights, principles, and the individual, the "morality of care" emphasizes responsibility, relationships, and context (Brabeck 37). While traditional, patriarchal approaches often employ brief, fabricated dilemmas to illustrate moral rules, the ethics of care perspective resists straightforward illustration in its attention to context. In other words, ethics of care is distinctly anti-universal in its approach, seeking to expose the problematically "reductive tendencies of 'grand theory,'" and develop a philosophy that, in contrast, "emphasize[s] the ethical irreducibility of specific situations" (Bowden 3). Margaret Walker goes so far as to claim that "when context is ignored or effaced in theorizing, what we get is irrelevant or bad theory: theory that does not connect with life; theory that distorts, rather than reveals and clarifies its subject matter; theory that becomes a pastime and even a competitive game for theory-makers independently of whether the theory enhances our understanding of its subject matter" (xiii). However, the kind of flexibility that Walker endorses can lead to theoretical instability, to an aporia at the heart of the ethics of care: care is both universal and inscrutable; it involves definitions and evaluation, yet eludes fixedness. The attention to context can make it difficult to discuss care outside of particular scenarios, which prompts Bowden to assert that "caring highlights the ways in which ethical practices outrun the theories that attempt to explain them" (2). In essence, at the heart of the ethics of care is a resistance to abstraction that can inhibit its own theorization.

My motivation for including this extended discussion of Kohlberg's Heinz dilemma and the subsequent evolution of ethics of care philosophy is twofold. First, I seek to provide a preliminary understanding of a philosophical model that is fundamental to my own investigation into the literary representation of care. In addition, I wish to underscore the role of narrative in the development and theorization of ethics of care philosophy. *Imagining Care* is premised on the indispensability of narrative for ethical philosophy, insisting that narrative literature has much to offer the enigmatic ethical theory based on care. Instrumental narratives like the Heinz dilemma have been vital tools for philosophical speculation and evaluation. I propose to invert the mode of inquiry, making literary narrative the primary subject, one that does its own speculating and evaluating, creating moral universes with the potential to address the insights of ethical philosophy. In other words, my perspective treats stories as the inquiring subject, rather than the instrumental device. I propose a dialogue, so to speak, in which stories, their narrators and protagonists, engage with philosophical issues.

Of course not all ethical philosophers relegate narrative to the position of subordinate exemplum. Some ethics of care scholars even promote the consideration of fiction as a means for exploring and understanding the intricacies of care relations. Hamington takes up this cause, arguing that "care is most adequately reflected in the stories of people's lives, where more is brought to light than the rules or outcomes of a given situation. Those interested in care would do well to investigate literature as well as first-person stories to discover the degree to which care flows through everyday experience" (35). Like Hamington, I contend that philosophy's emphasis on context and specificity makes literary writers valuable contributors to ethics of care debates in their creation of particular, everyday scenarios of dependence, responsibility, compassion, and care.[9] The challenges and losses portrayed in narrative literature illustrate the complex conditions of human life that the theories aim to apprehend. Indeed, literature can actually develop and amplify those theories. If narratives fabricated to demonstrate ethical dilemmas, such as the Heinz story, are problematically brief and morally pat in their depiction of subjects struggling with competing obligations, literature is elaborate, specific, and interpretively enigmatic enough to express the multiple, often irresolvable dilemmas of care, the simultaneous impossibility and necessity of responding to the needs of others. Ethics of care philosophers suggest that appropriate motives, as well as appropriate practice are necessary for "good" care. Literature shows its readers not only the rarity of the alignment of motive and labour, effect and affect, but the difficulty of exhaustively interpreting and evaluating such complicated and shifting impulses as motivation and intention. As the literary texts I analyse demonstrate, care relations can be at once positive and negative, progressive and regressive, sometimes both nurturing and hurtful, a potential for contradiction and duality that inhibits attempts to definitively theorize "quality" caregiving.

Despite the liberating potential of privileging care as fundamental for both human survival and ethical relations, the legacy of the burden of domestic labour borne by women throughout history complicates the feminist goals of ethics of care philosophy. Women's caring is often coerced, "a practice on which their survival depends" (Bowden 8). Though ethics of care philosophers as far back as Nel Noddings and Carol Gilligan have taken pains to stress care as a model for ethical relations that can, and should be adopted by men and women alike, actual care is performed primarily by women. Sarah Miller dismisses anxiety over enforced, gendered care as "unwarranted since the duty to care is an obligation by which all humans, not just female ones are bound" (145).

Nonetheless, many feminist philosophers remain wary of the romanticized notion of caring supplied by Noddings and others, suggesting that "current understanding of care as a feminine characteristic supports oppressive social systems" (Hoagland qtd. in Hamington 78). In response to the political ramifications of gendered obligations to care, many ethics of care philosophers expunge contentious care relations from their philosophical models, banishing subservience, self-sacrifice, overzealous care, and other forms of excessive involvement, insisting that "a firm sense of one's own boundaries is a precondition of sound caring for others" (Carse 104).[10] Still, anxiety over the burden of care persists in ethics of care philosophy.[11] Comparing ethics of care to Emmanuel Levinas' ethical theory, which stresses unending obligation, Ruth Groenhout sums up the hostility inspired by such encumbrance:

> I would like, at times, to live my own life, not to be continually at the service of the other. The notion of a realm of privacy, of individual freedom prior to responsibility to the other, is a deeply entrenched notion in our contemporary liberal society. The same criticism has been made of care; if care for the other is the basic human attitude, then there seems no space left for restricting care, for limiting my responsibilities to others in order to go about my own life in ways that would allow me to flourish. (86)[12]

The tension within feminist philosophy of care speaks to a long history of gendered domestic labour associated with care that has inspired feminists to both demand liberation from enforced domesticity and work for the elevation of women's labour. Typically the strategy for dealing with this tension is to stress that care need not be, indeed it *should not be* gendered. Men and women are equally dependent on care for survival and, therefore, equally obliged to provide care for others. The relational identity that is part of inherent dependency makes responsibility between subjects unavoidable. But the chasm between the realms of abstraction and prescription, on the one hand, and of performance and actualization, on the other, challenges the viability of egalitarian models that overlook the practical realities of everyday experiences of care. Though we may all be, philosophically, bound to others, obliged to care, as many of the literary texts I analyse demonstrate, the labour of care predominantly falls to women. Consequently, not all feminist scholars have embraced ethics of care philosophy as moral theory.

In their overview of ethics of care philosophy, Kittay and Feder do not shy away from the "harms and vulnerabilities that accrue to those who do dependency work" (3). Instead, they expose how private, domestic labour provided largely by women has significant social repercussions, in effect subsidizing the very neoliberal society that dismisses the inevitability of dependence and the value of care:

> The costs of caring for dependents are generally borne by individual families and sometimes by individual women, yet the social benefits of such care are distributed throughout society. While familial care robs the workforce of women whose skills and training are lost to the labor force, paid care always seems *too expensive*. And this despite the fact that those paid are paid poorly and generally work without the benefit other workers enjoy in industrialized nations. In law, we see little in the way of recognition of the crucial role of dependency work in our understanding of the public good. (Emphasis in original 3)

Feder, Kitty, and other feminist philosophers and sociologists, including Diemut Grace Bubeck, Janet Finch, and Dulcie Groves, emphasize the work involved in care. Bubeck, in particular, dispenses with idealistic visions of harmonious and reciprocal care, treating it instead as difficult labour that unavoidably aggravates and even generates power imbalances: "Unlike exchange for contracts, the usual paradigms in liberal social and political theory, caring is not mutually beneficial, but is an asymmetrical transaction of material benefits ... Hence, unless the carer is remunerated in some way (in-kind or paid), or the care she gives is reciprocated, she incurs a material net burden" (*Care* 167). This asymmetry appears frequently in literary explorations of care by Margaret Atwood, Michael Ignatieff, Alice Munro, and others. Depictions of particular relations of care in memoirs, stories, and novels, expose the labour and burden, the inequality and exploitation that are the liabilities, if not inevitabilities of caregiving. The highly imbalanced gender realities of care lend a political dimension to its study; despite efforts to de-gender care, to prescribe universal care, dependency work remains largely "women's work." In other words, once one takes the formidable power of social constructions of gender into account,

> caring emerges not so much as an expression of women's natural feelings of compassion and connectedness, as the psychological analyses suggest, but as an expression of women's position within a particular kind of society in which the twin forces of capitalism and patriarchy are at work. Caring, it appears, describes more than the universal feelings women have: it describes the specific kind of labor they perform in our society. (Graham 25)

For Hillary Graham, and the majority of ethics of care philosophers, the society they describe is distinctly American. As legal scholar Martha Fineman explains in her fascinating critique of American legal and political history, *The Autonomy Myth*, the United States is a nation built on myths of independence, autonomy, and revolutionary freedom. But what of care in Canada, a country with an encumbered colonial history that seems to resist totalizing narratives of national autonomy? To what degree is what Martha Fineman labels America's "autonomy myth" relevant to an analysis of Canadian literature and culture?

A Caring Nation?

Historians and philosophers have often characterized Canada as a caring nation[13] where collectivity and responsibility are deeply embedded within national history and culture, in contrast to Canada's individualistic, revolutionary neighbour to the south. Portrayals of Canada as a caring nation frequently reference the country's universal health care program, which contrasts starkly with America's private system of care,[14] a focus that conveniently omits the ample historical and political evidence that undermines the "caring nation" hypothesis, as I discuss in further detail below. For example, prominent Canadian philosopher Charles Taylor argues for the primacy of social programs, particularly health care, for Canadian identity, claiming that "Canadians ... see their political society as more committed to collective provision, over and against an American society that gives greater weight to individual initiative ... There are regional differences in Canada, but generally Canadians are proud of and happy with their social programs, especially health insurance, and find the relative absence of these in the U.S. disturbing" (220).

Economist Robert Evans makes a similar argument, claiming Canada's "system of universal public insurance for health care is by a considerable margin" not only "Canada's most successful and popular public program," but a measure of Canadian compassion and care, "an important symbol of community, a concrete representation of mutual support and concern. It expresses a fundamental equality of Canadians in the face of disease and death, and a commitment that the rest of us will help as far as we can" (Evans 21). Popular media reinforce the perspective of health care as an identifying and unifying force for Canadians. In November 2012, the *Globe and Mail* reported the results of a national poll that asked Canadians to rank "more than a dozen [national] symbols, achievements and attributes" (Cheadle). The response was overwhelming. Ninety-four per cent of 2,207 participants characterized universal health care as "an important source of collective pride – including 74 per cent who called it 'very important'" (Cheadle). In 2004 the CBC Television series *The Greatest Canadian* declared Tommy Douglas, the founder of Canadian Medicare, the greatest Canadian, based on a public nomination and voting process. Douglas placed first on a shortlist that included beloved athlete and activist Terry Fox, charismatic Prime Minister Pierre Trudeau, and Nobel Prize winner Frederick Banting. The popularity of Canadian health care is often treated as evidence of a larger national cultural preoccupation with care, compassion, and collectivism.

The frequent references to Canadian health care in discussions of Canadian identity and national pride correspond with a larger national mythology of Canada as a caring country founded on collectivism (Fairfield, Gwyn, Lipset, Madison, Manfredi, C. Taylor) and compassion (Jefferes, Taras), on tolerance (E. Mackey), and civility (Coleman). Variations on the theme of Canadian dependence, sensitivity, and collectivism recur across a variety of disciplines: from history and sociology to literary and cultural studies, one finds an emphasis on the isolation and vulnerability believed to stem from "frontier experience" (Lipset, *Revolution* 160; Frye 250), the victimization (Atwood, "Survival") and dependency (Angus) caused by colonialism, and the responsibility and civility of Loyalism (Angus, Lipset). According to these models, Canadian identity is the result of counterrevolutionary deference and the fulfilment of obligation.

More recent political developments are also incorporated into contemporary discussions of Canadian identity. For example, political scientist Christopher Manfredi argues that the Canadian Charter of Rights and Freedoms, introduced in 1982, illustrates the endurance of Canadian communitarianism in its divergence from its American counterpart, the Bill of Rights. Unlike the Bill of Rights, the Charter "protects the collective rights of linguistic minorities, aboriginal peoples, and multicultural groups [and] … does not expressly protect private property rights" (Manfredi 315). In other words, for Manfredi, the Charter reinforces the popular sense of "Canadian civic philosophy" as "one that articulates a way of life and a philosophy of pluralism within a framework of individual rights" (Fairfield, Harris, and Madison 3). This national commitment to both collectivism and liberal individualism is enshrined in Canada's multiculturalism policy, which legislates pluralism and tolerance. Philosopher Gary Madison rehearses the popular perception of Canadian multiculturalism as evidence of a national capacity for tolerance, assistance, and respect:[15] "The 'universal sense of citizenship' Canadians share is that of mutual recognition of rights and a respect for human differences (combined with a willingness to help others out when they fall into genuine need)" (Madison 61). This glowing appraisal of "universal" Canadian open-mindedness, which also gestures parenthetically towards the ethical benefits of Canadian health care policy, leads Madison to conclude that central to Canadian cultural identity "are a prominent respect for the rule of law, an emphasis on civic responsibility, a belief in reasonable argument and open discussion, and a commitment to civility and the spirit of compromise and accommodation. The Canadian philosophy is a moral philosophy geared to the democratic practice of human rights and based on the ethical principles of reciprocity and mutuality" (62). Madison's language evokes ethics of care philosophy with its emphasis on responsiveness, obligation, and reciprocity.

This purported national concern for human vulnerability would appear to make Canada a promising place for the study of ethics of care in action; the social safety net, universal health care, and a Charter attentive to collective rights seem like ideal mechanisms for fostering a culture of obligation and responsibility, in other words, a culture of care. However, the celebration of Canada's commitment to its most vulnerable citizens depends on a limited view of national history and policy. Cultural critics, including Daniel Coleman, Smaro Kamboureli, Eva Mackey, and Erin Manning, provide dissenting analyses that encourage readers' scepticism towards overly reverential interpretations of Canadian history and public policy that project a morally self-satisfied and moralistic national culture. The vision of Canada as a country built on respect and responsibility, tolerance and care is a mythological reading that obscures a serious legacy of exclusion, prejudice, and neglect. Manning contends that the "obsession with 'Canadian identity' perpetuates a violent discourse of national exclusion that is masked in the myth of Canadians as harmless, open, and generous people" (xvii). Indeed, critical and political discourses that celebrate Canada's tradition of "tolerance and justice," argues Mackey, ignore a national history marked by intolerance and injustice (2). In particular, discourses of Canadian benevolence depend on the obfuscation or revision of a long history of antagonistic relations between Canadian governments and the nation's Indigenous populations. Mackey describes the form and function of this fabricated harmony: "Canada's mythologised kindness to Aboriginal people was an important element in developing a national identity based on the notion of difference from the USA – a difference that was tied to the idea of Canadian tolerance. The contradiction is that this notion of Canada's tolerance coexisted with brutal policies of extermination and cultural genocide" (14). While Mackey focuses on the myth of Canadian tolerance, Daniel Coleman examines the discourse of Canadian "civility," outlining similar processes of nation building founded on a largely mythical national narrative of kindness and care (21). Though their terminologies differ, Mackey's and Coleman's work converges in a dedication to exposing the problematic excisions and exclusions necessary for prevailing popular narratives and symbols of Canadian cultural caring.

Late twentieth-century developments in Canadian politics further challenge the myth of Canada as a caring nation, especially as Canada adopts neoliberal practices that privilege the independent, active, able-bodied, young, wage-earning individual at the expense of the disabled, vulnerable and dependent, aged subject. Sociologist Stephen Katz's interrogation of shifting attitudes towards later life in Canada exposes the neoliberal critique of dependence and need:

> Most gerontological and policy discourses pose activity as the "positive" against which the "negative" forces of dependency, illness, and loneliness are arrayed … It is not just the medical and cultural images of an active old age that have become predominant, but also the ways in which all *dependent* non-labouring populations – unemployed, disabled, and retired – have become targets of state policies to "empower" and "activate" them. (Katz, emphasis added 136)

The emphasis on activity as empowering takes on distinctly moral overtones as responsibility for health and ability becomes individualized and privatized. Despite the fact that all of us experience periods of dependency,[16] most often at the beginning and end of life, the political and cultural discourses Katz identifies rewrite this inevitability, transforming human dependency into individual failure, an inability to properly manage and "activate" one's body.

Despite its avowed position as a cherished, identifying, and unifying national policy, Canadian health care perpetually faces funding crises, accusations of inadequacy, and neoliberal calls for increased privatization. Politicians frequently use demographic scare tactics to put the blame for Medicare's inadequacies on its dependent users, particularly the rapidly expanding elderly populations that, they claim, strain the system by overusing it. For example, in February 2012, the *Globe and Mail* reported on a speech delivered by Prime Minister Stephen Harper in Davos, Switzerland, that outlined how "Canada's aging population threatens our cherished social programs" (Friesen). Summarizing Harper's speech, the *Globe* suggested that aging baby boomers, with their "appetite for the pensions and health care they have been promised certainly will prove expensive" (Friesen). The language of the article is telling, implying as it does that users of social programs are exploiting resources, that their "appetites" are unseemly, casting dependent aging populations as gluttonous devourers of limited resources rather than vulnerable citizens whose needs will be met by a "caring" state committed to "mutual support and concern."

On 28 August 2007 the Ontario provincial government announced an "Aging at Home Strategy," which aims to allow, and one might argue, encourage "people to continue leading healthy and independent lives in their own homes" ("Ontario's Aging at Home Strategy"). Given the opportunity, many Canadians would choose independent living, but as a policy, this emphasis on home living and its attendant care transfers the burden of care from the public to the private sphere. The program is an explicit attempt to reserve health care services for other, non-elderly users. As the Ontario government website explains, "healthy and independent" seniors will be able to avoid "unnecessary visits to hospitals, which can ultimately reduce ER wait times" ("Aging at Home Strategy Expands"). Attempts to dissuade citizens from using health care is part of a process of "passive privatization" in Canada, which puts increasing pressure on the family as providers of care services (Madore 14). Fineman describes this dynamic in American attitudes towards private care in a manner highly relevant to a Canadian context. Fineman argues that the offloading of care onto the family, and most often onto women, creates a relationship of dependency and debt between the state and caregivers since private caregivers

> provide a subsidy to the larger society and its institutions. Far from being independent, the state and the market institutions that it protects and fosters are dependent on the caretaking labor that reproduces society and populates its institutions. Caretaking thus creates a "social debt," a debt that must be paid according to the principles of equality that demand that those receiving social benefits also share the costs when they are able. Far from exemplifying equal responsibility for dependency, however, our market institutions are "free-riders," appropriating the labour of the caretaker for their own purposes. (*Autonomy Myth* xvii)

Despite significant differences in our health care systems and national identities, Fineman's notion of the "autonomy myth" is relevant to both American and Canadian political and economic cultures. As the many literary narratives explored throughout *Imagining Care* demonstrate, the sense of shame, failure, and exclusion commonly associated with dependency is not unique to American culture. Increasingly, there is a significant overlap in the underlying neoliberal attitudes that construct dependency as exceptional, as a sign of weakness that can, and should be avoided through body management and psychological fortitude. According to the myth of autonomy, care is the exception, rather than the rule, making the caregiving relations necessitated by illness and impairment appear extra-ordinary as opposed to ordinary and ubiquitous.

I draw attention to the central, yet contested position of care within national cultural discourses to contextualize my own foray into Canadian literary care. The conflicting criticism on national identity suggests that the idea of Canada as a caring nation is a conveniently selective national mythology that often focuses on a particularly beloved social program, universal health care, in order to carve out a distinctly Canadian national ethos. Clearly, the idea of care is important to Canadian identity. But as I have demonstrated, care is a complicated, mutable concept. While the celebration of Canadian care relies on a straightforward, optimistic interpretation of care, the literature I examine offers a multivalenced view of this ostensibly Canadian characteristic. Canadian writers, including Atwood, David Chariandy, Ignatieff, Munro, and others implicitly encourage their readers to approach the myth of Canadian care with caution, replacing totalizing myths of Canada and its citizens as unified and identified by care with particular scenarios of complicated, often ambivalent relations of dependence and need. Literary representations of vulnerability and responsibility offered by these authors expose the myth of Canadian care in a different register from cultural criticism, depicting the day-to-day difficulties of care in the private realm of friends and family.

Narrative, Ethics, Care

Canada's shift from "state social intervention" to "community care," most commonly to home care (Guberman 76), coupled with increased longevity and the subsequent rise in age-related memory disorders, contributes to the growing demand for a range of private care activities. The emergence of the caregiver self-help genre attests to the growing number of self-identified caregivers seeking guidance. Popular instructional texts, such as Bart Mindszenthy and Michael Gorden's *Parenting Your Parents: Support Strategies for Meeting the Challenge of Aging in the Family* (2002) and Claire Berman's best-selling, *Caring for Yourself While Caring for Your Aging Parents: How to Help, How to Survive* (2001), now in its third edition, demonstrate the gap between the egalitarian ideals of philosophers like Benhabib, Fisher, Tronto, Held, Noddings, and S. Miller, and the dogmatic, often reductive insights offered to caregivers in "practical" handbooks, such as Mindszenthy and Gorden's, and Berman's. The magnitude of this gulf between philosophy, even philosophy that seeks to privilege relationality, and self-help pragmatism highlights the need for an investigation into the "middle ground" of caregiving, a space in which one can consider abstract ideals and prin-ciples alongside day-to-day experience. The ambiguity and complexity of caregiving scenarios depicted in literature, scenarios complicated by human desires for power, for attention, for affection, provide compel-ling territory for investigating both the satisfaction and connection, along with the ambivalence and unease produced by caregiving rela-tions. As the title of Berman's book, *Caring for Yourself While Caring for Your Aging Parents*, demonstrates, self-help texts fulfil a need for con-trition and care on the part of caregivers (see, as well, e.g., Hargrave's *Strength and Courage for Caregivers: 30 Hope-Filled Morning and Evening Reflections*; Abramson and Dunkin's *The Caregiver's Survival Handbook: How to Care for Your Aging Parent without Losing Yourself*; and Karr's *Tak-ing Time for Me: How Caregivers Can Effectively Deal with Stress*). These texts gesture towards the pain and struggle involved in providing care and the difficulty of "surviving" such an ordeal, while simulta-neously sublimating the more unsettling aspects of care relations, like resentment, anger, exploitation, under the guise of perky discourses of "blessings" and "fulfilment." The caregiver self-help genre is necessar-ily problematic because such texts attempt to prescribe motivations or attitudes of reception. Caregiving, with its difficult convergence of love and labour, evades dogmatic prescription and conclusive evaluation.

I conclude this opening with a return to the Heinz dilemma, which, for all of its problematic brevity, remains important for my study, not for its content, but for its form. My investigation into literary repre-sentations of caregiving stems from a deep conviction that narrative and ethics are irrevocably entwined. Thus, one of the major problems with the Heinz dilemma is the simplicity of its narrative. I posit that literature, that is to say, literary narratives as opposed to instrumental narratives carefully manufactured as ethical exempla, can convey ethi-cal dilemmas more meaningfully infused with the subjectivity and par-ticularity that complicate straightforward "right" or "superior" moral reasoning.

In Munro's story "My Mother's Dream," a colicky infant wreaks havoc on her begrudging, widowed mother's life, prohibiting her indulgence of her solitary source of pleasure, playing the violin. The story is the inspiration for the title of Naomi Morgenstern's thoughtful essay on ethics in Munro's work, "The Baby or the Violin? Ethics and Femininity in the Fiction of Alice Munro," which flaunts the obvious-ness of the ethical choice between a child and a musical instrument. However, both the essay and the story expose the complicated context that surrounds Morgenstern's question, which strategically flattens the ethics of Munro's work to appear much like the Heinz dilemma's central "theft or death" moral question. As Morgenstern makes clear, in "My Mother's Dream" and other stories, including "The Bear Came over the Mountain," Munro conjures ethical quandaries that refuse easy summary and solution, implying that the ethical dilemma itself is a false dichotomy that expunges the multitude of particularities and possibilities that make ethical action so challenging.

I have gathered here a selection of texts that allow readers to ponder particular aspects of care's challenges. Because caregiving memoirs deal with the everyday particularities of care in the most pronounced and sustained way, they are the focus of my first chapter. The exhausting, often demoralizing routines of care documented by Ian Brown and others lead to an investigation of issues central to *Imagining Care*, particularly the meaning of care, its role in identity and subjectivity, along with the risks of care and its potential limits. From here, I turn to the study of fictional representation. Margaret Atwood's work, particularly her collection *Moral Disorder*, offers a remarkable engagement with the caregiving obligations concomitant with familial attachment. Her book offers a compelling exploration of a character's attempts to escape the demands of care, and the repercussions that ensue. Atwood's stories from this collection are a touchstone for their treatment of the potential harms of care, a theme that informs much of the analysis that follows.

The succeeding chapters build on many of the issues raised in the Atwood analysis: witnessing and care in chapter 3, gender and power in chapters 4 and 5. Chapter 3 examines Ignatieff's novel, *Scar Tissue*, which depicts care as an all-encompassing activity, a dedication of one person to another that verges on the devotional and evokes Levinas' theory of fundamental, absolute responsibility. Chapters 4 and 5 further consider the potential harms involved in caregiving, examining stories by Munro that depict the disquieting aspects of care: the desire to dominate and exploit, the longing to flee and abandon those in need. These chapters provide a more sustained treatment of the highly gendered labour involved in providing care, and the power politics that result from inversions of responsibility, particularly when children are forced to provide care for their parents. Chapter 6 continues to explore the many ways difference informs the dynamics of care. This chapter considers David Chariandy's novel, *Soucouyant*, in tandem with Canada's official multiculturalism policy, the national discourses of accommodation and tolerance that often reinforce divisions and inequalities between so-called Canadian Canadians and the nation's "ethnic" populations. Chariandy's novel depicts a family stricken by the traumatic legacy of racist history, a legacy that at once amplifies the need for care and impedes it.

Throughout *Imagining Care* the claims of ethics of care philosophers and the boundaries and hierarchies of moral reasoning will play a role, but establishing or defending the position of "care" in moral theory is not my goal.[17]

Instead, this book grapples with the significance of care, both its giving and receiving, for subjectivity and selfhood, responding to the claim that responsibility, dependence, and care are integral for human identity. I strive neither to confirm care as the primary ethical relationship nor privilege it as the primary virtue in a virtue ethics framework. I leave philosophical schematics to the philosophers. Instead, I investigate literary representation to discover how caregiving can, might, and does function, and how that functioning, in all its literary multiplicity, ambiguity, and contradiction, relates to the ongoing discussion of care in ethical philosophy. My goal is to suggest that the richness of literary narratives can add to ethical philosophy, such that these two disciplines can together contribute to a fuller understanding of the ethical implications of the complicated relations accruing from care dynamics in a Canadian literary context. As these memoirs, stories, and novels suggest, caregiving is prone to shape shifting: one person's altruism can be another's narcissism, one person's compassion another's condescension. Canadian literature shows its readers Canadian care, and often its denial in action, furnishing readers with particular characters struggling in particular caregiving situations, depicting in stark terms the ethical quandaries arising from attempts to respond to the needs of others.

1 Embedded and Embodied: Caregiving, Life Writing, and the Myth of the Autonomous Individual

Ian Brown's memoir, *The Boy in the Moon,* which recounts the difficult life of Brown's disabled son, Walker, opens with two epigraphs that establish the author's competing ethical impulses. The first quotation, from Sophocles' *Oedipus Rex,* emphasizes difference and suffering. In it, the Choragos laments Oedipus' self-inflicted wounds:

> What madness came upon you, what daemon
> Leaped on your life with heavier
> Punishment than a mortal man can bear?
> No: I cannot even
> Look at you, poor ruined one.
> And I would speak, question, ponder,
> If I were able. No.
> You make me shudder.

The Choragos, the removed commentator, gives voice to the audience's mixture of horror and sympathy. Oedipus, having suffered beyond what "man can bear," wears the marks of his psychological agony on his "ruined" body, a ruination that, ultimately, overpowers the sympathetic urge to understand. The Choragos "would" seek to comprehend the source of Oedipus' pain, but the sight of Oedipus' body provokes a physical reaction, a "shudder" that pre-empts inquiry or connection. The epigraph evokes the torment of witnessing a "mad" and "ruined" subject whose suffering is beyond comprehension and at the same time conveys the distance that such difference creates. The Choragos' alienation is generated by dismay, even disgust, but also by narrative structure: Oedipus the character is removed from the

Choragos, who occupies a liminal space between the drama and the audience, and even further removed from us, the viewers, existing, as he does, exclusively within the dramatic realm. What kind of caring relations can exist between audiences and characters?, the epigraph implies. If Brown's disabled son is the ruined Oedipus, burdened but remote, is Brown the helpless, shuddering Choragos? Are readers of his memoir the spectators of tragedy, seeking catharsis in dramatic suffering? The epigraph sets the stage, with its dramatic referent, for a tragic tale of distant, incomprehensible, yet affecting suffering. The allusion makes Walker at once a tragic hero and a distressing creature, a figure more object than subject.

The second epigraph takes a very different tack, shifting from tragedy to comedy, ancient to modern, verse to prose, in a statement from René Goscinny, best known as the co-creator of the *Asterix* comic series: "I like imbeciles. I like their candour. But, to be modest, one is always the imbecile of someone." The epigram reverses the defamiliarization of the *Oedipus Rex* quotation, universalizing disability, dissolving, albeit somewhat ironically, the boundaries between "normal" and "abnormal," between the sophisticate and the "imbecile." Unlike the Sophocles passage, which points out the insurmountable barrier between witness and other, Goscinny deflates such grandiose assumptions with comedy. In the Goscinny quotation, suffering is replaced with "candour," "madness" with informality, bluntness, and honesty. In this second epigraph it is less clear who is disadvantaged, implying that author, witness, and caregiver Ian Brown is not so very different from his disabled, dependent son Walker, and perhaps neither are his readers.

This chapter examines auto/biographical stories of familial caregiving in Canada: memoirs written by authors providing care for disabled children or parents. I begin my exploration of literature and the ethics of care with life writing because this genre directly and explicitly addresses the meaning, obligations, and boundaries of care, provoking ethical questions that help frame this project. These texts set the stage for deeper considerations of key issues, particularly the impact of responsibility and dependency on models of subjectivity and identity that follow in later chapters. In illness and disability memoirs, including Ian Brown's *The Boy in the Moon*, Miriam Edelson's *My Journey with Jake*, Heather Menzies' *Enter Mourning*, and Irena Karafilly's *The Stranger in the Plumed Hat*, caregiving authors struggle to depict and comprehend loved ones existing beyond the realm of narrative ability.

These texts test the ethical parameters of life writing, particularly the rights and responsibilities of what G. Thomas Couser calls "somatography," that is, memoirs that recount the experience of "living *with*, loving, or knowing intimately someone" with an "odd or anomalous" body, a perspective he differentiates from the less ethically delicate "autosomatography," which concerns "what it's like to have or to *be*, to live in or *as*, a particular body – indeed, a body that is usually odd or anomalous" (*Signifying Bodies*, emphasis in original 2).[1] Somatographies authored by caregiving family members of the afflicted offer explorations of care poised between philosophy and fiction, depicting the experiences of caregiving, both rewarding and grim, that ethics of care philosophers aim to introduce to abstract philosophy. Although fiction and life writing employ narrative, life writing depends on the veracity of lived experience for potency and effect.[2] The life-writing genre carries a different ethical weight than fiction in its representation of actual persons and scenarios, raising issues of fidelity, consent, and exploitation. The intimacy of family memoirs results in particular narrative and ethical concerns; such texts are "inherently unstable" because they inevitably "oscillate between biography and autobiography" (Couser, *Vulnerable Subjects* 56).[3] In this chapter I examine two kinds of somatography: stories told by parents of disabled children and stories told by adult children of disabled parents.[4] Each category demonstrates particular concerns within the practice and representation of care. Parents often struggle to comprehend and validate their child's difficult life (Brown, Edelson), while adult children can struggle to confront their mixed feelings about an ailing parent (Edwards, Federico, Karafilly, Menzies), the narrator's caregiving complicated by unresolved family tensions. These two varieties of life writing raise important and often troubling questions about the ethics of care: What is the caregiving author's responsibility to the disabled subject? What do such accounts seek to accomplish and whom do they benefit? All of these authors have witnessed the extremity of human vulnerability, the fragility of corporeality, and the often impossible, yet necessary demands such vulnerability imposes. As a result, somatographies often evoke both the difficulty of care and the obstinacy of its limits.

Life Writing, Disability, Care

Like many of the subjects of disability biographies, Walker Brown is incapable not only of authoring his own autobiography, but also of consenting to his father's portrayal. Yet, even consensual collaboration undertaken by subjects with equivalent abilities has historically been a source of anxiety for critics and readers alike. The question of who holds the pen, so to speak, dominates discussions by both collaborative writing critics and the collaborating authors themselves. The prospect of collaboratively authored literature has often provoked unease in critics and readers, demonstrated by the "persistent need to 'decollaborate' these works, to parse the collective text into the separate contributions of two or more individual authors" (York, *Rethinking* 7). Misgivings about literary collaboration are perhaps the predictable result of the glorification of the solitary, individual (masculine) author, the literary genius independently creating great works. As a result, collaborative writing is "monstrously subversive" (*Rethinking* 9) in much the same way as disability since both invoke the spectre of dependency, threatening the illusion of autonomous, independent, productive agents: "collaboration, whether by women or men, has often been figured as female passivity, sentimentality, and weakness" (13).[5] The power of the "normative single-author paradigm" that Lorraine York identifies (14) is evident in each of the somatographies I examine, texts that represent a relationship as experienced and imagined by a single participant. Although these texts depict care, relationality, and embeddedness, they have the potential to reinscribe autonomy and independence in their singular signature.

The authorial absence of the care receiving subject of these autobiographical texts brings questions of licence and fidelity to the fore. Leigh Gilmore describes such ethically fraught testimonials as limit-cases in her book, *The Limits of Autobiography*, drawing attention to particular texts that test the boundaries of self-representation. Gilmore's topics include, what she terms, "the auto/biographical demand" of life writing "in which the demands of autobiography (to tell my story) and the demands of biography (to tell your story) coincide" (72). As Gilmore points out, "in many ways, it is impossible to satisfy this double demand because it yokes together a series of related and unrequitable tasks. First, the auto/biographical demand entails an irresolvable narrative dilemma because it both divides and doubles the writing subject with respect to the task (whose story is this? mine? ours? how can I tell them all?)" (72).[6] This is the difficult demand that confronts many caregiving somatographers, particularly life writers representing ailing or deceased family members.

For Couser, "individuals with disabilities that preclude or interfere with self-representation" are "doubly vulnerable subjects" (*Signifying Bodies* 18), vulnerable to both physical and narrative domination or exploitation. As he explains, such exceptional vulnerability creates a particular "ethical dilemma":

> On the one hand, it is desirable for disability to be represented as it is actually experienced by particular human beings. When those individuals cannot or will not represent themselves, it can be of value to have their lives represented by others. So when autobiographical representation is not possible, there is great potential benefit in nonautobiographical representation. On the one hand, portraying people not able to speak for themselves (and, in some cases, not clearly able to grant meaningful consent) entails the risk of *mis*representing them without speaking for them (that is, advocating for them) or even speaking with them (that is, consulting them to learn their desires). (19)

Couser's analysis implies that somatographic subjects risk becoming instruments of laudable efforts to represent the marginalized. In the "inherently ventriloquistic" genre of "collaborative autobiography" ("Making" 220), in which a single author writes another's story, the convergence of authorship and authority becomes particularly problematic. There can be "danger" in this ventriloquism, in "attributing to the subject a voice and narrative not originating with him or her – and that he or she may not have edited" (220). But despite such difficulties, life writing can be an indispensable tool for exposing discrimination and exploitation, becoming, as Julia Swindells puts it, "the text of the oppressed" (qtd. in Anderson 103). By "articulating through one person's experience, experiences which may be representative of a particular marginalized group," auto/biography can provide the representation necessary for raising public and political awareness (Anderson 104). As a result, the danger of potential exploitation or misrepresentation must be weighed against the value of disability memoirs, which can convey the experience of disability to readers who might otherwise remain ignorant to the marginalization and penalization of the disabled. Couser terms somatography "*quality-of-life* writing," arguing that such texts "should be required reading for citizens in the world with underfunded, often inadequate, health care, with enormous technological capability to sustain life and repair bodies in the case of acute illness and injury but with very little commitment to accommodate and support chronic illness or disability" (*Signifying Bodies*, emphasis in original 14–15). Furthermore, within the particular context of caregiving somatography, one can argue that the reading public needs texts like Brown's in order to witness disability and care beyond stereotype, myth, and caricature, while remaining attentive to Walker's limited collaboration and the possibility of misrepresentation.

In addition to somatography's political potential, that is, its ability to raise awareness of disability among able-bodied citizens, I want to emphasize the philosophical potential of memoirs by caregivers since such texts necessarily depict the relationality of identity in process, the lives of each participant, both author and subject, narratively developed by his or her relationship with the other. The intrinsic narrative interdependence of writer and subject – the writer depends on the subject for "material," the subject on the writer for representation – works in tandem with the inevitable interrelationality that arises between caregivers and dependents. In this sense, caregiving memoirs dismantle the "the myth of autonomy" that Paul Eakin regards as endemic to autobiography and its criticism, which relies on an "illusion of self-determination: *I* write my story; *I* say who I am; *I* create my self" ("Relational," emphasis in original 63).[7] Such emphatic individualism poses a number of problems for life-writing scholars. As Leigh Gilmore explains, "the ubiquity of the individual as a trope of Western consciousness" obscures or even erases important aspects of context, the various conditions and relations that have shaped, even created, the seemingly autonomous subject (12). Gilmore ties "this habit of decontextualization" to "the issue of political representation, for the autobiographical self who is cut off from others, even as it stands for them, is a metaphor for the citizen. Once separated conceptually from a nation, a family, a place, and a branching set of contingencies, how does an individual recognize this disestablished self?" (12). Caregiving memoirs reverse this detachment, depicting the web of interdependencies responsible for identity and, in the case of many of these subjects, for survival. At their most ambitious and provocative, life writing about care can demonstrate the commonality of vulnerability and dependency, the fluidity of care-receiver and caregiver roles.

The wariness with which life-writing critics like Couser, Eakin, and Gilmore approach the illusion of autonomy perpetuated by auto/biography dovetails with ethics of care philosophy in a shared attention to the fallacy of individualism and the vulnerability inherent in embodiment. Maeve Cooke associates the failure "to acknowledge the self's embeddedness as constitutive of its identity" with a denial of the impact of bodily experience on selfhood, astutely linking "the idea of the self as *disembedded* ... with the idea of the self as *disembodied*" (emphasis in original 259). Only by obscuring embodiment and its attendant vulnerabilities can one sustain the impression of autonomy. Many disability theorists stress the temporariness of able-bodiedness, and Rosemarie Garland-Thomson goes so far as to assert that "disability is perhaps the essential characteristic of being human" ("Integrating Disability" 260). Somatography counters the processes of disassociation responsible for the marginalization of disability by drawing attention to the vulnerability of embodiment, depicting subjects distinctly embedded and embodied.

However, somatography's political and philosophical potential must be considered in tandem with literary traditions that deploy disability[8] as a narrative catalyst, or "prosthetic."[9] As disability theorists, such as Couser, Garland-Thomson, David Mitchell, Ato Quayson, and Sharon Snyder have demonstrated, the "extraordinary"[10] or "abnormal"[11] body has a narrative function in both everyday life and literary representation: disability is a narrative sign as much as a visual one. The body marked by disability carries, in Quayson's terms, an "excess of meaning" that invites or appears to demand interpretation and explanation (4). Narratives of inquiry, driven by the compulsion to interpret and communicate the nature of an afflicted, unfamiliar mode of existence, are part of a larger pattern of response to impairment, injury, and illness as marks of abnormality in need of narration. *The Boy in the Moon*'s subtitle, *A Father's Search for His Disabled Son*, announces the author's aim to locate, that is, to understand, explain, and represent Walker, implying, from the outset, that an absence guides the narrative. Walker, despite the moving portrait on the book's dust jacket that depicts a smiling boy wrapped in his father's arms, is apparently lost. Much of the book is concerned with demonstrating, often anxiously, why and how Walker counts as a person, why he has meaning and worth, in reaction to Brown's lingering doubts on the subject, his worrisome inkling that his son, who suffers pain, indignity, and anguish, and is largely unable to communicate with those around him, lacks the essential ingredients for selfhood. What is the meaning of such a helpless, cloistered, unarticulated life, asks Brown? Indeed, he asks, can such a life have any meaning at all?

This compulsion to know the story of a disability, to find out "What happened to *you*?" (Couser, *Signifying Bodies*, emphasis in original 16), and furthermore, What does your difference mean?, makes narrative representation an important and ethically charged aspect of disability studies. As Quayson explains,

> disability serves then to close the gap between representation and ethics, making visible the aesthetic field's relationship to the social situation of persons with disability in the real world … [T]he intervention of the literary representation is an intervention into a world that already situates disability within insistent framings and interpretations. The literary domain rather helps us to understand the complex *processes* of such framing and the ethical implications that derive from such processes. (Emphasis in original 24)

Quayson's nuanced attention to the intersection of representational and ethical concerns substantiates my conviction that literary representations of caregiving engage the broader ethical field of dependency and responsibility,[12] providing insight into the "insistent framings and interpretations" that typify social constructions of disability identity.

Caring for Disabled Children

The labour of care rarely leaves the foreground of somatographies since this labour is typically constant, exhausting, and overwhelming. This is particularly true in life writing by parents of "medically fragile" children, like Walker. "Medically fragile" is how Miriam Edelson's describes her son in *My Journey with Jake*, another memoir that provides a detailed account of the demands of care, including administering gastrostomy tube (or "G-tube") feedings and struggling with G-tube malfunction, patting Jake's chest several times a day to clear the mucus that interferes with his breathing, applying a Ventolin mask to dilate his bronchial tubes, and suctioning mucus from his nose and throat (81). Jake suffers from lissencephaly, a rare brain disorder – it literally means "smooth brain" – that severely inhibits his development: he cannot walk or talk, has difficulty swallowing and digesting, and is prone to life-threatening infections. The physical strain of caregiving is never absent from Edelson's account; indeed, her memoir includes her struggle with panic attacks and depression, the burnout that results from the colliding demands of paid labour (she works for the Canadian Auto Workers union), and family labour (105). However, her lengthy descriptions of stress, strain, and exhausting care work are tempered by frequent references to the satisfaction and rewards of caring for Jake: "Every little thing he can learn to do is a gift" (82); "He has given me purpose, passion. His smile lights up my heart and even the word *love* has new meaning: a tolerant, observing caring that asks little in return" (121). As anthropologist Janelle Taylor explains, drawing on Paul Ricoeur, human relationships rely on exchange, on both giving *and* receiving "gifts" (emphasis in original 320). Edelson inscribes this reciprocity into the caregiving dynamic by drawing attention to the many ways Jake bestows "gifts" on his caregiving mother. As a result, for Edelson "the meaning of [Jake's] life" is clear and enduring: he "enrich[es]" the author's life and leads her to "reinvent [her]self in ways [she] could never have imagined" (125). Her various articulations of Jake's remarkable effect emphasize the meaning of Jake's life: his significance is his incomparable impact on Edelson's existence.

Throughout Edelson's text, Jake supplies his caregiving mother and others with "meaning," "purpose," and "passion." The implication, I believe, is that this bestowal is actually a process of exchange, suggesting that Jake's life gains meaning due to his powerful effects on his many devoted caregivers, both familial and professional. As with many of the narratives of care I examine throughout this project, both fictional and non-fictional, identity and meaning for vulnerable subjects are often construed as the effect of *their effects* on others, what I call, identity as a *relational-effect*. This phrase is inspired by Eakin's adaptation of Antonio Damasio's description of the self as a "teller-effect," that is, the self as created and maintained via narrative communication ("What Are We Reading ...?" 129).[13] For those unable to create such a "teller-effect," the relational-effect is prominent and primary; without the ability to "tell" the self, vulnerable subjects rely on narration by others, those whose narratives intersect with the vulnerable in profound and constitutive ways. Often, and perhaps inevitably, the vulnerable subject's story becomes occluded by the caregiver's, whose socially unrecognized, typically unsupported labour begins to dominate the narrative.[14] Life writing about medically fragile children like Edelson's emphasizes the profound, positive effects of so much stress and toil. Brown, however, refuses this approach, acknowledging, but rejecting the habit of interpreting severely disabled children like Walker as "gifts," as life-enriching supplements. Instead, Brown longs to glimpse Walker's enigmatic subjectivity, to perceive *his* experience of disability, pain, and care. He wants to confirm that Walker has an identity beyond his relational-effect, that he has a distinct subjectivity, which, though impossible to comprehend, might somehow be discerned.

Although Ian Brown's memoir shares its generic categorization (somatography) with Edelson's *My Journey with Jake* and the other Canadian caregiving memoirs discussed below, Brown's book has enjoyed a significantly wider readership than its peers. As a well-established Canadian journalist with a major national newspaper (the *Globe and Mail*), Brown was already a minor celebrity prior to the publication of *The Boy in the Moon*. Excerpts from the book appeared in a series of weekly special reports in the *Globe and Mail* from 1 to 15 December in 2007, helping to guarantee the book a national readership that pushed it to number one on *Maclean's* non-fiction bestseller list when it finally appeared in 2010. Furthermore, *The Boy in the Moon* enjoyed a wide release, international press (including a favourable review in the *New York Times*), and garnered a number of literary awards, including the Charles Taylor Prize for Literary Non-Fiction, the Trillium Award, and the British Columbia National Book Award for Canadian Non-Fiction. As well, *The Boy in the Moon* had a prominent presence in the popular media, including a profile in the April 2010 issue of *O* magazine. The book's enormous success (best-seller status, admiring reviews, national awards) lend a particular weight and significance to its representation of its subject, Walker Brown, and the difficult care he requires to survive.[15] *The Boy in the Moon*'s acclaimed status confers a degree of authority, encouraging readers to regard its representation as an accurate, admirable depiction of disability and care. Unlike works published by Edelson, Menzies, and Karafilly, Brown's memoir has had a significant, widespread public impact and, therefore, a much greater potential to shape public opinion regarding its ethically charged material.

Although it has enjoyed a very different, laudatory public reception, Brown's *The Boy in the Moon* covers much of the same territory as less celebrated works, like Edelson's, immediately introducing readers to the strenuous, exhausting labour of care Walker demands on a daily, and nightly, basis. The routines of care are both "mundane" and "crucial" (1). Night feedings are particularly gruelling when Brown must carry his 8-year-old, 45-pound son down three flights of stairs to prepare a bottle (2). Delivering Walker's formula meal is a complex process of clamping, disconnecting, and reconnecting tubes, and operating a feeding pump to deliver sustenance via his G-tube (1–3). This feeding routine is preceded by a diaper change, which is, because of Walker's size and tendency to flail, "a task to be approached with all the delicacy of a munitions expert in a Bond movie defusing an atomic device" (4). The tasks themselves, exhausting, frustrating, and demoralizing as they may be, are conveyed with little emotional commentary. Brown makes it clear that *doing* is the "easy part" (3). The real strain of care is the ontological crisis it provokes, a crisis of comprehension and meaning that Brown cannot resolve, but merely absorb. In other words, if labour is the easy part, reflecting on this labour is the "hard part" (3). Brown struggles to "answer the questions Walker raises in my mind every time I pick him up. What is the value of a life like his – a life lived in the twilight, and often in pain? What is the cost of his life to those around him?" and "if Walker is so insubstantial, why does he feel so important? What is he trying to show me? All I really want to know is what goes on inside of his off-shaped head, in his jumped-up heart?" (3). Brown refuses to regard his son as a gift from God as some cardio-faciocutaneous syndrome (CFC) parents do. He rejects any religious or quasi-mystical interpretations of Walker's suffering, focusing instead on the concrete details of his day-to-day life, the unceasing, difficult schedules of care required to keep him alive and relatively healthy. And yet, beyond these everyday concerns, there is a larger philosophical concern that motivates Brown's project, a compulsive desire to locate meaning in Walker's life that I read as a kind of meta-caregiving. Brown's longing to apprehend his son's subjectivity haunts him throughout the text, his narration of Walker's life and care interspersed with questions of identity and meaning. For Brown, the burdens of the labour of care pale in comparison with the emotional and psychological strain of witnessing subjects profoundly impaired from birth. The random genetic mutation responsible for Walker's severe impairment, pain, and vulnerability cast into relief the precariousness of able-bodiedness, of independence and autonomy, and this precariousness torments Brown, who struggles in vain to discover some meaningful way to interpret Walker's existence.

Brown is most distressed by his inkling that Walker's life might have no meaning or value within the culture at large, but also, and more distressingly for Brown, within his own ontological framework. Brown is preoccupied by the prospect of Walker's point of view, a perspective Walker is unable to communicate. Brown longs to know "what the routines meant to him" (48); in other words, he wishes he could understand how Walker perceives his father's care. Most prominent is Brown's desire to confirm that Walker *has* a discernible subjectivity: "What went on inside that thickened skin, behind that swollen heart?

… What I cared about was whether he had a sense of himself, an inner life. Sometimes it seemed like the most urgent question of all" (48). The urgency of this question is apparent in its recurrence throughout the text, the enigma of Walker's subjectivity hovering throughout representations of the family's daily routines. Brown's most pressing "care" is to know Walker's impression of all the labours made on his behalf. Labour, the easy part, is not where Brown locates his care, but rather in the knowing, in recognition. A photo of Walker at sunset during a cottage vacation, reproduced in the book, holds special meaning since it recalls "the first place I ever imagined him to have an inner life, a life private from the rest of us" (59). The need to detect some private, separate self reflects the conflation of autonomy and selfhood common to life writing, as discussed above. As the author of Walker's biography, which is, at the same time his own autobiography, Brown is not immune to this ideology of autonomy; indeed, the anxiety Walker provokes often stems from Brown's professed inability to comprehend or even discern any separate, or "private" aspect of Walker's existence. The absoluteness of Walker's dependency thwarts the possibility of separateness or communication that might hint at his particular experience of the world. Without such evidence of subjectivity, Brown is troubled by the problem of Walker's value. The questions of meaning and value that open the memoir introduce the text's affecting "search" for Walker. However, as Lisa Watt points out in her review of *The Boy in the Moon*, Brown's investigation into Walker's "value," "replicat[es]the dominance and hegemony of pervasive ideas around 'cognitive ability' and 'normalcy,' thereby denying the value of Walker and persons like him as human beings" (88). Brown searches for Walker within epistemological and ontological frameworks that cannot accommodate mute, vulnerable, wholly dependent subjects, lending the quest a mournful, even elegiac tone since the reader gets the sense that the Walker that Brown is searching for will not be found.

However, the memoir incorporates alternative perspectives on the significance of Walker's life. Brown's wife, Johanna Schneller, detects an intangible, unrecognizable, but nonetheless inherent and indisputable value in Walker's existence, drawing attention to the able-bodied assumptions that make Walker's meaning and value open for debate in the first place. She admits she does not know "what Walker's value is to the world" (182), and rejects the idea that his worth is based merely on his effect: "I'm not sure I agree that his lasting value is to have touched people … I don't think his life should only have value because he makes other people feel more contented with their own lives. I think his life should have a value of its own" (182). Her scepticism suggests a resistance to Brown's desire to discover Walker's significance, since intrinsic value needs no discovery. This implied critique of the book's underlying ontological quest gets to the heart of the ethical implications of somatographies, like Brown's, in which the depiction of vulnerable subjects and their care can become explications that implicitly *devalue* the disabled in their very attempt to locate and prove their value. Brown's text, from its opening epigraphs, which contrast strangeness and familiarity, struggles to situate Walker between the two poles of unknowing and knowing, which risks transforming Walker into a philosophical problem, a perspective that proves disastrous for fictional characters, as I discuss further in chapter 3.

The impossibility of understanding Walker evokes the "disability as hermeneutical impasse" category of disability representation Quayson finds typical in literature (52). Disability's "excess of meaning," which calls out for explanation, for narrative, confounds Brown, and the "hermeneutical impasse" that is Walker's subjectivity results in numerous, at times extravagant attempts to locate an epistemological framework able to contain and explain Walker's problematic existence. For example, Brown arranges DNA testing in the hope that such tests will pinpoint the imperfection responsible for Walker's condition, but the results are inconclusive. He visits Canadian and American families caring for members with CFC, but the meetings provide little solace or insight. A trip to the French L'Arche Community for the disabled run by Jean Vanier is inspiring, but Brown cannot accept Vanier's faith-based interpretation of disability as a reminder of universal frailty and weakness (187). Vanier's comments echo ethics of care philosophy in their emphasis on fragility and dependence as universal human experiences: "We begin in fragility," he tells Brown, "we grow up, we are fragile and strong at the same time, and then we go into the process of weakening" (208). Vanier observes that Brown has awakened to universal vulnerability in his experiences with Walker, in his ability to admit his own inadequacy (208). But Brown disputes the possibility that Western culture could undergo the massive ideological transformation necessary to perceive dependence, fragility, and weakness as inevitable and even acceptable and, as a result, returns home from his many journeys still "searching" for his son.

Near the end of *The Boy in the Moon*, Brown offers three similes to represent Walker. The first two, Walker "as lens ... through which to see the world more sharply" (242) and Walker as "a mirror reflecting much back, my choices included" (286), envision Walker as a means for apprehending the world and oneself. In the first, Walker's transparency assures his value as an ocular aid, but traps him in the role of medium able to focus relations between subjects and their environments. He functions, in this figure and the next, as a kind of para-subject, as an appendage, a device, one valued only for his usefulness to others. The lens, like the mirror, requires a gazing subject to fulfil its function, returning Walker to the effect-value Schneller had previously rejected for her son.[16] In positioning Walker as an apparatus of the gaze, Brown highlights Walker's role in determining the meaning of the world and its subjects, if not his own identity; his disability focuses or reflects Brown's, and by implication, the reader's, understanding of ability, independence, and autonomy. Brown's association between Walker and visual examination also invokes the history of disabled people as attractions "on display … visually conspicuous while politically and socially erased" (Garland-Thomson, "The Politics of Staring" 56). And while Brown's similes position Walker as a tool for examining, rather than as an object of examination, the role of the inquiring gaze remains primary, emphasizing the association between disability and curiosity, investigation, and explanation.

However, Brown's third figuration is different. Taking his cue from Wallace Stevens' poem "Anecdote of the Jar," which he reproduces in its entirety, Brown proposes, "Walker is like the vessel Wallace Stevens wrote about" (286). The jar in Stevens' poem remains enigmatic but powerful: its "[gray] and bare presence" on a Tennessee Hill transforms "the slovenly wilderness" around it. Set against the jar, the wilderness is "no longer wild." The jar takes "dominion everywhere," despite its emptiness, its stasis and silence. It is "like nothing else in Tennessee," and the poem suggests that this singularity has a profound impact. Brown's analogy between Walker and the grey, bare jar that commands the world around it reinforces the sense that Walker's difference is irrevocable, his opacity obdurate, while his influence and power are beyond measure. Brown seems to find comfort in this conception of his inscrutable son: Walker himself cannot be known or "found" as Brown would like, but he can be witnessed. In *The Boy in the Moon*, caregiving functions as a process of discovery; care's most important activities are not physical and laborious, but rather philosophical and illuminating. The book itself is both an artefact of care and an act of care since, within Brown's framework, investigation and analysis are the most significant labours that love demands.

Yet, despite the book's devotion to philosophical inquiry, personal reflection, and imaginary feats, it concludes with a scene of caring practice that is devastating in its honesty and resignation. Waiting for Walker's MRI, Brown wheels his son up and down the hospital corridors for three hours. Finally, the two rest, Brown sitting down, Walker standing nearby. Without warning, Walker swoons, falling into his father's arms, his eyes and limbs twitching in what Brown recognizes as the signs of a seizure. This is the first time Walker has had such an attack, and Brown can see his son's fear and helplessness. He holds Walker as he shudders and his eyes twitch, searching for his father's gaze. The intimacy of the event, Walker's extreme vulnerability, the closeness of his convulsing body, provoke a vision of Walker's fragile mortality:

> I held him in my arms as quietly as I could, and I thought: this is what it will be like if he dies. It will be like this. There was nothing much to do. I didn't fear it. I was already as close as I could be to him; there was no space between my son and me, no gap or air, not expectation or disappointment, no failure or success: only what he was, a swooned boy, my silent sometimes laughing companion, and my son. I knew I loved him, and I knew he knew it. I held that sweetness in my arms and waited for whatever was going to happen next. We did that together. (288)

This final image of connected bodies eschews the search that has guided Brown's text, implying that tactile experience, haptic connection provides a kind of knowledge that exceeds the results of his various intellectual inquiries. Walker's identity beyond the interrelational cannot be articulated, but his unassimilable difference is no longer a source of distress for Brown. Connections – familial ("my son"), physical ("there was no space between my son and me"), and metaphysical ("[I] waited for whatever was going to happen next. We did that together") – become primary and consoling. "I" becomes "we." In some sense, Brown's search is over; Walker has been located where he has always been. He is himself: unknown yet familiar, distant yet intimate, incomprehensible yet invaluable. In this brief scene, Brown evokes an experience of care that achieves a delicate balance of devotion and respect, dependence and autonomy, realizing, if only for a moment, the vision of relationality imagined by ethics of care philosophers: that of self and other existing for and through each other. In the end, Brown evokes his disabled son's identity as far more than a "relational-effect," that is, as determined primarily through his effect on others. Instead, Brown conveys the alterity of the other without recourse to familiarization or explanation, acknowledging, respecting, even embracing difference.

Caring for Disabled Parents

Unlike memoirs by parents, which stress devotion and love despite the labour and struggle of care, memoirs by adults caring for aging, ill, and disabled parents often reflect the ambivalence that results from an unwelcome reversal of roles. In many of these somatographies, adult children harbour deep misgivings about their new role as caregiver, misgivings rarely articulated by parents of disabled children. The caregiving experience can unearth buried grudges and resentment in adult children who have been disappointed by their parents' care, or lack thereof; parents rarely express feelings of resentment. Brown, for example, may admit to feeling frustrated, hopeless, overwhelmed, but like Edelson, he never doubts his child's entitlement to care and affection. Such doubts are common among memoirs documenting the experience of caring for aging parents: in Caterina Edward's *Finding Rose*, Meg Federico's *Welcome to the Departure Lounge*, Irena Karafilly's *The Stranger in the Plumed Hat*, and Heather Menzies' *Enter Mourning*, one encounters strained, if not outright abusive childhood relationships recalled by conflicted caregiving authors. These daughters,[17] forced into the role of caregiver, express ambivalence about their new position, one that calls for the kind, attentive caregiving they were often denied as children. All four texts represent a highly gendered dynamic of care, mothers and daughters struggling not only with private histories, but also with cultural norms that associate femininity with care, naturalizing the difficult labour necessitated by illness and disability.[18] These authors suffer twin pressures: as children of the afflicted they are expected to assume responsibility for their parent; as *female* children of the afflicted they are expected to be eager and devoted caregivers. The weight of personal and societal expectations is apparent in their discordant responses to their parent's new vulnerability. Memories of childhood suffering resurface to haunt these caregivers as they confront new familial dynamics and responsibility. As a result, some memoirs can convey a sense of reckoning, even vengeance, as tales of a parent's past harms and present needs reside in uneasy narrative proximity.

Caterina Edwards seems committed to settling scores in her memoir, *Finding Rosa: A Mother with Alzheimer's, A Daughter in Search of the Past*, which documents both her mother, Rosa's seemingly pathological cruelty to her daughter prior to her illness and Edwards' dutiful caregiving during her mother's dementia. Edwards recounts Rosa's incessant insults and accusations, physical abuse, and destruction of her clothing. For Edwards, Rosa's dementia provides an occasion for power, the opportunity to manufacture the kind of maternal relations she has always longed for. Not only does Rosa's illness generate a new intimacy between Edwards and her mother, but her mother's sudden helplessness precipitated by dementia also initiates a new freedom of expression for Edwards. As Edwards explains, writing has been a means of self-protection throughout her life: "That was why I told stories ... to make a space for myself. To erect a wall against my mother" (247). Her mother's vulnerability in later life increases the potency of Edwards' storytelling as her strategy transforms from defensive to offensive, her writing a chance to expose, even accuse her mother. Edwards is well aware of this new liberty and the fact that her mother would disapprove of her project: "I suspect that my mother unconsciously feared that one day I would write about her, that I would do what I am doing – exposing her secrets to the world. She'd be enraged if she were still her old self, enraged at the inevitable betrayal. She'd let out a high-pitched, wordless scream, throw a dish, land a random blow. Then, worse, the torrent of abuse of words, the unstoppable insults" (247).

There is no question that the text is non-consensual and non-collaborative and Couser's concerns regarding the ethics of representing "doubly vulnerable subjects" come to the fore in Edwards' text. The non-consensual nature of this memoir produces an uncomfortable position for the reader who is implicitly asked to balance various forms of victimization (the daughter's) and betrayal (the mother's). The text implies a hierarchy of suffering, suggesting that mistreatment in childhood legitimizes non-consensual representations that explicitly betray the wishes of the memoir's debilitated subject. As a result, there emerges a privileging of dependence: the vulnerability of the child set against the vulnerability of the aging and infirm. The language of competition and struggle proliferates. Caregiving for her Sicilian-Canadian father-in-law is an out-and-out battle: "You can let go now," she tells him, "because you got what you wanted ... You've won" (165). Similarly, Edwards submits to her mother's need for care: "I gave in; I shouldered my charge" (136). The book's final image employs an allusion to Jacob wrestling the angel to characterize her relationship with her mother during the final months of her life: "I hung on to her until she blessed me" (333),[19] a demanding hold that proves fruitful when, a few months before her death, Rosa responds to her daughter's kiss in kind and thanks her "for everything you have done for me" (333). Edwards is finally victorious in her struggle for reciprocity in care, a victory that is explicitly aligned with the production of her caregiving memoir: "She blessed me, she passed away, but I still hung on. For years … Until I knew her. Until I wrote this book" (334).

For Edwards, caregiving involves submission, labour, and duty. Nonetheless, she describes revelatory moments with her ailing mother, moments in which physical intimacy is set against an accentuation of the alienation between them: "Managing Mum's physical care, ensuring that she was clean, safe, fed, properly medicated, and reasonably calm brought me closer to her and farther away" (318). Edwards describes how she comes to know and accept her mother's body in its dependency, a "physical intimacy" that is "mocked by the growing mental estrangement" (319). This alienation is countered by the text itself, which is a nostalgic search for Rosa's hidden history and identity. Much like Brown, Edwards longs to know her mysterious, frustrating, disappearing mother. Significantly, as Edwards explains in the book's prologue, it is her mother's frailty, observing her "mind, then her body, fail," that motivates her desire to "know her … to know the woman she used to be" (1). Rosa's "failure," her disability, stimulates her daughter's narrative investigation: once again, illness and disability demand narrative explanation. What follows Edwards' prologue is a combination of caregiving narrative and recreated family history. Edwards counters her mother's refusal and then later, inability, to provide a personal history with a combination of research and fabrication. In Edwards' text writing about caring for her mother becomes an opportunity for self-care, providing a therapeutic testimonial that can obscure its ostensible subject, in this case, Rosa.

In Edwards', Menzies', and Federico's memoirs, the strain of caregiving goes hand-in-hand with the lingering pain of childhood mistreatment. All three conclude with the death of the mother whose inadequate parenting has complicated the duty to care. These memoirs speak *for* the vulnerable subjects at their centres with claims of accuracy and truth, and sometimes, vindication. Narrativization functions as an act of redemption, a disabled other providing opportunities for self-examination, and identity resolution. Such memoirs raise a difficult and uncomfortable question: Are adult offspring obligated to care for parents who have failed in their own obligation to care? And furthermore, adapting Wayne Booth's question in *The Company We Keep*, what are the author's responsibilities to those vulnerable subjects whose lives (and often deaths) are used as life writing "material" (130)?[20] Does one's answer to the first question determine one's answer to the second? And furthermore, is it ethically responsible to work through these questions in a public forum?

The "opportunities" offered by mothers with dementia are ample for caregiving daughters seeking a long-coveted bond. Not all struggles for connection are as dramatic or combative as Edwards'. In *Enter Mourning*, Heather Menzies depicts her cultivation of a cherished intimacy with her ailing mother, Elizabeth, via the routines of care. For Menzies, caregiving provides respite from a life spent "chasing after Mum's love" (40). While her siblings maintain their distance from their mother, Menzies gives herself over to the duties of care, framing the resulting closeness in metaphysical terms:

> The relationship itself leads ... And as our evolving relationship led, it took me far beyond the realm of quantifiable knowledge and meaning-making into an awareness of meaning beneath the surface of words and even the need for words. It opened me to the subtle flow of pure feeling, pure spirit. Somewhere along the way too, Mum and the meaningfulness of her life with "severe dementia" was no longer framed solely around her and her capabilities as free agent. It had been re-framed around us, and our relating to each other. (146–7)

Demonstrating her love for her mother in ways denied her as a child, Menzies sees herself becoming "fused" with her mother (159).

Menzies eagerly adopts an epistemology based primarily on touch, gesture, and facial expression, one that allows her to apprehend her mother's love and appreciation through their "connection" (91). She professes to know her mother via the body: "If I stayed in touch, not looking for the old Mum, but opening myself instead to the new, using the touch of her skin in my hand, the look in her eye, her frowns, her sighs and smiles as my guide, I could know her still. I could know her by giving up my own familiar ways of knowing, and opening myself to unknowing too" (93). The memoir is an emotional account of Menzies experience caring for her mother from the time of her Alzheimer's diagnosis until her death. But it is difficult for the reader to reconcile the two mothers Menzies depicts: a healthy, if distant and unaffectionate mother, and the docile appreciative, disabled mother. In *Enter Mourning: A Memoir on Death, Dementia, and Coming Home*, as the title suggests, the emphasis is firmly placed on the experience of the caregiver. Care *receiving*, the text implies, is simply a mirror of giving, Elizabeth's experience implied in Menzies' descriptions of her own. Her mother's subjectivity, mysterious both before and after her illness (hurtfully so before her ailment), seems largely irrelevant to Menzies' project, which depends on her mother's obscurity. The narrative is premised on her mother as the object of Menzies' care, a cherished and somewhat responsive object perhaps, but an object nonetheless.

Menzies represents care as connection and intimacy, but her interpretation can only be one sided since her mother cannot offer her own perspective. As a result, Menzies appears to employ her mother's dementia, her new dependency to create the kind of relationship she has always longed for, one that suits her particular model of familial harmony, employing a neo-Buddhist perspective that venerates moments of being (91, 127, 194). The degree to which this relation of care is unlike any previous relational mode experienced in the family is evident in her siblings' reactions to Menzies' expectations and needs, which they find tiring, even irritating (127). Overall, Menzies' version of care is one that employs her object of care as a mirror able to reflect her own goodness, values, and worth back at her, recalling Brown's references to Walker as "a mirror reflecting … [Brown's] choices." Again and again, Menzies draws attention to her own sacrifice in her acts of care, but there is very little attention to her mother's experiences, to her pain, confusion, or impairment. Consequently, the reader gets no sense of her mother as a subject; instead she remains a diseased object, one whose cruel and selfish, even pathological parenting traumatized her children, particularly the author.

Yet how does one write of caregiving and its burdens without exploiting or obscuring the object of care and ignoring his or her subjectivity? Irena Karafilly's *The Stranger in the Plumed Hat* draws attention to this dilemma in its treatment of the limits of care, its belatedness, even flimsiness, in its account of aging, illness, and dementia. Like Edwards, Menzies, and others, Karafilly has a history of family discord; however, unlike those authors, Karafilly explores the ethical implications of her project by drawing attention to the risks of somatography:

> I can't help being aware of the irony that my current project has actually placed me in the improbable position of being torn between Art and the very subject that has inspired it! Though I have set out to tell my mother's story, it has recently come to me that what started as a purely therapeutic exercise

has willy-nilly become a consuming work of art continuously nourished by the suffering of its protagonist. To put it bluntly, I seem to be simultaneously exploiting my mother's ordeal and – irrationally, unfairly, balking at its endless exigencies. Ultimately, of course, the tension is not just between Art and Life, but between two kinds of duty. (207)

Karafilly's articulation of conflicting duties – a commitment to the representation of care, on the one hand, and to the actual subject receiving that care, on the other – lays bare the central ethical problems of somatographies by accentuating competing fidelities. Karafilly examines her own intentions, her motivations and satisfaction, acknowledging the difficulty of distinguishing between caregiver and care receiver in the assessment of benefits. Aware of the impotence of her care, that her gestures are unlikely to comfort her mother, she continues her labours nonetheless:

I promptly set about improving my mother's new room. I bought her a new comforter, a plant; a painting to hang over the bed, a smiling terracotta sun. I had no illusions about any of it making a difference to my mother, but human beings are nothing if not given to gestures ostensibly meant to benefit others, but in fact serving to alleviate their own desolation and sense of impotence. (197–8)

Throughout *The Stranger in the Plumed Hat*, this self-reflexive style produces a double-voiced narrator, one able to conjure her experiences while simultaneously critiquing her actions and their representation. As a result, Karafilly is able to convey the pain, struggle, and rewards of caregiving while at the same time challenging her own characterizations. Karafilly frankly examines her own motivations for and satisfaction from her mother's care, recognizing the risks of the reminiscence and re-creation involved in life writing: "It is easy to love in retrospect; love earnestly, perfectly, while staring into the abyss" (36). In some ways, her mother's dementia makes caregiving easier since the condition diminishes her mother's agency until she is no longer "a threat to [Karafilly's] independence" (64).

Karafilly explains that her mother's medicalization increases her tolerance for her mother: "I don't know why it should be so; why a medical diagnosis, however tentative, seems to legitimize behavior that had only recently seemed unacceptable. Or, to turn the question around, why can't we be equally generous, equally tolerant, when a medical

label does not yet seem to be available?" (64). Much like Edwards'
and Menzies', Karafilly's account of her mother's dependence provides opportunities for intimacy, control, sacrifice, and affection. Yet,
Karafilly expresses misgivings about her role of life writer. Karafilly's
explicit attention to the conflicting interests involved in telling the stories of vulnerable subjects makes space for ambivalence and unease, a
space other caregiving authors tend to stock with images of handhold-
ing and embraces. Karafilly's remarks address the central dilemmas of
care: How does one reconcile the needs of the self and the needs of the
other? How can one balance between care and sacrifice?

For all of these authors there is another important question: How
to care for one who has failed to care for you? Karafilly finds solace in
confronting her own conflicted response to her mother's illness and
dependence, acknowledging that even as "love and ... pity" for her
mother flow through her "like a deep, tortuous river," "subterranean
fires of anger and resentment" also continue to burn within her (206).
I see a correlation between this self-reflexive attention to irresolvable
affective dissonance and the book's concluding image, which resists
resolution and satisfaction, the palatable aspects of care. Among these
memoirs of dementia by caregiving adult children, Karafilly's is the
only one that does not conclude with the parent's death followed by
comforting reflections. Her mother still exists at the book's end, drasti-
cally altered, but alive, a subject continuing to experience the world
around her. The memoir's final image is one of suspension: Karafilly's
mother's hand is "raised, trembling," a gesture severed from conventional communication (240). The raised hand "only looks like" a signal
of "farewell" or "benediction" (240). As Karafilly explains, her mother
no longer knows the word goodbye, "but she still smiles on being
kissed, and makes small kissing noises with her puckered mouth. It is,
I reflect, likely to be the very last gift my mother will relinquish. I know
she doesn't understand who we are" (239–40). But this lack of recognition and linguistic comprehension does not diminish the power of
this final gesture, a final "gift" that demonstrates her mother's care. As
Janelle Taylor argues, the emphasis on "recognition" as a precursor for
subject-status has dire consequences for those coping with dementia.
Taylor describes the frustration of her own experience as the daughter
of an Alzheimer's sufferer, terrorized by the recurring question uttered
by well-meaning interlocutors: "Does she recognize you?" According to
Taylor, this question speaks to the "erosion of personhood" that many
regard as concomitant with dementia and its debilitations; if those with

dementia are unable to "'recognize' people, words, and things," they lose their claim to "social and political 'recognition'" (333). Taylor's premise helps explain the horror commonly associated with Alzheimer's and the care it demands, suggesting that representations of the disease tend to rely on the conventions of "Gothic" or "zombie" stories in which

> the body may continue to live, but the person with Alzheimer's is dead, gone, no longer there, no longer a person. He or she does not know your name, does not "recognize" you, therefore cannot "care" about you, but you must "care" for him or her – and such "care" is conceived as an unending toil of unrelieved grimness. Such narratives are not "mere" stories. A caregiver's judgment that a person with dementia is "socially dead" does very real harm, when it leads them to ignore the person with dementia, or to treat him or her in dehumanizing ways. (322)

Karafilly's conclusion upends these conventions in its attention to the gifts, the care that flows between mother and daughter. Her representation counters "Gothic" and "zombie" stories of dementia by emphasizing presence rather than absence, demonstrating the persistence of her mother's being, the persistence of care. Karafilly's final image incorporates subjectivity and otherness, knowing and not-knowing, evoking care relations as reciprocal encounters that may defy rational comprehension, but profoundly register intimacy and personhood nonetheless.

Alternative Strategies

To conclude, I want to consider alternative discourses within the life-writing genre, discourses that simultaneously represent and reconfigure the experiences and meaning of care. In novelist Miriam Toews' unusual memoir, *Swing Low: A Life*, an autobiography of Mel Toews written by his daughter, and Sarah Leavitt's graphic memoir, *Tangles: A Story about Alzheimer's, My Mother, and Me*, the authors represent ailing parents as subjects disabled by illness. In these texts, the single perspective that typically characterizes caregiving memoirs, including *The Boy in the Moon*, *Enter Mourning*, and *The Stranger in the Plumed Hat*, is reconfigured by textual strategies that draw attention to the care-receiver's subjectivity.

In *Swing Low*, narrative itself serves as care for Toews' mentally ill father. Without claiming comprehension of his illness and its effects,

Toews imagines her father's perspective, recounting the story of his lifelong struggle with severe bipolar disorder in the first person. Toews' prologue clarifies both her aim in composing the book – to contradict her father's belief that his life was a failure – along with the book's genesis – at the end of his life her father asked her to "write things down for him," asking her to write in his voice so he could more readily recognize his own life (xiii). During his final depressive episode, which ended with his suicide, Toews began "filling up pages of yellow legal notepads with writing from his own point of view so he could understand it when he read it to himself" (xiii). She continues the practice after his death, regarding it as a "natural extension of the writing I'd done for him in the hospital, and a way, though not a perfect one, of hearing what my father might have talked about if he'd ever allow himself to. If he'd ever thought it would matter to anybody" (xiii). Consequently, *Swing Low* does not so much represent care as embody it, the book itself functioning as a final act of caregiving, a continuation of the care practice initiated during Mel's most severe period of illness. As Toews' foreword explains, and the body of the text makes strikingly clear, Mel's was a life lived largely in silence, an adaptive strategy adopted early in his life. His enduring silences – he sometimes went months without speaking to his family – are obvious emblems of suffering, both Mel's own and that of his neglected wife and daughters. As a result, Toews' inscription of Mel's voice manages to be at once a gift or tribute to her father and a therapeutic re-evaluation of her father's life that assists her in acknowledging a subjectivity that was largely hidden during her father's lifetime. Writing in her father's voice forces Toews to imagine herself as another. Her less-than-flattering portraits of herself as a child and a young woman responding to her father's periods of depression suggest a privileging of the other, an adoption of an ethical perspective that leads to a new acceptance of her father's often frustrating, painful opacity.

Swing Low is very clearly Mel's story, and Toews has described the scrupulous research she undertook in order to verify that "everything that happens in the book really did happen. *Every* single thing" ("It Gets under the Skin," emphasis in original 123). This prioritization of the verifiable leads her to label the book non-fiction, despite the fact that she has fabricated her father's voice (123). Despite this carefulness, ethical complications remain since, though Mel asked her to write for him in the hospital, Toews acknowledges that her father would have been troubled by her book: "By dragging some of the awful details into the light of day, they become much less frightening. I have to admit, my father didn't feel the same way, but he found a way to alleviate his pain, and so have I" (Toews, *Swing Low* xiv). Toews' struggle to provide care for both herself and her father speaks to a problem frequently depicted in both caregiving life writing and fiction: conflicting needs and limited resources as impediments to mutually beneficial care.

In *Tangles*, Sarah Leavitt uses the graphic memoir to represent her experiences of caring for her mother, Midge, who suffers from Alzheimer's. The genre, with its combination of image and text, provides a compelling approach to life writing, one that allows Leavitt to visualize her experiences as caregiver and her mother's experiences as care receiver literally side-by-side. Leavitt refuses to shy away from the demoralizing, even repugnant aspects of caregiving, such as dealing with her mother's incontinence, while at the same time conveying the comforting intimacy that care affords, as when she holds her mother's hand during walks, or they share silly, private jokes. Often Leavitt depicts her feelings of competence and helplessness in quick succession: A panel depicting a smiling Sarah in a nurse's uniform with the caption "Sometimes I felt like the calmest, most capable nurse," is followed by one of her hunched and sickened profile and a very different caption: "Other times I thought I might throw up from the smell of urine or shit" (110). This quick oscillation that continues throughout the text allows Leavitt to maintain an ambiguous, even ambivalent attitude towards care, to represent multiple experiences without synthesis.

In *Tangles*, Midge exists as a visible subject, both literally – she is a defined image drawn in black ink on a white background – and figuratively – she seems to exist beyond Leavitt's descriptions since she is able to occupy her own, wordless frames. Despite the reader's awareness of Leavitt's position as sole creator of the text (both its words and images), the repeated depiction of Midge as a solitary figure on an otherwise blank page (42, 91), along with reproductions of her handwriting (46, 69), and dialogue (61, 64, 82, 88), manage to represent her as a subject distinct from her caregivers, and visually emphasize the distance and isolation imposed by her disease. These graphic strategies accentuate the transient, the enigmatic, the non-narrative observation or interaction. The medium allows Leavitt to embrace anecdotes and vignettes and dispense with the kind of totalizing narrative structure that is characteristic of the non-graphic memoir. According to Theresa Tensuan, graphic narratives, or comics, are typically episodic, rather than epic in structure, allowing authors to include small events, communication, recollections, and ruminations that may not correspond with a larger narrative project (950). In other words, comics permit the author, and by extension the reader, to meander, to "loiter," as Tensuan puts it (951). The structure of the comic, composed as it is by separate frames at once joined and separated by "gutters," the formal term for the spaces between comic frames, facilitates an aesthetic "limbo," a liminality that encourages narrative multiplicity (950). The comic's cultivation of a meandering reading style persuades Tensuan to the term "loiterature" to describe graphic memoirs by Lynda Barry and Marjane Satrapi. "Loiterature," argues Mary Pat Brady, "forces the reader to look around, to linger and remember ... [by gesturing towards] the significance and sophistication of ... heretofore ignored and invalidated knowledges" (114). As "loiterature," graphic somatographies like Leavitt's allow, even encourage, readers "to linger and remember." As a result, *Tangles* achieves a measure of open-endedness, managing to narrate an illness that resists narrative coherence in its disordering of memory and identity without imposing consistency and resolution. The visual medium provides Leavitt with productive options: she can represent her mother, herself, her personal memories with text, images, or a combination of the two. At times, Leavitt employs images to communicate experiences of care, the pain and frustration of its limitations, without recourse to language. In many ways, dementia and the caregiving it requires are experiences beyond the scope of language, especially when the care receiver becomes unable to communicate through comprehensible speech. Leavitt's graphic memoir conveys the opacity of Midge's dementia, its fragmentation and multiplicity, its conflicting emotions, from both sides of the caregiving relationship. As Leavitt acknowledges, dependency can seem to erase personhood since "it gets hard to see someone as a person when they've become a list of needs: BATH, CLOTHES, BRUSH TEETH, WALK, FOOD, ETC" (Leavitt 84). However, her strategy of representation allows acknowledgment of moments of invisibility without perpetuating her mother's erasure. Midge's presence (literally and figuratively) and personhood are undeniable throughout *Tangles*, regardless of her abilities. Like Toews, Leavitt chooses a medium that permits her to highlight the subjectivity of the disabled subject. But while Toews must divide the text according to perspectives (her point of view in the foreword, her father's in the body of the text), Leavitt is able to oscillate and remain ambiguous, even ambivalent, in her representation of herself, her mother, and their relations of care.

Though life writing may have its roots in illusions of autonomy and vital individualism, memoirs of hardship and pain have a long history. As Arthur Frank explains, "Suffering has always animated life writing. During the nineteenth century, persons who had no other claim to public recognition wrote narratives of personal suffering – particularly captivity, slavery, war, and poverty – creating a publication niche and considerable readership. Today, illness and disability have displaced the nineteenth-century topics in popularity" (174). Couser stresses this recent shift in popularity, asserting that "only in the last quarter of a century or so have memoirs by anonymous individuals with anomalous bodies been widely read and critically acclaimed" (*Signifying Bodies* 3). These somatographic texts have the potential to challenge the "decontextualized," independent "I" of autobiography. Certainly there is no such "I" in these auto/biographies of illnesses and impairments, including dementia (Edwards, Karafilly, Leavitt, Menzies), cardiofaciocutaneous syndrome (Brown), and lissencephaly (Edelson). Indeed, because such texts function as autobiography and biography simultaneously, it is often difficult for the reader to distinguish a discrete, autonomous narrative subject. The caregiver and care-receiver's life stories are irrevocably intertwined, interdependent, and mutually constitutive. As a result, these texts, to varying degrees, draw attention to, even undermine or dismantle, the problematic mythologization of independence and autonomy that marginalizes and renders "deviants" all "those members of society who openly manifest the reality of dependency" (Fineman, "Masking Dependency" 216). Reading caregiving memoirs actually has the opposite effect, normalizing disability and dependency, making relations of care appear necessary for both survival and selfhood. In other words, these texts demonstrate that constellations of care are essential for existence and identity in disabled and able-bodied alike. Just as the "disabled body sharply recalls to the nondisabled the provisional and temporary nature of able-bodiedness and indeed of the social frameworks that undergird the suppositions of bodily normality" (Quayson 14), relations of care precipitated by extreme dependency recall the interrelationality of identity regardless of ability; the provisionality of able-bodiedness conjures the inevitability and necessity of care for all embodied subjects. Investigations of caregiving at the limit, that is, performances of care necessary not only for social identity and emotional well-being, but for basic survival, shed light on the everyday function of caregiving in all lives, disabled and able-bodied alike. Life writing about dependency enforced by illness and impairment grapples with the social frameworks linking identity with able-bodiedness, autobiography with autonomy, subjectivity with narrative ability, creating texts that can occasionally combine witnessing and testimony, at once imitating the Charagos' wild lament and Goscinny's impish declaration of the universality of "abnormality."

2 Moral Obligation, Disordered Care: The Ethics of Caregiving in Margaret Atwood's *Moral Disorder*

While life writing may be constrained by the ethics of fidelity and the author's sense of responsibility towards the actual people and scenarios he or she represents, in fiction the licence of fabrication often allows authors to explore unpalatable, socially unacceptable, or even illegal responses to vulnerability and dependency. In many of the Canadian stories and novels I analyse, the responsibility to care appears as a difficult, often overwhelming burden that characters seek to escape or evade. My discussion of the fiction of care begins with Margaret Atwood's 2006 collection of connected stories,[1] *Moral Disorder*. This collection grapples with the complicated ethics of obligation arising from a wide variety of caregiving scenarios, exposing the conflict between selfishness and sacrifice that can often arise within the praxis of care. While some stories were published earlier and separately, gathering them in this single collection produces a unified interrogation of the praxis of care. Indeed, the need for care dominates these stories: the narrator or protagonist cares for a variety of family members, friends, strangers, and even animals. But in these stories the demands of care are never quite met, and none of the characters thrive as a result of the care they receive. I read the collection as a literary contribution to ethics of care discourse that draws attention to the losses and harms that can come with obligation. In this chapter I explore how and why caregiving is so often hazardous in these stories and what the problematic situations these stories convey say about the larger philosophy of care, including but extending beyond their literary contribution.

Atwood and the Ethics of Fiction

Atwood herself has described "fiction writing" as "the guardian of the moral and ethical sense of the community," a form "through which we can see ourselves and the ways in which we behave towards each other, through which we can see others and judge ourselves" (*Second Words* 346). Many critics have drawn attention to the ethical dimensions of Atwood's works, which grapple with conflicts between witnessing and participation (Staines, Hollis), "engagement and escape" (McWilliams 130), art and life (Grace; York, "Over All"), and silence and storytelling (Merivale, Stein). Sexual politics have always been central to Atwood's fiction, and her early works, such as *The Edible Woman* and *Surfacing*, often depicted the "heterosexual relationship as warfare" (Somacarrera 49). As I discussed in the introduction, gender is a central concern for ethics of care theorists, many of whom are quick to draw attention to the determining force of gender in relations of care. Critics of the ethics of care philosophy argue that feminist celebrations of care threaten to reinforce gender roles that align women with the family, with service and subordination. For example, Raja Halwani highlights the potential for care to tip over into self-sacrifice or abuse, and the ways in which "caring is … often used to shield morally dubious activities from scrutiny" (Halwani 2). Philosopher Sarah Hoagland and others worry that the associations between women and caring implied by ethics of care theories such as Gilligan's risk reinforcing oppressive social systems. Indeed, women are particularly susceptible to exploitation since patriarchal culture has typically associated women with maternity, nurturing, and a "natural" predisposition to care work. Peta Bowden explains that many feminists criticize ethics of care philosophy and "stress the damage that female carers have suffered from the relations of domination and exploitation in which their caring has been practised, and argue that the feminine values of care are little more than the symptoms of subordination and dependency, weak ego boundaries, and an inability to act autonomously" (8). However, dismissing care as a mere reinforcement of limiting gender roles risks jettisoning the intimate labour necessary for survival and the affective bonds that are central to identity. The disparity between the philosophical obligation to care and women's actual encumbrance with dependency work can create an impasse for any woman seeking to be a caring subject, rather than subjected by caregiving.

The stories of *Moral Disorder* depict a protagonist mired in such a struggle, trying to find a balance between the trap of feminine domestic responsibility that threatens to engulf her and the drifting identity of a solitary existence devoid of care. While gender hierarchies and the debilitating "female" roles and expectations imposed upon the protagonist are fundamental to the many moral dilemmas of *Moral Disorder*, the collection also explores obligation as a human problem with the potential to transcend gender difference. Despite a shift from first- to third-person narration, I regard the stories as focusing on a single protagonist, interpreting the unnamed narrator of the early stories and "Nell" in the later stories as one and the same. The consistent chronology and familial organization throughout the stories reinforces such a reading. In the early stories, the unnamed narrator seeks to live a life of independent self-sufficiency divorced from responsibility and obligation, but discovers that she cannot avoid the demands of care. As she submits to such demands her identity becomes more visible: she is named, positioned as a sexual partner and stepmother to two young boys. The namelessness of the narrator in the early stories is a further representation of the malleability of subjectivity, especially for subjects labouring in enforced familial relations of care.

The struggle to avoid ethical responsibility in *Moral Disorder* echoes the interrogation of interrelational identity and ethical obligation in Atwood's 1981 novel *Bodily Harm*, which concerns a freelance journalist, Rennie Wilford, who flees a failed relationship, and a threatening home invasion for the "neutrality" and "invisibility" of work by taking a travel-writing assignment in the Caribbean (7). Notwithstanding Rennie's efforts to remain detached from her surroundings, she becomes enveloped in the island's dangerous political struggles. The narrative charts Rennie's inadvertent awakening to the consequences of relationality and responsibility, culminating in an extended, gruesome prison scene in which Rennie's cellmate is tortured. After the torturers depart, Rennie is left alone with the bleeding, abject body, which she seeks to avoid, "pick[ing] her way carefully around the outline of Lora, the puddle on the floor" (298). But despite her aversion, her desire "to throw up" (300), Rennie goes to the woman, the injured body's urgent need for care overpowering Rennie's visceral inclination to detachment. The novel pares ethical relations to their core, focusing on the primary, "bodily" demands made by one person on another. It concludes with this harrowing scene of the absolute perversion of care (torture, imprisonment, denial of sustenance) that initiates an awakening to responsibility. The obligation represented by this particular body becomes fundamental as Rennie draws a connection between the pulpy, repulsive object before her and a suffering subject: "it's the face of Lora after all, there's no such thing as a faceless stranger, every face is someone's, it has a name" (300). Rennie responds to this particular woman's need, despite her previous dislike of Lora, holding Lora's hand between her own: "She holds the hand, perfectly still, with all her strength. Surely, if she can only try hard enough, something will move and live again, something will get born" (300). In the novel's final pages, which alternate ambiguously between the wretched cell and Rennie's anticipated rescue, images of Lora's hand recur, a reminder of Rennie's obligation to others: like the "shape of a hand in hers ... like the afterglow of a match that's gone out. It will always be there now" (301). This is inescapable, unending ethical responsibility: "She will never be rescued. She has already been rescued. She is not exempt" (303). This final awakening to a lack of exemption signifies an acknowledgment of the kind of embeddedness and interrelationality that ethics of care philosophers stress as integral to subjectivity. But the violent catalyst that precipitates this awakening posits an unsettling correspondence between suffering and ethical insight.

Moral Disorder suggests that relational identity and the obligation it engenders may be both desirable and debilitating in its exploration of everyday, familial scenarios of need and care. To participate in the ethics of care, that is, to respond to the needs and demands of others is both necessary and dangerous; in these stories the self is often harmed by caring, but refusing the demands of care can also be harmful. Ethical response, Atwood suggests, involves a redistribution of suffering, reducing the pain of another via adoption of that pain. In *Moral Disorder* perfect compromise is impossible because pain, trauma, and obligation cannot be extinguished, only reassigned. Suffering is unavoidable, but transferable. Atwood's stories engage with the ethics of care by drawing attention to the harms concomitant with caregiving. Care and the relations it creates result in ethical aporias, impossible scenarios in which benefits and losses teeter back and forth, never achieving balance. This lack of balance is borne out in ethics of care discourse. Though many ethics of care critics may stress the "mutual recognition and realization, growth, development, protection" that caring relations can, and perhaps should foster (Benner et al. xiii), as Kittay, Bubeck, Held, and others make clear, entrenched power imbalances contribute to the denigration of care labour – what Kittay calls "dependency work" – and its labourers. Ethics of care philosophers must have a kind of double vision, conjuring a mode of being that incorporates relational identity while at the same time keeping a critical eye trained on the marginalizing, denigrating structures of care within a culture that idealizes autonomy and self-reliance. As Held explains, "the ethics of care envisions caring not as practiced under male domination, but as it should be practiced in postpatriarchal society, of which we do not yet have traditions or wide experience" (19). Without such a tradition, "harms and vulnerabilities ... accrue to those who do dependency work" (Kittay and Feder 3). Atwood's stories confront such "harms and vulnerabilities," evoking ethical quandaries in which characters feel compelled to choose between the self and the other.

Atwood's stories model a compelling theory of care relations as necessary and unavoidable, but also distressing and debilitating, thereby deepening readers' understanding of the difficulty of care in their depiction of particular, and particularly vexed scenarios of care. The stories engage with ethics of care philosophy, exposing the grim imperfection of care relations, the challenges and losses, the complex conditions of human life that philosophers of care aim to make sense of. In their detailed specificity, the stories provide the context, the relational dynamics that elude ethics of care philosophy despite its stress on the contextual, the particular.[2] Rather than simply exemplify philosophical positions, fiction like *Moral Disorder* deepens our understanding of care, its meanings and repercussions, contributing to its theorization by embodying the tensions inherent in "dependency work." In particular, Atwood's collection addresses the problem of responding to the suffering of others, rehearsing a central ethical dilemma: How does one reconcile the needs both of others and the self? Is the integration of such needs even possible? The text seems doubtful about the prospect of converging, mutually beneficial needs, suggesting there is inevitably a hierarchy, a subjugation of self or others. The collection's title points to the centrality of moral dilemmas in the text and provokes the questions, what is moral "order," and what are the effects of its disarray?

"Bad News" and Its Distribution

The opening story, "The Bad News," draws attention to the problems that arise in everyday experiences of suffering and helplessness that engage the desire to care, but provide no clear direction for action. Reporting on the pain of others "arrives in the form of the bad-news paper" (1), a document whose dire announcements have corporeal consequences: it "burns" the narrator's husband; it has "calories" and "it raises your blood pressure" (2). To expose oneself to its contents is to risk personal safety. Stories of distant assassinations and abuses of power, must be "absorb[ed]" by the narrator (2), helpless as she is to act on behalf of foreign sufferers. But bad news makes further demands; though the primary victims may be distant, the damage of such news produces new sufferers in the form of estranged witnesses, such as the narrator's husband, Tig. In effect, the damage is distributed between the narrator and Tig, and as a result, she cares for him by absorbing the "bad news" that pains him. *Moral Disorder*'s opening story quickly establishes care as an imperfect arrangement in which care can as easily increase pain as relieve it. For Atwood's narrator, giving care involves the absorption of another's pain, a strategy with distinct risks for the caregiver.

This first story introduces the strain of "embedded," "encumbered" identity (Held 15), and serves as the collection's touchstone, employing both realist and fabulist modes to draw attention to the central moral dilemmas that reappear throughout the stories. In this story the narrator is confronted by the pain of distant others, by suffering she is helpless to prevent or assuage. The story depicts the dilemma of ethical response: the protagonist feels the pressure to care for unseen others, but recognizes the impotence that comes with being aware of the suffering of distant others. She venomously rebukes those able to disengage from this suffering via abstraction:

> there's been bad news before, and we got through it. That's what people say, about things that happened before they were born, or while they were still thumb-sucking. I love this formulation: *We got through it*. It means dick shit when it's about any event you personally weren't there for, as if you'd joined some *We* club, pinned on some tacky plastic *We* badge, to qualify. (3)

Abstracting the suffering of others to the effects of large historical and political patterns is a strategy that protects the comfortable witness from involvement with the actual sufferings of others. Personal engagement, physical presence is, for the narrator, essential to ethical response. The story echoes Atwood's prose poem of the same title from 1992, which imagines "bad news" as a winged creature awaiting the mayhem and violence that will bring her to life (*Good Bones* 5).[3] *"Better them than you*, she whispers into your ear" as "you" read the paper (emphasis in original 5) – the same sentiments the narrator rails against in the story "The Bad News" and Rennie finds spurious in *Bodily Harm*. The story is like the poem in providing what Patricia Merivale describes as "both a riposte and a partial solution to the problem of living with 'Bad News'" (256). Though the story's narrator castigates those who cast aside the upsetting reports as insensitive and selfish, she is well aware of the limited options available to those wishing to engage with their contents. The situation echoes a famous line from Atwood's 1981 poem "Notes on a Poem That Can Never Be Written": "witness is what you must bear" (*True Stories* 69). Once again, in "The Bad News," the narrator is relegated to the role of impotent witness, protected from harm but freighted by guilt:

> We've dealt with the bad news, we've faced it head on, and we're all right. We have no wounds, no blood pours out of us, we aren't scorched. We have all of our shoes. The sun is shining, the birds are singing, there's no reason not to feel pretty good. The bad news comes from so far away, most of the time – the explosions, the oil spills, the genocides, the famines, all of that. There will be other news, later. There always is. We'll worry about it when it comes. (*Moral Disorder* 6)

A distant witness is helpless to alter disturbing events and though the narrator refuses to dismiss the suffering of others, she has no tools to affect it directly. Instead, she employs representation to call attention to suffering, making stories bear witness.

"The Bad News" concludes with an embedded story that recontextualizes the bad news, employing narrative to render it simultaneously universal, personal, and particular. The fable depicts the narrator in Roman-occupied Glanum in the third century when the barbarian invasion remains a distant threat, though rumours of the invader's cruel tactics – burning "wicker cages" filled with victims (9) – have begun to circulate. But such a remote danger is easy to cast aside; the luxury of distance allows the narrator to focus on the beauty of the day, with its flowering fruit trees and thyme-scented air. Distance is protection: "they're very far away. Even if they manage to cross the Rhine, even if they aren't slain in thousands, even if the river fails to run red with their blood, they won't get here for a long time. Not in our lifetime, perhaps. Glanum is in no danger, not yet" (9). "The Bad News" ends here, a fitting preface to the following stories, which depict characters grappling with danger, dependence, and responsibility both impending and remote. The Glanum story involves the transformation of abstract reports into a particular scenario. Bad news will impose itself despite the characters' efforts to ignore it; as we, the story's readers, know, the Barbarians do indeed come and the empire does fall. In a sense, the story dramatizes a shift in perspective from the impartial, abstract "justice morality" to the personal, particular morality of care. But Atwood complicates the simple moral lesson that particularity is necessary for ethics. In effect, "The Bad News" conjures a narrative of particularity to critique the shoulder-shrugging helplessness of those unmoved by media reports while at the same time suggesting that regardless of our attempts at empathy, care, and aid, human suffering and cruelty continues.

The "Art" and Labour of Care

The collection's second story, "The Art of Cooking and Serving," appeals directly to the service aspects of care, highlighting the often indistinguishable division between caregiving and care-taking. The narrator, now eleven, is forced to tend to her "expectant" mother whose "dangerous condition" demands constant aid and attention: "Something terrible might happen to her – something that might make her very ill – and it was all the more likely to happen if I myself did not pay proper attention" (12). Such "attention" involves a great deal of labour when the narrator and her mother are left alone at a remote summer house on an island while the narrator's father is away: she sweeps the floor, pumps the water, scrubs the clothes, weeds the garden, carries in the wood, "all against the background of my mother's alarming passivity" (15). Caring for her helpless, lethargic mother translates into constant, anxious toil; the threat of "the dangerous thing – whatever it was – [beginning] to happen" is terrifying and ominous (17). The narrator's responsibilities and obligations are overwhelming and alarming since she is unsure of how to implement her concern for her mother, how to enact her desire to protect her. The demands of care remain abstract; though the narrator's labour is apparent and substantial, there is little sense that her work is appropriate, appreciated, or even acknowledged.

The narrator's desire for principles and rules for care inspires the story's title, which refers to a care-taking guide that fascinates and comforts her (17). She is particularly distracted by the first two chapters of this guidebook, "The Servantless House" and "The House with a Servant," which provide "strict ideas on the proper conduct of life" (18). The narrator respects author Sarah Field Splint's sureness and control – "She had rules, she imposed order" (18) – and envies Splint's servant, who appears in photographs demonstrating appropriate attire for both daytime and dinner. She admires Splint for her ability to lay down clear, unalterable rules for behaviour, and the servant for having such rules to follow (19). Outside the ordered world of the "art of cooking and serving" text, the art of care is abstract, shifting, and often ineffectual. Actually giving care, the narrator discovers, with dismay, is demanding, often unrewarding labour.

The image on the 2006 hardcover edition of Atwood's collection points to the importance of the elusive, enticing vision of domestic care offered by Splint. The dust jacket features the photographs of the servant from the actual guidebook, *The Art of Cooking and Serving*. The images are side by side below the title, *Moral Disorder*, which appears in bold red type. The words and images hover over a faded and stained blue background, imitating the look of a well-worn book, hinting at the otherwise invisible labour of the posed servant in her impeccable daytime and dinner uniforms. The cover design illustrates a central tension within the stories between representations of ordered, recognizable, remunerated care, and the disordered, often unrecognized and ineffectual labour of care the narrator experiences.

Autonomy vs. Responsibility

Once the narrator's sister is born in the story "The Art of Cooking and Serving," the demands for care increase, heightening the conflict between her own desires and the needs of others. Her sister refuses to sleep, wailing endlessly the moment she is put down and the burdens of the infant's constant demands inscribe themselves on her mother's body: "From having been too fat, mother now became too thin. She was gaunt from lack of sleep, her hair dull, her eyes bruised-looking, her shoulders hunched over" (21). Maternal caregiving is materialized as a never-ending labour that distorts the female body, debilitating it through excess; "too fat" and then "too thin," the mother's body is determined by the needs of the child. The mother's vulnerability demands caregiving from the narrator, who consequently becomes what Kittay terms a "transparent self," "a self through whom the needs of another are discerned, a self that, when it looks to gauge its own needs, sees first the needs of another" (*Love's Labor* 51). As Kittay explains, the burdens of dependency work bleed outwards, creating "secondary dependency," that is, dependency in the dependency worker (46). Initially, the narrator responds to her mother's dependency, adopting the labour of rocking her sister and singing to her, as well as assisting with household chores (21). But over time she becomes irritated by such responsibilities and resists what Kittay describes as the "nested set of social relations" necessary to support dependency workers (70). Refusing to become a "transparent self" whose identity is fashioned by the needs of another, the narrator rejects her mother's call for assistance, seeking to replace "nested" social relations with a model of individualization that severs the ties of obligation: "'Why should I,'" the narrator replies to her mother's request for help. "'She's not *my* baby. I didn't have her. You did.' I'd never said anything this rude to her. Even as the words were coming out of my mouth I knew I'd gone too far, though all I'd done was spoken the truth, or part of it" (emphasis in original 23). Her outburst triggers a slap from her mother, but the narrator feels relieved and released rather than hurt or regretful. In her refusal of responsibility the narrator tries to reject the gendered burden of care, familial obligation, and insists on autonomy, which she associates with freedom, mystery, and magic. The story's final paragraph describes the narrator's flight from obligation in which she trades the drudgery of care for the magic of independence:

> I … felt set free, as if released from an enchantment. I was no longer compelled to do service. On the outside, I would still be helpful – I wouldn't be able to change that about myself. But another, more secret life spread out before me, unrolling like dark fabric. I too would soon go to the drive-in theatres, I too would eat popcorn. Already in spirit I was off and running – to the movies, to the skating rinks, to the swooning blue-lit dances, and to all sorts of other seductive and tawdry and frightening pleasures I could not yet begin to imagine. (23)

Autonomy comes with a price. To be free she must sever her bonds with her family; she must become selfish. The story's conclusion reflects the "disorder" at the heart of the collection, exposing the price of independence and freedom, those conditions so valued by North American culture. This moral choice is between the self and other(s), which *Moral Disorder* presents as an impossibly binaristic either/or proposition. Despite her fantasies of a life of carefree pleasure, the narrator realizes that she will be unable to choose this life at the exclusion of her life of obligation: she would still be helpful "on the outside"; she "wouldn't be able to change that about [her]self." Here Atwood complicates Kittay's "transparent self" by demonstrating its recalcitrant pull. Even in the act of selfish rebellion, the narrator's capacity to be helpful, to provide care, cannot be left behind.

These conflicting impulses imply the impossibility of integrating the needs of others and of the self; instead a hierarchy of care emerges. In the final moment of "The Art of Cooking and Serving," the narrator chooses herself over others, but acknowledges it as a "dark" choice with as yet unknown repercussions that promise to be "tawdry," "frightening," and pleasurable. She makes a self-consciously selfish choice, choosing to overlook prescribed gendered familial feelings in favour of the alluring freedom from obligation, a typically masculine prerogative: "I ought to have felt hurt, and I did. But I also felt set free" (23). Hers is not an "ordered" response to her mother's call for help. In turning away from obligation, the narrator is at once fleeing from and succumbing to a patriarchal system that erases a fundamental aspect of human identity, a contradictory tension that becomes increasingly problematic in the stories that follow.

In the third story, "The Headless Horseman," the narrator reflects on the repercussions of her refusal of dependence and responsibility. Her insistence on autonomy has resulted in an estrangement that she conveys with an image of a floating, detached existence: "I lived in a sort of a transparent balloon, drifting over the world without making much contact with it … the people I knew appeared to me at a different angle from the one at which they appeared to themselves … the reverse was also true. I was smaller to others, up there in my balloon, than I was to myself. I was also blurrier" (25).

In her attempt to protect herself from the "transparency" that threatened her in the "The Art of Cooking and Serving," the narrator remains barely visible, blurred by estrangement. The passage evokes identity as a function of human relations, which the narrator discovers only via her retreat from interconnection. Her subsequent difficulties call to mind philosopher Kelly Oliver's claim, drawn from Hegel's lord and bondsman metaphor, that dependence and independence are paradoxically entwined, each one producing the other: "It is only by acknowledging that I cannot possess others or the earth, that they are independent of me, that I can become *independent* through the acknowledgment of my dependence upon them" ("Subjectivity," emphasis in original 324). For Oliver, subjectivity results from recognizing one's simultaneous separateness from and obligation to the world:

> Subjectivity depends upon recognizing the independence of the world and others. More than this, one's own independence requires acknowledging one's indebtedness to the world and others ... [T]his dependent foundation of subjectivity brings with it an ethical obligation to the world and others. Dependence is not a sign of a lack of freedom or a lack of agency; and independence is not total disconnection from others and the earth. Insofar as subjectivity is produced in, and sustained by, our relation to the world and others, an ethical obligation lies at the heart of subjectivity itself. (324–5)

In these terms, the wilful estrangement of Atwood's narrator from the world and its responsibilities produces a predictable alienation and distortion of subjectivity. For Oliver, "subjectivity and humanity" depend on what she calls "response-ability," that is, "the ability to respond and be responded to" (*Witnessing* 91). The transformation of "responsibility" into "response-ability" enables a "double sense" of both "opening up the ability to respond – response-ability – and ethically obligating subjects to respond by virtue of their very subjectivity itself" (91). By avoiding engagement with others so far as she is able, the narrator disrupts her response-ability and with it her subjectivity; just as others are difficult to discern from her removed position, so too is she "blurred" by her detachment.

In "The Headless Horseman" the adult narrator, accompanying her sister to care for their now ailing mother, looks back at episodes of care and need in her sister's childhood. Ironically, this sister, whose infuriating demands helped inspire the narrator's turn away from responsibility and connection, recognizes the necessity of responding to others in need. The narrator recalls spying on her young sister and her friend, Leonie, as they conducted a tea party with dolls. She is mystified by the dutiful care they provide for the lopsided papier-mâché head the narrator made for a Halloween costume years earlier. But as her sister and Leonie explain, there is a distinct difference between affection and care:

> "We don't *like* him,' said my sister.
> "We're taking care of him," said Leonie.
> "He's sick," said my sister. "We're the nurses."
> "We're making him feel better," said Leonie. (Emphasis in original 36)

Her sister distinguishes care as separate from affection, perceiving care as a necessary chore. Although, in some sense, her younger sister achieves a compassion the narrator has become unable or unwilling to assume, this care, like most in the collection, is impotent. The obligated labour of care produces no tangible benefit; the inert head cannot absorb or appreciate the efforts made on its behalf. The narrator's sister recognizes the obligations of interdependence, the "response-ability" that "lies at the heart of subjectivity," but her efforts, like all attempts at care in Atwood's collection, remain stunted and dubious.

The narrator continues to resist the bonds of care as she ages into adulthood. The life of independence she longs for, one free of responsibility and commitments, is finally achieved in the collection's fifth story, "The Other Place," which depicts her "wander[ing]" around Vancouver, living a "dislocat[ed]" existence (77, 78). She loathes the prospect of feeling "trapped, stagnant" (78), and avoids dependence of any kind. She owns very little, has few friends, and her love affairs are purposely brief. She avoids and resists any commitments and responsibilities, fleeing at the first sign that demanding bonds are forming. And yet, despite all these efforts to ward off domesticity, she finds her "desire for fecklessness" competing with a "shameful desire" for a "normal" life of gendered family commitments (79–80). In the end, she finds herself responsible for an acquaintance, a friend of a friend, who begins appearing at her apartment. This man, Owen, a relative stranger, draws the narrator back into the world of relationality, compelling her to engage with his silent presence: "He had a desolation about him that I couldn't account for" (86); "He wasn't demanding anything from me, but he didn't seem to be offering anything either" (86–7). However, the narrator's description of Owen's lack of expectation is an oversight, since Owen demands her company and attention, and "his muteness" proves "more exhausting than any conversation might have been" (87). These silent evenings continue until Owen finally makes his testimony, obliging the narrator to be his listener, becoming what Sho-shana Felman calls an "involuntary witness" to his narrative of child-hood trauma (Felman and Laub 4). He relates the story of how his three older brothers tried to kill him when they were children by shutting him in a disused icebox (87). The narrator feels the urge to "respond in some emphatic way, declare a firm position, reach out a help-ing hand" (88), but she finds herself unable to say more than "that's terrible" (88). After this testimonial Owen never returns and the nar-rator imagines that he has used her to deposit his suffering: "possi-bly he'd done what he'd wanted to do: dropped off his anguish, left it with me like a package, in the mistaken belief that I would know what to do with it" (88). By imposing the role of witness on the narrator, Owen unwittingly initiates her reintroduction into the world of human involvement, and by extension, confirms her status as subject according to Oliver's model of witnessing.

Owen's traumatic tale clings to the narrator, who finds his suffer-ing converging with her own life in unexpected, unsettling ways. The image of "a little child being suffocated, or almost suffocated," an image of profound, almost deadly isolation, a child cut off from the world, becomes "inseparable" from her own memories of early adult-hood, a time of restless solitude. This solitary past remains divided from the life that follows, one of relationships and commitments, and continues to haunt her. In this "other place" her "dreaming self" "continues to wander, aimless, homeless, alone" (89). The isolation of independence she sought becomes a frightening entrapment, a life of permanent solitude that threatens to overtake her: "This is where I'll have to live, I think in the dream. I'll have to be all by myself, forever. I've missed the life that was supposed to be mine. I've shut myself off from it. I don't love anyone. Somewhere, in one of the rooms I haven't yet entered, a small child is imprisoned. It isn't crying or wailing, it stays completely silent, but I can feel its presence there" (89). In her frightening vision, there is no communication, neither responsibility nor "response-ability," only an unconfirmed awareness of distant, seemingly inevitable suffering. The fantasy of autonomy and inde-pendence has become a nightmare of helplessness and incarceration. This reversal evokes the central philosophy of the ethics of care: the human being as relational, and the giving and receiving of care as essential to both survival and identity. Without such connection, the narrator is stuck in "the other place," a place where, devoid of human relations, she herself becomes other.

"The Other Place" marks a transition in the narrative voice. It is the final story told by a first-person narrator before a set of four stories narrated in the third-person. This "I" that speaks throughout the first set of stories is eager to assert herself as autonomous, unencumbered, and unembedded, yet fearful isolation is the result. In the following four stories, "Monopoly," "Moral Disorder," "White Horse," and "The Entities," the protagonist is no longer nameless and no longer solitary. The third-person limited narrative perspective names the protagonist, "Nell," and situates her within a network of relationships. The more Nell engages with others, the more she is, often reluctantly, bound by obligations. And though her ambivalence towards the demands of others remains, she no longer flees responsibility. In many ways, this process follows the *Bildungsroman* path of development, demonstrating a transition from innocence and self-centredness to maturity and responsibility, and McWilliams considers the collection "Atwood's most elaborate renovation of the Bildungsroman yet" (129). Nell's development also connects the stories to the gendered path of moral development Gilligan outlines, in which the central transition is from egocentrism to "a reflective understanding of care as the most adequate guide of the resolution of conflicts in human relationships" (105). However, Nell registers this awakening to the inescapability of obligation as a disturbance, rather than enlightenment. The Nell stories illustrate the imperfections within relationships of care and the unsettling frequency with which they can transform into relationships of harm.

Messy Care, Ordered Destruction

The four stories narrate Nell's move from the city to a dilapidated farmhouse with her lover, Tig. As the pair accumulates domestic animals the repercussions of caregiving are exposed: sustenance and suffering in animal relations are often simultaneous, even interdependent. At the opening of "Moral Disorder," the second of the Nell stories, Nell and Tig sit and watch as their ducklings are scooped up by an owl and taken to her nest, where they are torn apart and fed to the young (116). The animal world displays the mercilessness of caregiving, exposing care as a redistribution of goods that is never simply positive and productive.

Initially, Nell is optimistic about the farm's promise of abundance and fertility. She imagines herself as a selfless provider who will generate sustenance for Tig and his two sons. She plants a garden, envisioning "an overflowing of fecundity," picturing herself at the centre as one of the "fruitful goddesses" Demeter or Pomona.[4] But her happy idyll overlooks the suffering within her mythic allusions: Demeter is as much a symbol of loss as abundance, since she is known primarily for the kidnapping of her daughter, Persephone, by Hades, god of the underworld. It is this abduction that leads Demeter to withhold her powers of fecundity, causing crops to whither and die. Her violence and pleading finally have an effect and her daughter is returned to her, but only for half of the year. The Demeter myth is fundamentally one of compromise; Demeter must settle for a reduction of her unhappiness, as opposed to its elimination, forced to share her daughter with her kidnapper.[5] As "Moral Disorder" continues, these undercurrents of the Demeter allusion become manifest in the loss and destruction that accompany fertility. As the local farmers ruefully put it, "if you're going to have livestock, you're going to have dead stock" (122).

Farm life vividly demonstrates that the ability to provide care has both responsibilities and risks. In "Moral Disorder" the needs of the truly dependent – domestic animals – lead to conflicting obligations in which the care for some means the suffering of others. Caring for animals proves to be exhausting, often bewildering labour in which the care is aimed at assisting a creature to thrive in order to allow for its destruction. "Susan the cow went away in a truck one day and came back frozen and dismembered," a process Nell imagines as a "magic trick" in reverse (131). The inverted "magic" of transforming "livestock" into "dead stock" culminates in the story's final scenes. When a lamb is rejected by its mother, Nell assumes its care, cradling and singing to the animal in spite of herself (135). But when the lamb grows strong and begins to challenge Tig, charging him when his back is turned (137–8), Tig convinces Nell that the animal is too dangerous to keep. Because the lamb trusts only Nell, it falls to her to lure the creature to the spot where Tig waits with a rope. As they lift the lamb into the trunk of their car he kicks, struggles, and bleats; Nell has become the abductor, like Hades stealing Persephone from her mother's company: "Nell felt as if they were kidnapping the lamb – tearing him away from home and family, holding him for ransom, except that there wouldn't be any ransom. He was doomed, for no crime except the crime of being himself" (138). They drive the lamb to the abattoir, a gruesome place where Nell discovers skinned cows' heads in barrels as she searches the premises for an employee. The space gives off "a sweet, heavy, clotted smell, a menstrual smell" (139), further aligning feminine fertility and destruction.

The double symbolism of blood as both a source of life and a sign of (often violent) death is grimly manifest in the slaughterhouse where animals are killed in order to sustain human life. This bloody compromise echoes the story's earlier depictions of uneven care, emphasizing the imperfect alignment of obligations in which one responsibility interferes with another, just as Nell's commitment to Tig's safety and welfare requires an abandonment of the lamb's care. Finally Nell locates the proprietor of the slaughterhouse, a man who appears "as in some old comic book about torturers in the Middle Ages … He had an apron on, or maybe it was just a piece of grey canvas tied around his middle. There were brown smears on it that must have been blood. In one hand he was holding an implement of some kind. Nell did not look closely at it" (140). The man responds to her cries of "hello" with "Help you?" (140). In his response help is recast as harm since his aid will involve the lamb's slaughter, a reversal of meaning that is like the inverted magic of Susan's dismemberment. This reversal of meaning resonates throughout the collection, exposing the repercussions of caring and caregiving, of countering artificially neat principles of justice-based approaches to morality with the "messy" details and particularities of care.[6]

The story concludes with an ironic neatness that depicts the unsettling alternative to disorder. The lamb returns from the slaughterhouse in a "white oblong cardboard box" (141), dismembered for consumption. Inside the box, Nell discovers the lamb's body has been "neatly arranged" into discrete parts: "tender pink chops, the two legs, the shanks and neck for stewing. There were two little kidneys, and a delicate heart" (141). Violence and destruction have produced a hitherto elusive order. Despite her sorrow, Nell cooks the lamb and enjoys the meal, regarding herself as a cannibal (141). The act of cannibalism represents the most extreme perversion of care since it involves destroying another for one's own sustenance. The farming stories undermine any hope of a moral order, or at the very least, ordered care, in their exposure of the destructive elements of caregiving. Care on the farm is provided with destruction specifically in mind, since farming's purpose is ultimately to transform animals into objects, imposing a deadly order. But Canadian culture does not regard such behaviour as immoral, quite the opposite. Indeed, Nell feels little regret while consuming her lamb, reflecting on her "cannibalism" with "odd detachment" (141). In the end, the ideal role Nell imagines for herself is one of grim responsibility. She envisions becoming a woman to be "called in emergencies," one who would "roll up her sleeves and dispense with sentimentality, and do whatever blood-soaked, bad-smelling thing had to be done" (141). That which "ha[s] to be done" is violent and repugnant, but necessary nonetheless. In "Moral Disorder" caregiving involves a hierarchy of needs, privileging particular others and unevenly distributing resources. Care involves devotion and "odd detachment" in equal measure. In her characteristically Gothic terms,[7] Atwood depicts cannibalism as a perverse aspect of care, sacrificial blood as the family's nourishment.

Storytelling as Caregiving

The collection's final two stories return to the first-person narrative voice, the narrator now a mature woman who has raised her own child and faces the needs of ailing parents. In "The Labrador Fiasco" and "The Boys at the Lab" the narrator is a self-conscious storyteller, reciting well-worn narratives to soothe first her father, and later, her mother. She tells both her parents stories they already know and cherish, confirming their knowledge, their pasts, in effect, their existence. The "Labrador fiasco" refers to a tale of doomed exploration that her father relishes for its proof of his own expertise. The "boys at the lab" are prominent characters from the narrator's mother's favourite memories, memories the narrator attempts to revive through storytelling. The narrator tells stories she heard as a child, recounting events she never witnessed, but absorbed through photographs and conversation. Storytelling appears as a species of care with the potential to restore subjectivity to the object of care; the narrator observes that "in the end, we'll all become stories"(188). If stories are indeed the matter of identity, telling and listening to stories represents an essential part of acknowledging, establishing, and even restoring subjectivity. *Moral Disorder*'s final stories depict characters at the end of their lives and the narrator's efforts to comfort, if not necessarily revivify the dying with stories integral to their identities. Afflicted by disease and disability, disoriented and detached from the world, the narrator's parents continue to respond to the narratives that have made them. By returning stories integral to her parents' subjectivity, the narrator finally fulfils the role of witness, using storytelling to give care. The narrator's storytelling seeks to restore what Oliver, building on Dori Laub, calls "the inner witness," the interactive sense of self necessary for thinking, talking and taking action as an agent (*Witnessing* 87). In this sense, having dialogic interaction with other people is what makes dialogue with oneself possible: "The inner witness, then, is the structure of subjectivity as address-ability itself, the structure of witnessing" (*Witnessing* 87). The narrator's mother's curious habit of writing in a diary that she would then methodically destroy (210–11) speaks to the power of the "inner witness"; writing one's story, even if it will be never read, attests to the *possibility* of a reader, a witness to confirm the subject's status. The narrator recites stories that she recognizes as essential to her parents' sense of self, thereby confirming their subjectivity both in returning the integral tale, and performing as a witness, assuring her auditors that she has been listening to their addresses throughout the years. The narrator recognizes the preservative effects of witnessing: "Simply being watched ... had a protective effect, and so I kept an eye on my parents. It made them safe" (210). Witnessing is a form of caregiving that preserves and respects the subjectivity of the other.

But, as usual in this collection, efforts at care are never exclusively consoling. In "The Labrador Fiasco" and "The Boys at the Lab," storytelling comforts the characters whose disabilities interfere with their subjectivity and at the same time provides the narrator, and the implied author, with the material necessary for her fiction. The storyteller is able to produce order and coherence out of the chaos of experience. At the collection's conclusion the narrator and implied author seem to converge in a distant observer whose watchful gaze is not so much protective or comforting as curious, even voyeuristic. In the end the narrator is an invisible witness, a transparent presence that casts doubt on her potential for caregiving. As she concludes the narration of her mother's past she must invent the stories her mother is no longer able to recall. As a result, "the fate" of the characters from her mother's stories is "now up to [her]" (223). In breaking through the diegesis to confront the reader with the necessity of narrative manufacture, the narrator exposes her multiplicity: she is not only a teller, but also a creator responsible for this final tale, and by implication, the entire collection. Her mother's brief mention of the presence of an "Indian from India" at the lab provokes the narrator to conjure the moment of this foreigner's uncomfortable arrival in the imposing Canadian wilderness (219). This final self-conscious storytelling echoes the Glanum story from "The Bad News," in which the narrator created a tale to rebuke those able to dismiss the pain of distant others. But here the creator is no longer a participant. Instead she is a secret, almost sinister observer and recorder of stories, watching events unfold like a spy:[8] "The Indian man looks back over his shoulder: he alone can sense me watching. But he doesn't know it's me: because he's nervous, because he's in a strange place" (225). Her shift from concerned witness to curious voyeur is a reorganization of priorities that makes her own satisfaction paramount.

Storytelling functions as care in *Moral Disorder*, but like all depictions of care in the collection, its effects are uneven and unpredictable. Care easily turns back on itself, good intentions manifested in self-serving action. Atwood's vision of care suggests a syllogism: care implies obligation and responsibility. Obligation implies inequality. Inequality implies harm. Therefore, care and harm are interrelated. But, according to philosophers of care, life, identity, and subjectivity are impossible without care and obligation.[9] If so, Atwood's "vicious circle" of care is unavoidable. Helping and hindering, liberating and burdening, care appears as part of an inescapable circle of dependence. Atwood's stories contribute to the discourse of care by embodying the particularities of the strife of care, the strain of dependency work, the messiness of care in action that so many critics have sought to illuminate through philosophical discourse. If philosophers of care attempt to provide guidelines for navigating the difficult, unpredictable terrain of responsibility and dependence, the ethical "ought," Atwood's stories show us the ethical "is," care incarnate, refusing to shy away from the competition and resentment, the danger and manipulation that are part of interrelational subjectivity. *Moral Disorder* confronts readers with the burden of responsibility, the pain of witnessing, the disorder of emotional attachment while simultaneously evoking the more disturbing alternatives: fecklessness, alienated detachment, and orderly dismemberment.

3 Caring for Relative Others: Alterity and Narrative in Michael Ignatieff's *Scar Tissue*

Like Atwood's *Moral Disorder*, there is a grim edge to caregiving in Michael Ignatieff's novel, *Scar Tissue*, a pessimistic sense that care and harm are closely related. Once again storytelling is integral to practices of care. However, in Atwood's stories the mysteries of care and ethical obligation are observed and explored, but rarely "solved" (indeed, solutions are not the goal, or at least, are understood to be a futile ambition), whereas solutions are the explicit purpose of the narrative in *Scar Tissue*. In Ignatieff's novel, care is inexorably bound to comprehension, a correlation at odds with the alterity of illness and mortality. The narrator's insistence on insight and understanding produces caregiving as an impossible responsibility that risks overlooking the practical needs resulting from illness and disability in its focus on philosophical analysis.

In this chapter I address the ethical implications of the novel's central relationship between the narrator and his ailing mother. In particular, I explore how the narrator's experience as caregiver affects his subjectivity by considering the novel in tandem with ethical theories that privilege witnessing, dependence, and interrelation as integral to survival and subjectivity. The narrator's reaction to ethical obligation presents a compelling test case for considering the confluence of responsibility and identity. In its self-conscious exploration of the painful, vexing convergence of theory and praxis in experiences of caregiving, the novel confronts the consequences of helplessness and responsibility, dependence and obligation.

Ignatieff's Politics of Care

Prior to 2006 Michael Ignatieff was a Harvard academic and a minor British celebrity known by many more for his TV appearances and his star-studded wedding guest list than for his political aspirations. But his entrance into Canadian politics in 2006 and ascendance to leader of the Liberal Party two years later gave him new visibility in his home country. Ignatieff's long absence from Canada – he lived outside the country for more than thirty years – was a primary source of criticism throughout his political career, often interpreted as a lack of attachment to Canada. In May 2009 the Conservative Party launched a series of attack ads that amplified these sentiments, depicting Ignatieff as a political outsider whose commitment to Canadian politics was new and untrustworthy. According to his opponents Ignatieff lacked dependability and experience, and they implied that he could not, or would not, meet the obligations demanded of a head of state. As their "Ignatieff: Just Visiting" advertisements claimed, "he's not in it for you or for Canada. He's just in it for himself" (*Ignatieff.me*). A glowing portrait of the author-turned-Liberal-leader that appeared in the *New York Times* provided Ignatieff with the opportunity to counter such depictions by emphasizing the satisfaction of engagement: "I'm [in Parliament] to be serious ... This is the only place I can be a participant, not a spectator. I've been a spectator, and now I'm in the boat fishing. That part of it, from a spiritual point of view, it feels good" (Konigsberg). However, accusations of self-involvement and disengagement haunted Ignatieff throughout his short-lived political career, which culminated in the dubious distinction of leading the Liberal Party during an election that produced the worst results in the party's history. As a result, he retired from politics in May 2011 and returned to academia.

In some sense, Ignatieff was easy prey for attacks questioning his sense of commitment since Ignatieff himself has explored the difficulty of ethical responsibility in his literary endeavours, both scholarly and fictional. Ignatieff's political aspirations initiated a new interest in his fiction,[1] often as a means of gaining insight into his notoriously elusive character. The year after he became leader of the Liberal Party, an overview of his novels and their plots appeared in the *Globe and Mail*, which insisted that one should resist the temptation to "read politics and autobiography into the three novels," while at the same time wondering whether Ignatieff "would echo the main character in *Scar Tissue* when he says about the books he has written, 'I know why they're no better than they are, whereas I can't begin to explain why I myself am no better than I am'" (Sutherland). The sense of inevitable failure present in this quotation runs throughout the novel, which treats the narrator's experience of caregiving as it recounts the narrative of his mother's illness and death.

Scar Tissue depicts a narrator struggling with the repercussions of problems that are the very opposite of the self-involvement and detachment derided by Ignatieff's political opponents. If, as Michael Stickings, Canadian correspondent for the *Guardian*, claims, Ignatieff's political weakness was his failure to "care deeply about this country," then Ignatieff's narrator's weakness might stem from caring too much. As Michael Valpy explains in his lengthy portrait of Ignatieff, which also appeared in the *Globe and Mail* in March 2009, many reviewers have interpreted the novel as autobiographical since Ignatieff's mother, Alison, died from Alzheimer's a year before its publication. But as Valpy points out, it was his brother, Andrew, not Michael, who was Alison's primary caregiver. By his own account, Ignatieff visited Andrew and Alison in Toronto once or twice a year (Valpy). Ignatieff seems to have preferred representation to participation, producing stories and articles about his mother's Alzheimer's that became a source of family conflict. In particular, Andrew has expressed his displeasure with Michael's quasi-voyeuristic treatment of the family's pain (Valpy). If, as Ignatieff claims, his writing about family is a "process of self-invention" (Valpy), then one might regard *Scar Tissue* as an effort to conjure the relations of care and responsibility that have disturbed and eluded him. Unlike his brother in the novel, who remains largely distant and unaffected throughout their mother's illness, the narrator struggles to locate a tenable position between spectatorship and participation as his mother's illness worsens, requiring more and more care.

Care and Redemption: Rescue Fantasies

The novel opens with the narrator's lament for the past, his reluctant reproduction of his memory of his mother's final moments of life, a recollection that plagues him with its meaninglessness. It is this haunting memory that provides the impetus for the narrative itself: he clings to the possibility that testimony may emancipate him, that storytelling may somehow "redeem this," and help him to "believe that the banal heartlessness of it all was not for nothing" (1). He longs to replace torturous recollections with comforting images of health, "when [his mother] was in her painting clothes, barefoot, sipping a beer, humming to herself, happy and far away. That is how she should be remembered" (1). The opening paragraph introduces both the narrative's subject and purpose: his vital, vibrant mother "must" be "rescue[d] from her dying, if such a thing can be done" (1). In this sense, the narrator engages storytelling as part of giving care, both to the person and her memory. Prefacing this opening remembrance is an epigraph by Milton: "So by this infirmity may I be perfected, by this completed. So in this darkness, may I be clothed in light." The lines introduce the novel's preoccupation with comprehension, the narrator's eagerness to shed light on the mysteries of illness and death. The quotation is a reference to Milton's blindness, thereby connecting Milton's hope for enlightenment through "infirmity" with the narrator's own redemptive quest for insight. The novel abounds with moments of self-reflexive vision, observations, gazes, and the language of eyes and blindness. Witnesses are often spectators, helpless to comprehend or assuage the suffering they observe. Whether produced by the uncomprehending stare of the narrating son or the mechanical gaze of medical equipment, in Ignatieff's novel sight fails to become the insight he desires. This failure of comprehension, which the narrator seeks to redress with his narrative of illness, a kind of fictional "pathography," in the terms of Anne Hunsaker Hawkins,[2] coincides with a perceived failure of care since, for the philosopher son, care depends on making sense of his mother's dementia-affected subjectivity. In his analysis of *Scar Tissue* as pathography, John Wiltshire stresses "meaning making" as a primary goal of the pathographic text since "mortal illness or medical crisis tends to represent the world's unmeaningness, its chaotic and incoherent quality, and this is a condition faced (though with differences) as much by the care-giver as by the patient. In the broadest sense, illness is the evacuation or stripping of meaning from both person and event. Under this duress, and challenged by this contingency, illness narratives are processes of meaning-creation" (413). For Wiltshire, "The need to create meaning, prevalent in the pathography in any case, becomes pressing when the patient, the very subject of the narrative, while apparently physically well enough, incarnates the disruption or bafflement of normal meaning-making activity, and seems in fact to be a different 'self' or to have lost the self that they were. The challenge of all illness experience may then perhaps be said to confront the pathographer of Alzheimer's with particular intensity" (413). *Scar Tissue* rehearses the "intensity" of Alzheimer's resistance to narrative meaning in painful detail as the narrator struggles repeatedly to transform the "unmeaningness" of his mother's illness into something comprehensible. However, this narrow interpretation of "meaning" and care as dependent on understanding relies on the possibility of an ordered comprehension that is at odds with the disordered obscurity of dementia, initiating a frustrated longing for impossible transformation that exacerbates his suffering and alienation.

The unnamed narrator's redemptive narrative quest reflects alchemical desires: the longing to transform suffering into philosophical meaning, mystery into clear truths, incomprehension and confusion into knowledge and insight. In this chapter I argue that the novel's recurring images of blindness[3] and sight reflect the narrator's consuming urge to redeem pain through narrative knowledge. But, I argue, in his desire to see and comprehend, the narrator risks transgressing the ethical obligation to respect alterity.[4] As Wendy Roy explains, "his own narrative, presented with the best of intentions, is thus revealed as patently inadequate in capturing the nuances of her life story" (48). I take Roy's characterization further to suggest that not only is the narrator's story "inadequate" in its efforts to re-create the mother's narrative, but in its obsessive quest for complete understanding it risks a kind of violence to both its subjects (mother and son). The narrator's obsessive need to penetrate his mother's alterity culminates in an absorption of otherness, an alienation from the world and a manic pursuit of "selflessness," what he calls "the strange joy of being utterly alone" (176). As he approaches the incomprehensible (dementia, illness, mortality), he retreats from interactions with others, severing the ties of witnessing and responsibility that Oliver regards as integral for subjectivity. I argue that the narrator's belief in care as comprehension results in obsessive, frustrated efforts at "adequation," Emmanuel Levinas' term for "the process by which the Other is rendered intelligible ('seen') through representation" (Meffan and Worthington 134). Caring for his ailing mother, the narrator confronts a dilemma: he can either deny dementia's unintelligibility and the alterity it imposes upon its victim, or he can lose himself in the mystery of illness, the alterity of mortality. The spuriousness of the duality is irrelevant to the narrator who remains trapped by an epistemological craving that sees him progress from denying alterity to absorbing it. His goal is to represent alterity and "redeem" it with narrative; but alterity cannot be comprehended or salvaged. Instead, the other's alterity when determined by dementia becomes increasingly assertive, confounding, and distressing, and rather than rendering the other intelligible, the narrator instead seems to absorb unintelligibility, becoming increasingly estranged from those around him. He observes his mother's illness and death, but his witnessing is single-minded, the desire for comprehension diminishing opportunities for the respectful, sympathetic listening that is fundamental to processes of testimonial.

Trauma, Witnessing, and Narrative Comprehension

As critics such as Cathy Caruth, Shoshana Felman, Dori Laub, and Kelly Oliver have demonstrated, the witness occupies an integral role in the process of coming to terms with trauma. Trauma, the experience beyond comprehension that returns to haunt its victim, is connected to storytelling since it is, in Caruth's terms, "always the story of a wound that cries out, that addresses us in the attempt to tell us of a reality or truth that is not otherwise available" (*Unclaimed* 4). The difficulty of "knowing" trauma is integral to the dynamic of the witness and the survivor. The victim must tell "not only the reality of the violent event but also the reality of the way that its violence has not yet been fully known" (*Unclaimed* 6). In a sense, a tolerance of incomprehensibility is vital for the witness since the traumatic experience is one that surpasses understanding and can only be expressed and interpreted obliquely. Victims tell stories in order to survive. As Dori Laub explains, "there is, in each survivor, an imperative need to *tell* and thus to come to *know* one's story, unimpeded by ghosts from the past against which one has to protect oneself. One has to know one's buried truth in order to be able to live one's life" (emphasis in original 63). But witnessing is a daunting, even disturbing responsibility since it involves listening to suffering that can be neither discarded nor transformed. In other words, the witness can become a vehicle, hollowed by his or her role as receptacle for another's pain. Levinas constructs the witness as such a hollow instrument of the other, one who "testifies to what was said by himself. For he has said 'Here I am!' before the Other; and from the fact that before the Other he recognizes the responsibility which is incumbent on himself, he has manifested what the face of the Other signified for him" (*Ethics and Infinity* 109).[5] Levinas' exacting vision of the survivor/witness relationship echoes his larger claims regarding the ethical responsibilities of the subject, the all-encompassing obligation of the self to the vulnerable other. For Levinas, subjectivity is predicated on obligation and debt, reflecting his belief that selfhood is attached to an awareness of responsibility. Such obligation can be refused, but the refusal brings its own repercussions: "The other haunts our ontological existence and keeps the psyche awake, in a state of vigilant insomnia. Even though we are ontologically free to refuse the other, we remain forever accused, with a bad conscience" (Levinas and Kearney 27–8). *Scar Tissue* depicts both the demands of obligation concomitant with selfhood, and the torment that results from the impossibility of meeting those demands.

Oliver adopts Levinas' association of subjectivity with responsibility to buttress her claim that witnessing occupies a central position within the creation and maintenance of human identity, or as she puts it, "witnessing is the essential dynamic of all subjectivity, its constitutive event and process" (*Witnessing* 7). For Oliver and others, witnessing is primarily an act of attention, of listening and accepting, an attestation of presence before the other that confirms the subjectivities of both the witness and the other. She refutes theories that insist upon the autonomy of subjectivity, claiming, against "Enlightenment notions of autonomy," that "our subjectivity or our sense of self or agency is dependent on relations with others"; in other words, autonomy is "an illusion" (*Witnessing* 4). But Ignatieff's narrator depends on "Enlightenment notions of autonomy," a belief in the primacy of independence for subjectivity that makes him particularly vulnerable when relations of dependency and care intrude on his fantasy of independence. The belief in an enlightened self runs aground in experiences of trauma and witnessing.

Central to trauma and its treatment is "its enigmatic core: the delay or incompletion in knowing, or even in seeing, an overwhelming occurrence that then remains, in its insistent return, absolutely *true* to the event" (Caruth, "Trauma," emphasis in original 5). It is this inscrutability, this belatedness and unpredictability that plagues Ignatieff's narrator, whose witnessing of his mother's suffering and death caused by a particularly disorienting illness, transfers the trauma of illness to the victim's caregiver. Despite all his efforts to organize and interpret the narratives of his family life and the suffering of his loved ones, he is frustrated by the inevitable incongruence that results. Shoshana Felman explains, "As a relation to events, testimony seems to be composed of bits and pieces of a memory that has been overwhelmed by occurrences that have not settled into understanding or remembrance, acts that cannot be constructed as knowledge nor assimilated into full cognition, events in excess of our frames of reference. What the testimony does not offer, however, is a completed statement, a totalizable account of these events" (Felman and Laub 5).

Ignatieff's narrator sets himself the impossible task of discovering and delivering just such a "completed statement." He seeks such "assimilated," "full cognition" in a variety of ways, adopting various philosophical poses in hopes of an epistemological fit. But the inassimilable illness thwarts his every attempt at comprehension.

Seeing Suffering: The Caring Eye

Scar Tissue's narrator wants witnessing to perform an empirical function, to produce knowledge of the value and meaning of the damaged body before him via the workings of sight. He appeals to what Foucault identifies, in *The Birth of the Clinic*, as the "suzerainty of the gaze" (4), a glorification of the visual stemming from nineteenth-century medicine. Foucault traces the effects of this empiricism on pathological discourse, that is, the assumption that "illness is articulated exactly on the body" (4), a focus on physical clues and signs that ignores, even silences the suffering subject. Within this relatively new medical discourse, "the eye becomes the depository and source of clarity; it has the power to bring a truth to light that it receives only to the extent that it has brought it to light; as it opens, the eye first opens the truth: a flexion that marks the transition from the world of classical clarity – from the 'enlightenment' – to the nineteenth century" (xiii). The belief in such a penetrating, enlightening gaze haunts Ignatieff's narrator whose philosophical training conditions him to seek logic and rational answers, to satisfy "philosophy's love of tidiness" (Goldman 814).[6] According to these models, the medical gaze should enlighten and explain by exposing hidden truths: "The residence of truth in the dark centre of things is linked, paradoxically, to this sovereign power of the empirical gaze that turns their darkness into light" (Foucault xiii–xiv). The metaphorical image of knowledge as a light shone on a "dark centre" recalls *Scar Tissue*'s epigraph, Milton's hope that illness may provoke illumination. According to this empirical ethos, care, particularly medical care, involves looking, seeing, knowing. In other words, caregiving involves illuminating the darkness of illness with the bright, clear light of diagnosis.

Many illnesses have an element of impenetrability, but dementing diseases such as Alzheimer's produce a particularly persistent, and often devastating obscurity. Alzheimer's and its attendant dementia provoke anxiety as harbingers of memory loss and the erosion of identity. In *Scar Tissue*, despite the narrator's desire for comprehension, gazes rarely glimpse truth or clarity; instead, knowledge is repeatedly thwarted by the opacity of the disease. Though the majority of people who reach old age will not suffer from dementia, awareness of its debilitating power casts a heavy shadow. The aversion to dementia provokes Christine Cassel, former president of the American College of Physicians, to label "dementing illness ... the single most powerful factor in the negative attitudes about aging that occur in our society and throughout the world ... The stereotype of the elderly person as inevitably 'losing it' is an enormous barrier to progress in productive aging" (x). Alzheimer's and other illnesses causing dementia are alarming for their ability to disassemble, even eradicate memory, rendering subjects strangers to themselves and those who care for them. Ignatieff's narrator grapples with the profound impenetrability of dementia, which eventually overtakes his mother, his family history, and his personal identity in a cover of darkness that no inquiring gaze can penetrate.

Such obscurity and strangeness can have repercussions for practices of care. Philosophers of care tend to see the care relation as one of reciprocity and equality. Nel Noddings, one of the first to broach the subject of care from a feminist perspective, puts great value on the "responsiveness" of the cared-for who "accept[s] the gift" of care ("The Cared-For" 33). The "one-caring" addresses the "cared-for" as a "subject – not as an object to be manipulated" (33). For Noddings, and others,[7] caregiving enriches the life of the cared-for, who responds appropriately: "The responsive cared-for, in the fullness of the caring relation, feels the recognition of freedom and grows under its expansive support" (33–4). But of course such reciprocity is often impossible when providing care for victims of dementia. In *Scar Tissue* the narrator's mother can provide little acknowledgment of, let alone appreciation for, the care she receives. Even before the most dramatic symptoms of Alzheimer's have appeared, she feels alienated by the illness: "I am alone," she says, "not piteously, but in the unemotional voice she used of old when facing up to disagreeable realities" (49), sitting on the porch with her son. As the disease progresses, the narrator's mother often ignores his efforts at care and eventually ceases to recognize him as her son. Noddings insists that "a caring relation requires the engrossment and motivational displacement of the one-caring, and it requires the recognition and spontaneous response of the cared-for" ("The Cared-For" 38). Engrossment without response risks becoming self-sacrifice, which can undermine the caregiver's own selfhood. As ethics of care philosophers have noted, Noddings' definitions of care are problematic, particularly in their tacit reinforcement of traditional gender roles, but they are useful for interpreting performances of care in Ignatieff's novel. Engrossment is key in this text; to engross is "to absorb or engage the whole attention or all the faculties of" ("Engross," def. 6), and it is this total engagement that threatens to engulf the narrator. But despite his preoccupation with his mother's illness and its effects, his focus remains primarily introspective, making his engrossment an obsessive attention to his own relation to the sick and deceased, and the personal repercussions of these family changes. Dementia provides the occasion for uncanny vision, a distorted sight in which the object of the gaze is at once distinctly familiar and at the same time strange and incomprehensible. The impotence of the gaze to provide insight, knowledge, or assistance is a recurring trope in Ignatieff's novel, a pattern of frustrated empiricism that unsettles the narrator's philosophical foundations.

A preoccupation with knowledge and self-preservation appears early in the novel. Reflecting on the family's history of late-life dementia, the narrator employs an image of time-lapse ballistic photography to describe the movement of fate: "I think of it as a bullet leaving a smoking chamber, perforating the flesh of our ancestors, exiting in a spray and resuming its flight toward the expectant canopy of our skin. Thanks to genetics, we can see the bullet coming, estimate its likely impact and the path it will cut through our viscera. We can even calculate the pattern of the exit spray. The one thing we cannot do is duck" (6). The image illustrates the novel's ongoing tension between seeing and knowing, observing and understanding. The narrator longs for the impossible – to duck the bullet – and it is this impotence, this simultaneous seeing and blindness that plague him. He imagines the "new clairvoyance" of genetics, the ability to predict who will inherit diseases without the means to cure them (7). In addition to genetic "clairvoyance," there are many medical gazes able to predict the future. The narrator's brother, a neurologist, arranges for X-rays, CAT scans, and PET scans, imaging intended to show "where we are. How much time there is" (54). The narrator has misgivings about subjecting his ill mother to medical scrutiny, and he watches with dismay as she is led "naked and uncomprehending into a tiled room and sealed inside a machine" that will "measure cerebral activity" (55). The machine produces images of the neurochemical movement within her brain: "bright blue for the skull casing, red for the cerebral lobes, purple for the tracer" (55). The medical gaze is all seeing, producing a Foucauldian penetration of its object. But this gaze is at once all-powerful and impotent, since it provides awareness without any promise of amelioration. The gaze of the PET or CAT scans provides images without insight; the colourful scans of the narrator's mother's brain remain mere images, devoid of meaning since initially the narrative offers the readers no interpretation. This is the effect of the medical gaze, as Foucault explains: "The observing gaze refrains from intervening: it is silent and gestureless. Observation leaves things as they are; there is nothing hidden to it in what is given" (107).

Later, when a specialist attempts to provide the missing interpretation, the explanations are impersonal and unhelpful: "Your wife will be dead in three years" (57), she tells the narrator's father. The narrator is unsatisfied with the pronouncement since the diagnosis fails to account for the particularities of his mother as a subject, as more than a dehumanized "case," or object of scans. "You keep telling me what has been lost, and I keep telling you something remains" (58), he tells the doctor. But her response returns the conversation to the limited insight of the diagnostic gaze: "I just see what I see," she informs him, "from the clinical point of view" (58), the circular defence omitting knowledge and understanding, producing a proliferation of gazes without meaning. The narrator continues to resist this clinical vision of his mother, insisting that what the scans fail to record is that his "mother's true self remains intact at the surface of her being, like a feather resting on the surface tension of a glass of water" (58). The conflict between these two visions, the starkly clinical scans and the poetically ambiguous image of vulnerability, share a figurative approach to the other, both representing the patient indirectly. The doctor relies on metonymic interpretation, allowing scans to replace the person, while the narrator conjures a simile to represent his mother's identity. While different, both analyses attempt to encapsulate a subject in a particular visual image, transforming an absolute other into a relative other, a form of adequation, the other rendered intelligible through figurative representation.

Though Ignatieff's narrator rages against the dehumanizing clinical gaze, he, too, is removed from scenes of suffering. For example, early in the novel, while his mother is still living at home with his father, the narrator refrains from intervening as he witnesses his parents grapple with the painful, day-to-day struggles of both caregiving and care receiving. Awoken by scuffling noises in the next room, the narrator rises from bed and follows his parents from a distance as they shuffle their way down the stairs. He pauses at the landing and watches unseen as his parents begin to struggle at the front door: "At first I thought they were embracing … [but] she was fighting to break free of his grip" (74). He observes his mother's efforts to strike his father, their desperate thrashing transformed into theatre for a secret audience: they become "like two figures in a tragedy" (75) eventually falling to the floor with a groan. Throughout it all, the narrator remains hidden: "Too late to stop them, too late to lift them up, I stood on the stairs watching my parents sobbing on all fours in the dark" (75). The scene is an arresting demonstration of vulnerability and suffering that inspires a kind of inverted voyeurism in which the narrator spies on his parents not for pleasure, but for pain. He watches as a spectator, divorced from the drama that unfolds, grimly aware of, as well as somehow sequestered by, his inability to alter or assist those before him.

However, as the novel continues, the narrator shifts from uncomprehending spectator transfixed by the mysteries of illness and mortality, by the fallibility of the body and mind, into an obsessively devoted caregiver whose sense of self converges with the subject of his care. Initially, he perceives his mother as an afflicted other, but once his father dies and his mother is moved into an assisted-living facility, the narrator pledges his life to caring for her. His life is so singular in its purpose of providing care that he eventually abandons his obligations to his wife and children in order to assist his mother. He even has an affair with his mother's "intuitive," "gift[ed]" nurse (110), Miranda, following which he leaves his wife and children to live in a shabby apartment a stone's throw from his mother's new accommodation.

The narrowing of his focus extends to his professional life as well. He spends all semester teaching a single text, *King Lear*, in his philosophy class.[8] The play resonates with the narrator's philosophical inquiry into vision and recognition and his thwarted efforts to order and identify love, to see and know the intangible. In his discussions of Shakespeare's play, the narrator emphasizes the relational formation of identity, comparing Lear's final reach for Cordelia to "infants" who "grab a finger when it is extended to them. This is the primary identification process: the elementary awareness of an otherness to be reached for and held" (165). But his interpretation is ironic in light of his own experiences of care. Reaching out to comfort the other remains a challenge for the narrator whose own impulses have frequently prevented him from embracing his ailing mother, the incomprehensible other. For him, the other's alterity is a nagging problem that he longs to solve. For Ignatieff's narrator, "primary identification" goes far beyond comfort and care. The narrator's description of elemental responsibility echoes Kelly Oliver's insights regarding the relational structure of identity, what she labels, our "response-ability," that is, our human ability to witness and react to the needs of others ("Subjectivity" 327).

For Oliver, "It is the possibility of address and response that sustains psychic life and the subject's sense of its subjective agency … If the possibility of address is annihilated, then subjectivity is also annihilated" (327). But the narrator's interpretation of responsibility as the need to penetrate and assimilate otherness transgresses the role of responsible witness and becomes an impossible quest triggering his own descent into pathological alterity. In his mother's dementia he sees his own dissolution. When his mother eventually fails to recognize him, the narrator conjures an image of a famous ocean liner, the *Andrea Doria*, sinking "down through the ocean with its lights left on, blazing through the dark. The eyes that do not see, the eyes that have no memory, the eyes that are dead. I had arrived at the moment, long foretold, hopelessly prepared for, when Mother took the step beyond her self and moved into the world of death with her eyes open" (166). The mother's gaze is devoid of reason and knowing, and the son looks at her with no comprehension of her experience or subjectivity. She has moved "beyond her self," a severing of the ties of recognition, of response-ability and responsibility necessary for human identity, moving her into a remote space of isolation and alterity.

The narrator's mother's inability to recognize her son initiates a similar process of deterioration in the narrator himself, who begins to doubt his own identity as a result. Her inability to identify him becomes a personal dissolution and he senses that he is "all in pieces inside her; name, face, texture of skin, shape of my eyes, all tumbling over and over in the darkness of her mind" (163). Denied communication and insight, the narrator mimics his mother's removal from relational identity. After his mother's death, the narrator embarks on a crazed philosophical project examining the condition of "selflessness," attempting, in the process, to initiate his own freedom from selfhood. It is notable that his project explores an attitude often associated with the performance of care, that is, the selfless attention to the needs of another. But for the narrator, in accordance with his attitude towards illness and loss throughout the novel, his approach to selflessness is a self-reflexive inquiry into the personal repercussions of tragedy. This solipsism has a powerful antecedent when, shortly after his mother's diagnosis, the narrator conducts a morbid lecture on illness and death with his mother in the audience. The narrator cannot understand why his mother flees the auditorium as soon as the lecture concludes. He insists that his lecture was "about [his] own death, not hers," but his wife is more perceptive: "I don't care what you thought you were doing. Think about what it sounded like to her. You were saying to her, 'You are going to struggle, and it won't make all that much difference because you are going to die, and all of us are going to have to accept that'" (69–70). This solipsism recurs in his philosophy of "selflessness." His attempt to adopt his mother's pathology, to exist without selfhood, is an attempt to flee from responsibility by denying his very response-ability. As a self-less creature he is removed from the relational identity that comes with human dependence and obligation. His flight from others becomes a joy-fully manic escape as he transforms his disposal of interrelation and iden-tity into a quest for "purity" (176). "Selflessness" is the name he assigns to the manuscript documenting his growing obsession "with people vanish-ing, people walking out of their own lives" (174). He describes the project "filling the empty place in my day which had once been taken up in the nursing home," but also insists that the writing is in no way "a compensa-tion for anything, or … a working out of some unresolved emotion" (176) (unlike the novel itself, which is meant to redeem). Instead, he acknowl-edges only "enormous relief that the long ordeal was over. I suddenly felt the strange joy of being utterly alone" (176). The referent of "ordeal" has many possibilities: care for his mother; obligations to his wife, his girlfriend, his children – all of these responsibilities must be discarded to achieve the pureness of being he seeks. But the example he provides for "selflessness" and the "fullness of pure being," is one of degradation. He describes author Malcolm Lowry's final experience of "fullness" as he lay dying in an incontinent "heap," acknowledging that the silencing of the self came "at the cost of [Lowry's] sanity" (176). The narrator's failure to comprehend the illness and suffering he has witnessed (his mother's ill-ness, the deaths of both his parents) leads him to seek a territory beyond comprehension, going so far as to embrace the debasement that coin-cides with complete alienation. He longs to find a way to live without the knowledge or understanding that have failed him, without human connection, without response-ability and the obligation it engenders.

But the obsession does not last and he looks back on his "manic trea-tise" with embarrassment once he has abandoned his quest (179). He continues to live in his "efficiency apartment" from which he can "see the nursing home and [his] mother's room, now dark" (192). Despite such keen sight into the outside world, he has trouble recognizing or even discerning his own reflection since his "eyes have disappeared" (193). Instead he sees only "the shadows of two former faces" which hover "behind the outlines of my jaw, my eye, and my forehead. Now at last, as I look at the night reflections in the glass, I see Mother, Father, the faces of the dead" (193). In his attention to the details of his mother's deterioration his own identity has blurred so profoundly that he cannot distinguish himself from the former objects of his care. For the narrator, care is an all-encompassing dedication that hollows the caregiver, transforming him into a receptacle for another's needs, desire, even identity. This profound amalgamation leaves him struggling to carve out a discrete space of identity once the object of care has departed, wondering, "What was mine? What was the margin beyond inheritance?" (193). He longs, still, for enlightening vision.

Despite all his investigations, the blindness remains, blindness to identity, physicality, the "truth" hidden within the body. In his "dream of the transparent body" (194), he recalls the 1950s products, "The Visible Man" and "The Visible Woman," plastic models of the human body with transparent skin that allowed the user to both see and touch the internal organs. But this fantasy of transparency is possible only with imitations and the imagination. In his dealings with the living, empiricism fails him. His longing for comprehension butts up against the opacity of the body and its machinations, the mysterious interconnections of genetics and environment, history, identity, and biology. His desire to *know* the self and its inner recesses results in a refusal of the figurative; he wants all things to be as they appear, to avoid the slipperiness, the imprecision of metaphors and symbols, to "be done with metaphors … to see the thing itself" (194). This longing for the open, "visible" body is a desire for the literal, a trading of mystery and alterity for clarity and familiarity, and most importantly, for *knowledge*.

But time, change, and illness thwart perfectible knowledge. The novel's final pages address the problem of unknowing head on, encapsulating the desire for illumination, the frustration of ignorance, and the obsession with preserving the past. The narrator recalls a vivid scene from his time as caregiver when he brought his ailing mother a photograph of himself as a child, ostensibly to comfort her, though his desire for recognition and validation is apparent. But his mother's response to the gift is shockingly vicious:

> I wanted to pin this picture up on the bulletin board beside my mother's bed. I had already laid the pin in the centre of the top margin of the picture when I placed the photo in her hand. She held it there for a second and stared carefully at this image of a child who was once her son. Then with sudden, savage deliberation, she removed the pin and jabbed at the picture, puncturing both of my eyes. (198)

The narrator's interpretation is quick but shifting, changing in accordance with his philosophical perspective: "there was not a shadow of a doubt as to what she intended. It had been a blinding. Now, of course, I understand. If you hold the picture up to the light, radiant illumination streams through the eyes. It is the light streaming from the terrain beyond the gates of truth" (198). The narrator reincorporates his mother's expression of anger, confusion, resentment, appreciation, frustration – the list can go on and on, so mysterious is dementia – into his own themes of concealment and revelation, falsity and truth, protecting him from the opacity of alterity. The narrator's responses to the punctured photograph reflect his belief in limitless illumination and insight, his refusal to acknowledge the alterity of illness. Once again, an expression of care, giving his mother a photograph of her young son, initiates a process of self-reflection. In effect, the mother's illness functions as a catalyst igniting the flames of self-interpretation. It is not the image's eyes, but "my" eyes that are wounded by the pin. The narrator envisions his own future when he witnesses his mother's suffering.

The novel's final paragraphs treat the self and its miserable fate: "This room will soon become a prison. The doors will be locked … The faces of my wife, my children and my brother will blur, decompose and then reform into the image of jailers. My own hands, my own face, my own thoughts will seem alien to me" (199). In effect, his care for his mother becomes an exercise in gathering knowledge. Despite the defacement of the narrator's portrait, it is the mother whose image becomes distorted and then lost as the narrator effectively uses her suffering to anticipate his own. When he looks at her, it is his own fate, his own struggles and desires he apprehends. In this sense, the mother's photographic blinding suggests a profound and painful insight into her son's blind attention, an uncanny awareness of the implications of his care. His mother's story, which he promised to deliver at the novel's outset, has become his own narrative, his obsession with family inheritance[9] initiating the conflation of "she" and "I." The novel's final lines address the meaning the narrator has fashioned from his mother's illness, the conviction that he too will face the uncharted terrain of dementia's alterity. But even this vision of personal otherness incorporates what is known and understood; his projection of dementia transforms the familiar spaces of his childhood into the mysterious place of mental illness: "The night is warm. My feet are bare and the sidewalks will be dry and warm under my toes. I will walk out to the end of the railway line … I will see the lights of Alton and hear voices beckon … My fate has come to meet me. My voyage has begun" (199). In this sense, the narrator's blink-ered attention to his mother's care is part of a quest for self-discovery.

For Ignatieff's narrator, care is an all-encompassing activity, a dedi-cation of one person to another that verges on the devotional and pro-vokes Wiltshire to characterize the relationship as "pathological" (418). Certainly such devotion has serious consequences for the caregiver and the various relationships that contribute to his identity. Care becomes suspect as the narrator's attention to his mother becomes an exclusive focus, an inquiring gaze into his mother's illness that transforms into solipsism after her death, undermining feminist visions of care as mutu-ally beneficial. As we have seen, ethics of care philosophers, including Virginia Held, Eva Kittay, Nel Noddings, and others, typically regard caring as involving labour and relationships, as relational practices that emphasize mutual recognition and development, foster well-being, social bonds, cooperation, and as the productive result of human inter-dependency. However, Ignatieff's narrator approaches caregiving not as a means towards "well-being," but as an occasion for inquiry and exploration, regarding his mother's alterity as a "philosophical prob-lem" in need of an impossible solution (53), or, in other words, a story in need of redemption, as he explains in the novel's opening pages.

Though caring involves both givers and receivers, reciprocity is often limited by ability, and for many philosophers of care the emphasis is primarily on the needs of the other.[10] In her definition of "care," Diemut Bubeck describes it as "fundamentally other-directed and beneficial to others" ("Justice" 160). Care is a "labor, an attitude and a virtue," writes Eva Kittay ("When Caring Is Just" 259). Maurice Hamington concurs: care is *"committed to the flourishing and growth of individuals yet acknowledges our interconnectedness and interdependence"* (emphasis in original 3). But such unflagging commitment to the other can be at odds with modern glorifications of personal independence, making both dependence and devotion into identity handicaps. The struggle between caring devotion and self-protection appears repeatedly in *Scar Tissue* as the narrator attempts to negotiate the expectations of care as a "morally appropriate reaction to another's needs" (S. Miller 142). For Derek Attridge, encountering the other involves the "impossibility of finding general rules or schemata to account fully for him or her … the experience is an encounter with the limits of one's power to think and to judge, a challenge to one's capacities as a rational agent" (24). And though one may not comprehend or know the other, he or she will make demands, demands of responsibility and obligation that often exceed the capacities of the self. In *Scar Tissue* the narrator encounters the alterity of his closest relative, and the ensuing relations of dependence and responsibility challenge his own sense of self.

In *Camera Lucida*, Roland Barthes explores the uncanny status of the photograph, which evokes past and present simultaneously, allowing one to be at once object and subject: "the Photograph is the advent of myself as other: a cunning dissociation of consciousness from identity" (12). For Barthes, the photograph produces a kind of double vision as the viewer witnesses both the image and its genetic referents, the subject and its relations: "The Photograph is like old age: even in its splendor, it disincarnates the face, manifests its genetic essence" (105). As a result, photographs can provoke vertigo: seeing oneself in a photograph produces a blurring as one experiences being "neither subject nor object but a subject who feels he is becoming an object ... a microversion of death" (14). Though they are different genres, *Camera Lucida* and *Scar Tissue* share a mournful, reflective tone. Like the fictional conceit of Ignatieff's novel, Barthes wrote *Camera Lucida* in response to his mother's death. Encountering a photograph of his mother as a child Barthes "shudder[s] over a catastrophe which has already occurred. Whether or not the subject is already dead, every photograph is this catastrophe" (96). Photographs conjure death in their attestation of what "has been" and is no longer. There are echoes of Barthes in Ignatieff's unease with photographic traces, to which he confesses in his family memoir, *The Russian Album*, published six years prior to *Scar Tissue*. In *The Russian Album* he contrasts recollection with photographic evidence, lionizing the former as restorative, denigrating the latter as merely documentary: "Memory heals the scars of time," he writes, "photography documents the wounds" (7). *Scar Tissue* appears to continue this dichotomous interpretation: setting out to heal through narrative remembrance, it eventually stumbles over untreatable photographic wounds. In this case the "wounding" is literalized in the punctured eyes of the narrator's photographic self, an injury that speaks to the impotence of recollection to heal the wounds of dementia, a condition that manifests itself in the dismantling of memory. The defaced photograph calls attention to that which the narrator (like the author) would prefer to forget: that some wounds persist, deep and unhealable, refusing all efforts at care and repair. There are, perhaps, some wounds that demand our respect and nothing more.

4 "Parodies of Love": Demands of Care in Alice Munro

... helplessness ... was revealed as the most obscene thing there could be
– Munro, "Heirs of the Living Body"

If Ignatieff's novel is an effort to heal the unhealable, an exercise that leads to a dawning awareness of the indelibility of the wounds of time and illness, Alice Munro's stories conjure narratives of illness and disability outside any comprehensive epistemological framework. There are no narrative claims for healing or recovery in these stories, only attempts at investigation and exploration absent of recuperative goals. Here iteration is not a means towards comprehension but only a chance to tell what cannot be understood, or even fathomed: the exhausting, often appalling demands of corporeality. In this chapter and the following I explore bleaker features of caregiving, examining stories that depict highly ambiguous relations of care, in which the alignment of motive and action defies the hopeful interpretations supplied by philosophers such as Held, Noddings, and Kittay. In stories such as "The Peace of Utrecht," "Winter Wind," and others, the relentless cry of the sufferer often overwhelms the caregiving witness and the burden of response becomes an insufferable weight the caregiver seeks to avoid. Munro's fiction asks us to consider the ethically vexed dynamics of care through situations in which the impulses and "right" actions of care can appear in direct opposition.

Munro's Literature of Care

Munro, who turned 80 in 2011, has a writing career spanning six decades, culminating in the Nobel prize for literature in 2013. Her early works, particularly the connected short story collections *Lives of Girls and Women* (1971) and *Who Do You Think You Are?* (1978) garnered much critical attention as feminist explorations of identity that provocatively scrutinize the politics of gender and art. Critics have stressed Munro's commitment to the everyday lives of women, her unflinching investigations into the by turns suffocating and satisfying world of the domestic (Howells; Rasporich; Redekop; York, *Other Side*).[1] This preoccupation with gender, power, and responsibility has revealed itself in stories that depict women confronting ethical dilemmas in which the needs of the self come into conflict with the needs of the other, that is, stories rife with depictions of conflicted care. A number of critics have examined the ethical implications of Munro's work, in particular what the stories suggest about a writer's responsibility to her "material," both the work of fiction itself and the actual world that has inspired it.[2] Robert McGill considers the crises of responsibility in Munro's stories, teasing out the "relationship between ethical writing and ethical living" in "Material" ("Daringly Out") and the meaning of fidelity in "The Bear Came over the Mountain" ("No Nation"). Tracy Ware and Dennis Duffy examine another aspect of fidelity in their respective analyses of Munro's "Meneseteung," a story that unsettles the historical fiction genre by raising questions about the fiction writer's "responsibility to history" (Ware, "And They May" 68). While many Munro scholars explore the ambiguities arising from her self-reflexive narrative techniques that draw attention to fiction's art and artifice,[3] my own perspective is closer to that of Naomi Morgenstern, who analyses in Munro "crises of responsibility generated by ethical relations" (72). Morgenstern stresses the productive indeterminacy of Munro's writing, arguing that "her narrators and central characters provocatively resist final acts of judgment, leaving readers confronted by the complexities and impossibilities that characterize the ethical" (79). This chapter builds on Morgenstern's assertion, focusing on a particular, and particularly charged, ethical relationship in Munro's fiction, namely, the affiliation between caregivers and their charges.

In "Day of the Butterfly" (1968), a gift bestowed on an unpopular girl, Myra, becomes a socially valuable performance of care after Myra's social status surges when she is hospitalized for leukemia. On the opposite end of the benefits spectrum, in "A Queer Streak" (1986), Violet, the careful, pristine toiler who maintains the household for her slovenly sisters and parents, gives up the chance for marriage and escape in order to devote herself, martyrlike, to the very relatives who have spoiled her hopes of happiness. Violet's capitulation reaches a religious pitch as she regards succumbing to her family's needs as righteous surrender: "To give in. To give up. Care for them. Live for others" (232). The equation is clear: her devotion to her family is a renunciation of her own needs and desires. The extremism of her perspective is a chilling inversion of the ideal of mutually beneficial care, of "intertwined" interests, of care models based on an egalitarian balance of labour and benefits, egoism and altruism (Held 12).

Again and again in Munro's stories, both the feelings and actions of care appear as oppressive burdens borne by obliged caregivers. In "Monsieur, les Deux Chapeaux" (1986), 13-year-old Colin experiences a disturbing epiphany when he learns that his accidental gunfire has not, in fact, struck and killed his eccentric younger brother: watching out for Ross, Colin realizes, will "be his job for life" (83). Prior to the news of Ross' safety, Colin experienced a disorienting sense of elation as he considered the sudden disappearance of obligation signified by his brother's imagined death, the sense that "his life had split open, and nothing had to be figured out anymore" (82). As philosopher Annika Thiem explains, the inescapable, impossible responsibility experienced by the subject in response to the other's vulnerability and mortality can inspire murderous impulses: "While the other's demand cannot be silenced, the other's life remains precarious; the other can be killed. The other's death is not only a possibility but also a temptation" (105). Assured of Ross' health, Colin feels "dizzy and sick with the force of things coming back to life, the chaos and emotion" (83) of the rushing return of the duty to care. Emotional attachment and the dependence and obligation it engenders are repeatedly explored in Munro's work, including the stories "Memorial" (1974), "The Ottawa Valley" (1974), "Spelling" (1978), "Mrs Cross and Mrs Kidd" (1982), "Friend of My Youth" (1990), "Open Secrets" (1994), "The Bear Came over the Mountain" (2001), and "Queenie" (2001). In all of these stories, shifting allegiances and dependencies inspire ethical problems without clear resolutions. Even when caregiving roles are adopted voluntarily, the imbalances of power inherent to dependency work lead to resentment, exploitation, and distress.

In these stories, relations of care are frequently complicated by the introduction of a new character whose caregiving or dependency upsets established relational hierarchies.[4] For example, in "Mrs Cross and Mrs Kidd," a close bond develops between the title characters during their stay in a nursing home. However, their friendship and mutual devotion are interrupted by the arrival of Jack, a stroke victim confined to a wheelchair. Mrs Cross' attention shifts exclusively to Jack, the demands of his care estranging her from her friend. Mrs Cross' dedication continues until a new, younger woman, Charlotte, arrives and usurps Mrs Cross' position as Jack's caregiver. Mrs Kidd remains faithful to her friend and tries to help her recover from Jack's rejection and the loss of her role as caregiver. When Mrs Cross is too exhausted to walk, Mrs Kidd offers her own wheelchair, despite her own exhaustion, and she has barely delivered Mrs Cross to her room before she collapses. Mrs Kidd's care for her friend manifests as a transferal of resources and energy that leaves her helpless and incapacitated, prostrate on the hallway floor, "pray[ing] no nosy person would come along until she could recover her strength" (180). Throughout the story, relations of care shift according to gender, ability, and age,[5] reflecting the interaction of various forms of marginalization;[6] the power-prerogatives of masculinity, mobility, and youth interact to determine caregiving hierarchies. From Mrs Kidd's perspective, Charlotte, dutifully stationed at Jack's elbow, is "itching to be somebody's slave" (174), and she assumes that Jack will tire of the younger woman's obsequiousness since "slaves cost more than they were worth. In the end, people's devotion hung like rocks around your neck" (174). But Jack seems to feel no such weight under Charlotte's ministrations. Indeed, quite the opposite: given the opportunity, he aligns himself exclusively with Charlotte, rejecting his previous caregiver.

The story depicts the ease with which one caregiver is traded for another, suggesting an absence of reciprocity between caregivers and recipients of care, the obligation of the former far outstripping any commitment by the latter. As affection and alliances are developed and abandoned throughout the story there is a persistent hierarchy among caring subjects. As in many of Munro's stories, caregiving initiates, or perhaps merely exposes, power relations among subjects. Even in "Mrs Cross and Mrs Kidd," which is unusual in its depiction of an empowered dependent, there is an obvious correlation between authority and caregiving, since it is Charlotte's relative youth and ability that allow her to usurp Mrs Cross' position. Power hierarchies are ubiquitous and dangerous, lurking within all dynamics of care, whether familial or professional, private or public, voluntary or coerced. Munro's stories frequently blur such caregiving positions, evoking dependency work as a duplicitous, volatile, even sinister phenomenon that inevitably affects not only relations between subjects, but subjectivity itself as characters come to confront the conflict between the limitless vulnerability and demands of human dependency and the limited capacity of human response. Ethical responsibility destabilizes the subject – it "separates me from myself" (Blanchot 25); it unsettles the autonomous subject by exposing his subjugation to the other, his status as "hostage" to the other's needs (Levinas, *Otherwise* 117) – a disturbance that causes characters to recoil from, evade, disavow responsibility even as they continue to perform the actions of care. In Munro's fiction characters come to glimpse the acute vulnerability of the other and the impossible demand such vulnerability represents, evoking the hostility of Levinasian ethics: "For Levinas ... the ethical subject emerges in response to an accusation" (Thiem 113). The discomfiting extremism of this perspective, its overtones of "moral masochism" (112), is central to the ethical disturbances arising in Munro's work; it is this very struggle between the oppressive demands of the "hostaging" other and the (impossible) desire for separation and unencumbered identity that haunts Munro's characters. In Levinas' terms, "to be oneself, the state of being a hostage, is always to have one degree of responsibility more, the responsibility for the responsibility of the other" (*Otherwise* 117). The tension between caring and withholding in these stories presents the reader with the impossibility of "good" or "ethical" care, evoking a central clash between responsibility and self-preservation as the bleak heart of caregiving. These stories repeatedly put ethics of care to the test, demonstrating in practical terms the banal and essential, crushing, and empowering responsibility of one person for another.

Mothers and Daughters: Inversions of Care

The ethical quandary created by familial obligation announces itself early in Munro's oeuvre. In the final story of her first collection, a story Munro considered an important landmark in her literary career,[7] the ominous demands of care are immediately prominent. The story's central characters, narrator Helen and her sister Maddy, have a shared history of reluctant caregiving for their invalid mother, their "Gothic Mother" whose "raw and supplicating" cries for help continue to haunt Helen long after her mother's death ("The Peace of Utrecht" 200).[8] Their mother's needs create a shared past that separates rather than binds the sisters, locking each into private memories of humiliation and inadequacy. The story opens onto this gulf:

> I am afraid – very likely we are both afraid – that when the moment comes to say goodbye, unless we are very quick to kiss, and fervently mockingly squeeze each other's shoulders, we will have to look straight into the desert that is between us and acknowledge that we are not merely indifferent; at heart we reject each other, and as for that past we make so much of sharing we do not really share it at all, each of us keeping it jealously to herself, thinking privately that the other has turned alien, and forfeited her claim. (192)

This opening passage evokes what Shoshana Felman terms the "scandal" of illness,[9] the shame and outrage that stem from "the eruption of an evil that is radically incurable – is itself somehow a philosophical and ethical correlative of a situation *with no cure*, and of a radical human condition of exposure and vulnerability" (Felman and Laub, emphasis in original 4–5). For the sisters at the centre of Munro's story, the shared experience of witnessing their mother's suffering and helplessness and the supplication that resulted are part of a traumatic history that both long to escape. Their shared humiliation as children of an afflicted, bizarre, even monstrous mother is a history of shame, fear, and cruelty that is at once engrossing and repellent. Helen, entering the house after many years away, expects to hear "the cry for help – undisguised, oh, shamefully undisguised and raw and supplicating … A cry repeated so often, and, things being as they were, so uselessly, that Maddy and I recognized it only as one of those household sounds which must be dealt with, so that worse may not follow" (201–2). The mother's cries are "shameful" in their blatancy, laying bare her "scandalous" illness, her helplessness and need. The mother's disease eviscerates the construct of autonomy and self-sufficiency.

In Munro's work anxiety frequently attends moments of dependency, as the epigraph for this chapter demonstrates. The quotation appears in "Heirs of the Living Body," a story in which multiple forms of dependence and vulnerability confront the young narrator, Del Jordan. There is the vulnerability of the mortal body, painfully apparent in the story's various corpses, which include a cow and Del's Uncle Craig, whose funeral provokes the story's climax. There is also the cognitive vulnerability, demonstrated by Del's cousin, Mary Agnes, who, though "not an idiot," the narrator assures the reader, suffers developmental delays on account of being "deprived of oxygen in the birth canal" ("Heirs" 43, 44). This is the explanation supplied by Del's mother, an explanation Del finds disturbing in its randomness: "I shied away from the implication that this was something that could happen to anyone, that I myself might have been blunted, all by lack of some namable, measurable, ordinary thing, like oxygen" (44). The possibility of association, of being like Mary Agnes, is a recurrent source of distress for Del since Mary Agnes' exaggerated vulnerability is a reminder of Del's own vulnerability, which she longs to deny. When her mother tells her how Mary Agnes was molested by five local boys who lured her to the fairgrounds where they "took off all her clothes and left her lying on the cold mud" (47), it is not the fact that this abuse caused a bout of bronchitis that nearly killed Mary Agnes that disturbs Del. Rather, it is the public exposure that makes her sick and reminds of her own moment of ignominy: "Having to be naked myself, the thought of being naked, stabbed me with shame in the pit of my stomach. Every time I thought of the doctor pulling down my pants and jabbing the needle in my buttocks, for smallpox, I felt outraged, frantic, unbearably, almost exquisitely humiliated" (47).

The anxiety attending moments of vulnerability is captured in Del's reaction to her Uncle's funeral. When Mary Agnes refuses to view the Uncle's corpse, Del bites Mary Agnes' arm in a moment of rapturous violence, an animalistic assertion of dominance – she tastes Mary Agnes' blood – that she experiences as "pure freedom" (63). She expects this unruly and hateful act to alienate her from her family, effectively liberating her from all future responsibilities. But, to her disappointment, she is simultaneously blamed and forgiven for her cruelty, an experience that produces a new, "peculiar shame" (63). This shame is more invasive and overpowering than the previous sensation; it goes "far beyond" her "former shame of nakedness; now it was as if not the naked body but all the organs inside it – stomach, heart, lungs, liver – were laid bare and helpless," a sensation that reminds her of being tickled "beyond endurance," a "horrible, voluptuous feeling of exposure, of impotence, of self-betrayal" (63). The experience ushers her into a distressing awareness of mortality, vulnerability, and the bitter knowledge that "to be made of flesh was humiliation" (63). Her revelation culminates in a grim epiphany: "helplessness … was revealed as the most obscene thing there could be" (64). Her new comprehension of the adult world of social codes and constructs is a comprehension of appalling vulnerability, of dependence as both unavoidable and repellent.

Helplessness, she realizes, despite its inevitability, must be hidden from view along with other indecent, corporeal habits.

Helplessness, like violence, sex, and bodily functions, is evidence of base needs and desires that must be concealed whenever possible to avoid shame and scandal. In their effort to skirt the taint of such indignity, the sisters in "The Peace of Utrecht" "grew cunning" over the course of their mother's illness, learning to enact "parodies of love" that concealed their "cold solicitude" (201).[10] But this show of care, the narration suggests, is transparent, since care without feeling fails to nourish: "we took away from her our anger and impatience and disgust, took all emotion away from our dealings with her, as you might take away meat from a prisoner to weaken him, till he died" (201). Many ethics of care theorists have insisted on the proper alignment of motive and action necessary for effective care. Munro's prisoner simile takes the association of feeling and action one step further, implying that the denial of emotion is actually a denial of care, a denial of sustenance that is in fact the opposite of care. In this story and others, Munro divulges the repercussions of uneven, ambiguous care, the paltry all-too-human responses to obligation and need that cast doubt on the viability of care as a superior ethical alternative to justice-oriented models.

Dependency, Attachment, and the Flight from Responsibility

The urge to withhold, to deny affection, is another symptom of the shame of familial attachments, according to Judith Butler, who interprets the "adult sense of humiliation when confronted with the earliest objects of love – parents, guardians, siblings, and so on – the sense of belated indignation in which one claims, 'I couldn't possibly love such a person'" as a response to the extreme dependency and attachment necessary for survival in early life (*Psychic* 8). The child has no option but to love his or her caregiver since "a child's love is prior to judgment and decision; a child tended and nursed in a 'good enough' way will love, and only later stand a chance of discriminating among those he or she loves ... [T]here is no possibility of not loving, where love is bound up with the requirements for life. The child does not know to what he/she attaches; yet the infant as well as the child must attach in order to persist in and as itself" (8). This unavoidable attachment is both known and unknown by the child, both existing and denied, and it is this "partial denial" of primary attachment that is necessary for the emergence of the subject (8). But this enforced attachment haunts the subject in adulthood as the subject comes to confront these childhood figures of love. The memory of childhood attachment is saturated with humiliation and scandal that threaten subjectivity: "The 'I' is thus fundamentally threatened by the specter of this (impossible) love's reappearance and remains condemned to reenact that love unconsciously, repeatedly reliving and displacing that scandal, that impossibility, orchestrating that threat to one's sense of 'I'" (8–9). Thus, the sisters in "The Peace of Utrecht" are doubly afflicted, forced to confront the "scandal" of their love for the mother, and at the same time made to witness the shamefulness of her dependence that forces them to become responsible for, in Felman's terms, the "radical human condition of exposure and vulnerability" (Felman and Laub 5).

As in *Scar Tissue*, "The Peace Of Utrecht" involves a reversal of roles in which illness transforms a parent into a dependent. Ailsa Cox sums up Maddy and Helen's joint response to their mother's increasing helplessness: they have "formed a partnership, reversing the power relationship between the generations. Their mother has been managed like a child, robbed of her adult autonomy by muscular and vocal paralysis" (22). But their partnership is based on shame and resentment, and the narration pays little attention to the subjectivity of the afflicted. For both characters there is an impulse to flee the needs of the vulnerable other their mother has become, though only the narrator is successful on this count, a success experienced as "a secret, guilty estrangement" (203). The desire to flee, even to injure the demanding other has precedent. In Thiem's account of Levinas, she draws attention to the conflict "at the heart of the subject formation" (106–7), namely, "the struggle between the call of the other and the temptation to forsake the other" (107). Freedom from responsibility is possible, Munro's story suggests, but it comes with a price; dependency produces an either/or distribution of benefits, allowing the caregiver or the care receiver to achieve satisfaction and fullness, omitting the possibility of conjoined interests. While the narrator removes herself from the scene of suffering, Maddy remains in the family home, finally succumbing to her own desire for freedom by institutionalizing their mother against her wishes. The narrator discovers Maddy's effort at escaping the burdens of care near the story's conclusion when their aunt eagerly divulges Maddy's betrayal, telling how Maddy lured her mother into the hospital where she abandoned her to medical care, the temptation to forsake the other proving irresistible. Aunt Annie testifies to the mother's suffering, a testimony the narrator wishes "not to be told," while at the same time anticipating the story of her mother's downfall: "what I would be told I already knew, I had always known" (210). For both sisters their mother's impossible needs remain inescapable even after her death, haunting the failed caregivers in their memories of resentment and humiliation. Maddy is trapped by guilt for her attempt at independence, an ironic turn in which her striving for unburdened autonomy has left her suffocated. "I couldn't go on ... I wanted my life" (212), she says, defending her actions to the narrator; yet she remains unable to take control (213), that is, to be responsible only for herself, despite the narrator's urging, and the story closes with her desperate, questioning appeal: "But why can't I, Helen? *Why can't I?*" (emphasis in original 213). Concluding with a rhetorical question may be further evidence that ultimately the locus of an ethics of care resides not in the answers to questions but in the very kinds of questions that are articulated in fictional narratives, questions that expose the provisionality of an ethics of care. This concluding, repeated question evokes the double bind of relational identity and the care it requires: caregivers suffer either the resentment and exhaustion of impossible responsibility or the guilt and regret of shirking one's obligation to the other's demands. Maddy's agonizing desire for autonomy is futile if one keeps in mind the theories of subjectivity supplied by Butler, Levinas, Oliver, and others, which, though varied, share an assertion that subjectivity is impossible without subordination and responsibility. In other words, there is no "my" life, no "I" without the call of the other. In this sense, the characters are doubly obstructed: first by structures of care that pit caregivers and dependents in an oppositional struggle, and second by the consequences of this struggle, the rejection of the dependent that omits the opportunities for witnessing and responsibility central to subjectivity. The story's open-ended conclusion suggests an impasse within the ethics of care, unresolvability as the legacy of responsibility and dependency.

In Munro's stories the demanding, relentless call of the other shakes the foundations of subjectivity; it provokes "an encounter with the frayed edge of meaning" (Morgenstern 88), with vulnerabilities and dependencies that outpace the abilities and comprehension of the responsive subject. Such an encounter inevitably affects the subject in profound, unsettling ways. Writing of Munro's story "Meneseteung," Morgenstern suggests that the protagonist is permanently disturbed by the bizarre call of the other: she "will never be the same again" (75). The call of the other is an "animal" cry of need, a "cry from beyond," at once human and animal, within and outside of language (78). The cry summons the subject to the realm of responsibility and obligation to a consciousness beyond comprehension, one that is strange, even threatening. Such is the cry that haunts Helen upon her return to her family home. Raw, useless, and shameful, the mother's cry is barely human to Helen, blending, as we have seen, with other "household sounds which must be dealt with, so that worse may not follow" (200–1). The call of the other, in this case, a close relative distorted and estranged by illness, inspires exclusively negative emotions: disgust tinged with guilt. Significantly, it is the sound of the cry that haunts the narrator, rather than memories of its human source – indeed there is very little description of the mother in the story and no sense of her perspective; her suffering remains entirely external, perceived through the lens of the resentful daughters as strange and unsightly. It is the narrator's failure to care "appropriately," to feel or act responsibly that clings to her. Both sisters are unable to rid themselves of the lost other's demands for care, the cries that they were unable, or unwilling to answer.

In "The Peace of Utrecht" and other stories, characters are frequently summoned by the call of the other, a call at once insistent and repugnant, a call that portends the realignment of personal structures of power. In heeding the call of the incapacitated other, the subject becomes both omnipotent and subservient; she has all of the ability and mobility the afflicted lacks, but in exchange for such relative privilege she becomes a kind of handmaiden. This rearrangement of authority and responsibility is particularly apparent in the story "Winter Wind," which deals, like "The Peace of Utrecht," with a reversal of familial roles – in this case, a child responsible for her disabled mother. The young protagonist's duty to care for both her mother specifically, and the household more generally, provides a responsibility that she resents and resists, yet secretly enjoys since authority brings freedom from the rules of childhood. In the story a blizzard prevents the narrator from returning to her rural home, where her invalid mother awaits. Instead, she is forced to stay with her tidy, doting grandmother and great aunt. At first, the order and warmth of the house are a welcome respite from home where "the only warm room there was the kitchen; we had a wood stove. My brother brought in wood, and left tracks of dirty snow on the linoleum; I swore at him. Dirt and chaos threatened all the time. My mother often had to lie down on the couch, and tell her grievances" ("Winter" 193).

But after a few days of clean and ordered living at her grandmother's house, the narrator is eager to return to her laborious and chaotic household. The power and authority of her responsibility call her home:

> My mother objected to things, but in a way I had the upper hand of her. After all, it was I who heated tubs of water on the stove and hauled the washing machine from the porch and did the washing, once a week; I who scrubbed the floor, and with an ill grace made her endless cups of tea. So I could say *shit* when I emptied the dustpan into the stove and some dirt went on the lid; I could say that I meant to have lovers and use birth control and never have any children … The loud argumentative scandalous person I was at home had not much more to do with my real self than the discreet unrevealing person I was in my grandmother's house, but judging both as roles it can be seen that the first had more scope. I did not get tired of it so easily, in fact I did not get tired of it at all. (202)

Here, scandalousness is an ironic pose, one of many the narrator adopts to suit her surroundings: at home she exploits her unusual empowerment in order to be outrageous; in public she adopts a demure aspect to avoid attention. In the end, "comfort palls" and the narrator is willing to give up all the pleasures and amenities of her grandmother's house "in order to be able to drop my coat where I chose, leave the room without having to say where I was going, read with my feet in the oven, if I liked" (202). The subordination demanded at her grandmother's house, that is, the enforced role of child, of dependent, is too cumbersome for the story's narrator. Once she has discovered the pleasures of control and domination, she cannot tolerate their loss. The needs of others have become her bargaining chips: the one who sweeps the floors can say what she pleases.

"Winter Wind" and "The Peace of Utrecht" provide visions of the irrevocable havoc initiated by reversals of responsibility (children forced to provide care for parents). In these stories and others, there is a sense of the traumatic repercussions of the consuming obligations initiated by illness and disability that plague both those who accept *and* reject the responsibilities of care. Munro conjures scenarios of caregiving that augment models of care provided by Nel Noddings, Carol Gilligan, and others that tie caring to engrossment, engagement, and harmony. While the positivity of such protocols has been tempered in more recent writings on care, with Eva Kittay, for example, conceding there is an "inequality of power endemic to dependency relations" (*Love's Labor* 33), philosophers of care consistently stress the undeniable "reality of human dependence" (Held 10) that makes care, both giving and receiving it, primary to human existence. And yet the inevitability of dependency is no assurance of harmonious care, and Munro's stories evoke the improbability, perhaps even impossibility, of mutually beneficial care. Relational identity and subjectivity based on responsibility cannot ensure responsiveness, and the desires to protect and destroy appear as part of the same ethical ontology. Caring certainly has the potential to "foster well-being in the midst of change, crisis, vulnerability, or suffering" (Benner et al. xiii); it may indeed involve an "intertertwin[ing]" of the caregiver and care-receiver's interests (Held 12) and be "committed to the flourishing and growth of individuals" in a manner that "acknowledges our interconnectedness and interdependence" (Hamington 3). It may be the case that "the fact of human vulnerability and frailty ... must function in our very conception of ourselves as subjects and moral agents" (Kittay and Feder 3); yet the undeniable anxiety and condescension precipitated by human dependency beyond the predictable periods of limited ability (childhood and advanced old age)[11] speak to the difficulty of valuing care and acknowledging fundamental human dependence and responsibility in a culture that celebrates autonomy and independence. Munro's fiction demonstrates how the "shamefulness" of vulnerability and need, the "scandal" of illness and disability tarnish the labour of care, tainting both providers and receivers of care.

The "Scandal" of Illness and Vulnerability: Care's Power Politics

As we have seen in the work of Atwood, Ignatieff, and others, care incarnate, that is, practical rather than abstract care, is infrequently, if ever harmonious; instead it is conflicted, competitive, even threatening and destructive. Even those philosophers who propose care as the ideal ethical framework for human relations acknowledge the problem of reconciling the association of dependence with weakness, a status with serious political consequences, with the promotion of care as a viable ethical model. As Benner and others observe, "caregivers are stained with shame because our society rejects any concept of interdependence" (Benner et al. xv). This "stain" is difficult, if not impossible to avoid in practical scenarios of care, despite efforts to rehabilitate the labour of caregiving.

Relationships of care and the needs that precede them inevitably expose structures of power and the many instances of caregiving depicted in Munro's stories are no exception. In these stories women gain power via caregiving, a power often leached from the receiver. The stories reveal power as a limited resource among women, one that is rarely shared, more often traded, borrowed, stolen. Munro's fiction suggests that caregiving relations are distinctly gendered, depicting the very limited and limiting means to power available to women. Caregiving women in these stories gain power by employing their authority and influence in ways that fail to correspond to patriarchal fantasies of selfless, nurturing femininity. The stories undermine claims, such as Nancy Chodorow's, that women are more empathetic than men. In these stories, the burdens of care tend to impede rather than provoke empathy, inciting resentment, exhaustion, a closing down of the affection and sympathetic identification necessary for empathetic response. It is worth noting that empathy itself is not without its critics suspicious of the ethical significance associated with affective response. For example, Suzanne Keen is dubious of the "empathy-altruism" hypothesis that assumes empathy leads to self-betterment.[12] As Keen explains in her treatment of affective reading practices, empathy, which implies an adoption of another's suffering, can actually provoke a "turning away from the provocative condition of the other," a rejection of empathetic distress (4). This problematic over-arousal of empathy is the cause of "compassion fatigue,"[13] a common affliction among medical caregivers and the like, leading, in the extreme, to outright rejection of the sufferer: "Too much empathy can lead to an aversion to the victims or to the source of information" (19). As Keen makes clear, even affective response is no guarantee of assistance: "While empathy has been demonstrated to contribute to moral reasoning and to altered attitudes about members of out-groups, it does not inevitably lead to just actions undertaken on behalf of others" (22). Keen's analysis casts doubt on straightforward cause-and-effect relationships between feelings and actions, between "caring about" and "caring for." In Munro's stories both affect and action are multiple, unpredictable, unreliable, even contradictory. As familial structures of care and responsibility are upset by illness and disability, the duty to care, both "about" and "for" becomes an exhausting assignment.

In Held's vision of care, "those who conscientiously care for others are not seeking primarily to further their own *individual* interests; their interests are intertwined with the persons they care for" (emphasis in original 12). Like Atwood's stories, Munro's fiction complicates the hope of such well-aligned motivations, depicting the day-to-day struggles of practical care, care imbalanced by human emotion. Munro's stories cast doubt on the possibility of "conscientious" care in their representation of the repercussions of care for both givers and receivers. In these stories relations of care are necessarily relations of power, a corollary that impedes the balance and harmony associated with successful care. Visions of harmonious relations between caregivers and care receivers are stripped away to reveal the repercussions of subjectivities constituted by power relations that evoke a Foucauldian vision of human relations in which we are all "both victims and agents within systems of domination" (Sawicki 10). Judith Butler expands on the "double aspect of subjection" that seems to "lead to a vicious circle: the agency of the subject appears to be an effect of its subordination. Any effort to oppose that subordination will necessarily presuppose and reinvoke it" (*Psychic* 12). Within Butler's model, with its echoes of Foucault and Levinas, the subject does not exist prior to power relations: "Power not only *acts on* a subject but in a transitive sense, *enacts* the subject into being. As a condition, power precedes the subject" (emphasis in original 13). The relational model of identity favoured by ethics of care theorists chafes against such a Foucauldian view, the former relying on the universality of dependence and care, the latter stressing the foundational structures of dominance and subordination. In a sense these two interpretations of human relations and the tension between them, between the impulse to assist and the impulse to dominate, reflect the ethical dilemmas at work within Munro's fiction.

Throughout Munro's early work, in stories like "The Peace of Utrecht," "Winter Wind," as well as others, such as, "The Ottawa Valley" (1974), "Spelling" (1978), "A Queer Streak" (1986), and "Goodness and Mercy" (1990), one finds reversals of caregiving roles, young women saddled with the responsibility to care for older family members. Munro's attention to power dynamics in mother-daughter relations turns Sara Ruddick's theory of maternal knowledge on its head. Anticipating Carol Gilligan's notion of "a different voice," Ruddick argues in favour of love-based knowledge gleaned through maternal devotion ("Remarks" 252). Ruddick is unflinching in assessing the unavoidable inequality within relations of care. "Rather than depending upon an illusory state of equality," Ruddick argues, mothers "aim to fight as they live, within communities that attend to and survive shifting differences in power" (253). Although Ruddick's claims are somewhat dated, their influence should not be underestimated. Held, herself a formative philosopher of care, cites Ruddick's 1980 essay, "Maternal Thinking," as the location of "the beginnings of the ethics of care" (Held 26). Held elaborates Ruddick's position, which elevates maternal experience, making it the ideal situation for fostering a moral outlook that favours peace. Both Held and Ruddick recognize that "mothering" which "aims to preserve the life and foster the growth of particular children and to have these children develop into acceptable persons" remains an ideal (Held 26). As Held notes, "the actual feelings of mothers are highly ambivalent and often hostile toward the children for whom they care, but a commitment to the practice and goals of mothering provides standards to be heeded" (26). Ruddick's theory relies on what Peta Bowden terms "attentive love," that is, on "emotionally engaged attention as an ethical activity that depends on responsiveness to the unique particularity of another person" (109). But in Munro's stories, the inversion of familial roles upsets a conventional morality of love, exposing an underbelly of desire for power, control, exclusion, and dominance that Ruddick seeks to exclude from feminine morality. In these stories of daughters forced to care for their mothers, the ideals of "maternal thinking" appear irrelevant to characters burdened by unexpected, unwanted responsibilities. As much as the ideals of feeling expressed by Ruddick represent a novel and potentially constructive approach to human relations, the practical burdens of dependency and obligation overwhelm the possibility of collaborative cooperation and positive love. For these characters forced to become dependency workers, the labour of care far outweighs its positive affective potential. The language of love and affection is largely absent from stories like "The Peace of Utrecht"; instead there is a shame, guilt, repulsion.[14] If, as Kelly Oliver suggests, "love is an ethics of differences that thrives on the adventure of otherness" (*Witnessing* 20), the adventure, for these children and young women, has become too wild, verging on nightmare. Stories like Alice Munro's "The Peace of Utrecht" and "Winter Wind" depict characters forced to move beyond clichés and platitudes of love, far beyond the manicured terrain of affection and respect, to the hinterlands of resentment and anger where the absolute otherness of loved ones becomes distressingly apparent.

5 Caregiving and Caretaking: Affective Economies in Alice Munro

The recurrent depiction of women grappling with the needs of others and the dubious empowerment such responsibility engenders, draws attention to the formative role of gender in larger discussions of the philosophy of care. As we have seen, the legacy of ethics of care scholarship is largely feminist and recuperative, that is to say it seeks to legitimize and elevate so-called feminine morality. In other words, ethics of care philosophy is largely committed to celebrating female experience and relationships. But, as many critics point out, and Alice Munro's stories demonstrate, the gendering of caregiving has serious ethical and political implications. The inevitable realignment of power structures that accompany dependency and obligation arising from illness and impairment has serious consequences for characters in Munro's fiction. Opportunities for dominance and control are rare for many characters, and the empowerment that attends one person's dependence on another can represent both stifling responsibility and a new chance for empowering authority. Exploring the gendered implications of care relations involving the rearrangement of responsibility, Munro's stories conjure dilemmas central to the philosophy of care: namely, how can women balance the demands of others with self-preservation in a culture that encourages and celebrates female selflessness? Indeed, does the recognition of identity as relational and responsibility as fundamental have serious risks for women? Do caregivers risk succumbing to patriarchal scripts of female subservience loathsome to women seeking to escape the bonds of domesticity? Munro's stories confront these and other ethical questions in their exploration of relations of dependency and care, exposing the disquieting aspects of care: the desire to dominate and exploit, the longing to flee and abandon those in need.

The unnerving aspects of caregiving that preoccupy Munro's fiction bear some resemblance to the negative implications of compassion that Lauren Berlant and others expose and analyse in her collection *Compassion: The Culture and Politics of an Emotion*. Berlant's investigation into the term suggests asymmetry is at the heart of compassion, both in its definition and practice. Berlant draws attention to the distance and power imbalance the term connotes: "In operation, compassion is a term denoting privilege: the sufferer is *over there*. You, the compassionate one, have a resource that would alleviate someone else's suffering" ("Introduction," emphasis in original 4). Compassion endows the compassionate subject with the pleasure of means, that is, the capacity to endow or withhold. It supplies the opportunity for self-satisfied rescue; it "measures one's value ... in terms of the demonstrated capacity not to turn one's head away but to embrace a sense of obligation to remember what one has seen and, in response to that haunting, to become involved in a story of rescue or amelioration: to take a sad song and make it better" ("Introduction" 7). Consequently, there is an "undertone" to compassion (9), since the relationship relies on inequality. There is always the possibility of denial:

> scenes of vulnerability produce a desire to withhold compassionate attachment, to be irritated by the scene of suffering in some way. Repeatedly, we witness someone's desire to not connect, sympathize, or recognize an obligation to the sufferer; to refuse engagement with the scene or to minimize its effects; to misread it conveniently; to snuff or drown it out with pedantically shaped phrases or carefully designed apartheids; not to rescue or help; to go on blithely without conscience; to feel bad for the sufferers, but only so that they will go away quickly. (9–10)

Munro's stories refuse to shy away from such "undertones" in their depictions of care, exploring the "desire to withhold," the refusal to engage with those in need. As Berlant suggests, opportunities for rescue offer subjects the power of choice, whereas caring response, according to both ethics of care philosophers and relational identity theorists like Kelly Oliver, is built into the mechanics of subjectivity as responseability. Training in compassionate action runs alongside what Berlant identifies as "training in aversion," since "when we are taught, from the time that we are taught anything, to measure the scale of pain and attachment, to feel *appropriately* compassionate, we are being trained in stinginess, in not caring, in not knowing what we know about the claim on us to act" ("Introduction," emphasis in original10). And although ethics of care philosophers stress the obligation to care as primary to existence and subjectivity, Munro's stories suggest that care and compassion are not so far removed from one another, that the compulsion to care is less compelling than we might wish, that calculation and choice play an unmistakable role in caring relations. The distinct pleasure of "rescuing" gained through care coupled with the perhaps unconscious impulse to withhold or limit care function in tandem within these portraits of conflicted, even sinister caregiving.

Such unsettling affective economies,[1] that is, systems of exchange that employ affective response as currency, are particularly obvious in Munro's many stories involving paid caregivers, typically "practical nurses," providing in-home care for ill or disabled patients. In her book on Munro, Ailsa Cox notes the preponderance of "conniving nurses" in Munro's fiction, paid caregivers "who insinuate themselves with their patient's relatives, taking charge where there is disorder and imposing a more rational, up-to-date lifestyle on the families they have colonized" (52). Cox's language is significant. In characterizing the nurse as a colonialist, she evokes imperialist relations, implying domination, exploitation, and destruction, characteristics quite antithetical to those associated with care, namely, assistance, sensitivity, and responsibility. The irony of this characterization is significant since, as health care critics, such as Jennifer Parks make clear, home care workers are often at risk of exploitation by employers (9). Munro's stories, on the other hand, tend to stress the potentially threatening authority of the capable home health care worker within families disrupted by illness and disability. Cox's figurative language highlights a particular structure at work within nursing relations in Munro's work, exposing the patterns of self-interested exchange that dominate and determine affective economies.

This chapter considers the gendered labour underpinning affective economies in Munro's stories involving professional caregiving, which depict women struggling to balance the demands of others with self-protection in a culture that idealizes and promotes female selflessness. Within these stories of caregiving, to recognize identity as relational, and responsibility as fundamental, founding principles of ethics of care theory, is to risk succumbing to patriarchal scripts of female subservience and dependence abhorrent to female characters seeking to escape the binds of domesticity.

Caregiving, Caretaking: Gifts and Thefts

The "giving" of care involves "taking" as well, in the form of money in many cases, but there are more intangible gains as well. The power gained by dealing with those aspects of the body that others deny or reject (blood, pus, urine, excrement) puts the nurse in a tenuous position of power (Bowden 115): her familiarity with the abject makes her at once knowledgeable and dangerous. It is no coincidence that the nurses in Munro's fiction are often threatening, enigmatic, potentially "conniving" figures. Munro's stories blend the "giving" and "taking" elements of care in their depictions of duplicitous nurses whose intentions are often shrouded and vaguely threatening.

The terminology of care-"giving" and "taking" provides a useful entry point for attending to the precariousness of care. Though "give" and "take" are opposing verbs, the former denoting donation, the latter receipt, once compounded with "care," their clear opposition begins to blur. Lexically, "caretakers" have existed at least a hundred years longer than "caregivers." According to the *OED*, a "caretaker" is "one who takes care of a thing, place, or person; one put in charge of anything" ("caretaker," def. a) The power implications are clear: to "take" care is to take charge, to adopt a position of power over the person or object cared for. The non-discrimination of the term is significant; anything, anywhere, anyone may be the object of the caretaker's attention. The colloquial, contemporary usage of the term accentuates the site of care since "caretaker" is now most commonly applied to those engaged in property maintenance. As the roots of the compound term imply, caretakers are likely to "take" something tangible, some payment in exchange for their labour.[2] The objectification of the care recipient in such scenarios is glaring in the term's verb form, which derives from the noun "caretaker" via back formation and omits the human recipient from the act of caretaking. To caretake is to "take charge of, watch over, and keep in order (a house, estate, business premises, etc.) in the absence of the owner or customary occupants" ("caretake"). Furthermore, the back-formation responsible for the verb form "caretake" implies a lexical hierarchy that privileges the caretaker over both the practice of care and its recipients: "caretakers" existed prior to "caretaking." The recent substitution of "caretaker" for the term "janitor," represents a shift in register that may help explain the emergence of the term "caregiver" in the United States in 1966 to denote "a person, typically either a professional or close relative, who looks after a child, elderly person, invalid, etc." ("caregiver"). Notably, only people receive "caregiving," unlike the object recipients of "caretaking." The caregiver is not "put in charge of anything" like the caretaker, but rather he or she attends to "the needs of others, esp. those unable to look after themselves adequately" ("caregiving" *OED*).

The caregiver responds to perceived need while a caretaker is handed responsibility. The power implications of "caregiver" are dispersed and subtle, lacking the transparent hierarchy of caretaking, which involves one person put into a position of maintenance and responsibility. Caregiving does not, by definition, necessitate payment, training, assignment, or supervision. Its lexical development suggests the need for terminology denoting care work and connoting ethical commitment. The caregiver responds to another's needs rather than merely assuming responsibility for upkeep and oversight. Caregivers offer attention and concern, implying decency, selflessness, responsibility, even affection; one "gives" care to infants, the elderly, the disabled, and "takes" nothing away from the recipient. The development of "caregiving," both the term and the practice, emphasizes the association of dependency work with the heroism of love, duty, and honour, banishing the unsavoury aspects of care, its labour, costs, and burdens. The new term masks the many ways "caregiving" can resemble "caretaking," in particular, the opportunities it provides for objectification, reimbursement, and hazardous power imbalances. The lexical distinction between the terms speaks to a desire to maintain ideological distinctions between love and work, distinctions that Munro's fiction refuses to maintain.

In her recurring depictions of paid care labourers, Munro blurs boundaries between caregiving and caretaking. In stories like "Jesse and Meribeth" (1986), "Floating Bridge" (2001), "Queenie" (2001), "Runaway" (2004), "Soon" (2004), and "Hired Girl" (2006), untrained women are paid to care for people and spaces simultaneously, drawing attention to the shifting motivations and arrangements that accompany caregiving. The ambiguous caregiver/caretaker figures within these stories are often at once necessary and threatening, undermining romanticized visions of caregiving by bringing to the fore the vexed labour involved in ostensible acts of love. In "Queenie," the title character runs away with Mr Vorguilla after caring for his ailing wife. While living together, Queenie appears a powerless victim of Mr Vorguilla's obsessive jealousy when he torments her into making false confessions of secret flirtations. But when Queenie abandons him, Mr Vorguilla is bereft, made helpless and pathetic by the loss since he has grown dependent on her household labour and affection. The blurring of care-taking and caregiving is especially pronounced in the story "Runaway," which centres on a young woman, Carla, who does domestic work for her neighbour, Sylvia, while Sylvia's husband is dying. Carla's presence provides comfort to Sylvia in her time of grief, her domestic labour providing inadvertent care. Meanwhile, Carla incorporates the dying man's invalidism into fantasies of sexual harassment she concocts in order to amuse and arouse her husband, Clark. All three of the story's primary characters, Carla, Clark, and Sylvia, long for some form of care while at the same time resenting and avoiding the position of caregiver. Sylvia depends on Carla's labour and humour; Carla depends on Sylvia's assistance and advice; Clark depends on Carla's domestic work and attention. But none willingly adopt the role of caregiver. When Sylvia greets Carla after her return from a vacation in Greece, the "indescribable bond [that] had seemed to grow up between them, and had consoled her in the awful months" of her husband's fatal illness has disappeared (20). Carla, Sylvia discovers, is "not at all the calm bright spirit, the carefree and generous creature who had kept her company in Greece" and whose presence she has been eagerly anticipating (21). When Carla finally explains her sullen demeanour, purging her despair over Clark's cruelty in a "noisy fit" that Sylvia finds "appall[ing]" (22), Sylvia's affection and admiration dissolve. She has her own cares to attend to and worry over, and Carla's display of grief and pain repels Sylvia, denuding Carla of her value: "with every moment of this show of misery, the girl made herself more ordinary" (22).

In "Runaway," the glimpse of another's helplessness and need kills affection and desire; the labour of caregiving is onerous and undesirable, and all of the characters seek to avoid its burdens. Throughout the story the labour of care is repeatedly mistaken for the performance of affection and kindness, caretaking masquerading as caregiving. The sinister antitheses of caring – jealousy, cruelty, selfishness – haunt the story's brief moments of comfort and consolation. In "Runaway," receiving care is seductive and addictive and those who interfere with or threaten the benefits of care must be eliminated. The utter lack of reciprocity in the story's relations of care results in paranoid, dangerous dependents who must protect their focal position in their caregiver's life, sometimes at all costs. The story's conclusion, in which Carla comes to believe that Clark has killed her beloved goat, Flora, as retribution for her near abandonment, evokes a world determined by a miserly emotional economy in which comfort and happiness are paid for by suffering and sadness. As a result, the story exposes the fragile tissue that separates caring from its opposites. Carla's suspicions surrounding the goat's demise ensure her cooperation with Clark's desires and demands (46); fear and helplessness keep her tethered to him, keep her giving care. "Runaway" suggests that scenarios of so-called care are easily destabilized by the selfish motivations seething beneath the surface of caregiving. Carla maintains her equilibrium despite her frightful suspicions only by restricting her thoughts to the shallowest of concerns. Her belief that Clark has slaughtered the goat out of revenge becomes a "murderous needle somewhere in her lungs" that can be avoided only by "breathing carefully" (46). Despite her efforts, the "needle" remains a palpable threat, a painful suspicion that cannot be forgotten. In "Runaway," Clark's awareness of his need for Carla spurs him to terrible lengths to guarantee her attention and assistance. His need for her could potentially transfer power to Carla, but she is blinded by her own need to arrange her life around him. Her escape from the marriage is foiled by her recognition of her dependence on him; on the bus to Toronto she anticipates the emptiness that awaits her new life without Clark: "what would she care about? How would she know that she was alive? … [W]hat would she put in his place? What else – who else – would ever be so vivid a challenge?" (34). Carla's identity as caretaker evaporates without a subject to care for, and panicking at the anticipated void, she begs to be let off the bus. In the power struggle between Carla and Clark, Carla surrenders to her dependence on Clark's dependency and is punished for her transgressive, if fleeting desire to be free of the burdens of care.

As one might imagine, ethics of care philosophers tend not to advocate care performed under such coercive conditions. According to Held, "a caring person not only has the appropriate motivations in responding to others or in providing care but also participates adeptly in effective practices of care" (4). From such a perspective, care in these stories is rarely "effective." But the balance of appropriate motivation and practice is difficult to strike, and Bubeck argues that "there are good reasons for keeping the meeting of a particular type of need and the expression of love distinct, while acknowledging that they may often coincide (especially in the private sphere)" ("Justice" 166). Munro's stories concur with Bubeck, suggesting in their exposure of selfishness and fear, jealousy and cruelty that the ideal Held and others promote and strive for is complicated by the vicissitudes of human self-interest. Munro's stories depict a multitude of caregivers tending to elderly, disabled, and ill characters in a variety of situations, familial and professional, voluntary and enforced, that frequently mutate and converge. Throughout these scenarios of care, love and devotion are countered by an equal share of resentment and exploitation, deception, and manipulation.

Nursing: Woman's "Natural" Profession

Dependency and care are inescapably implicated in power relations. As Munro's stories demonstrate, there can be no purely benign empowerment since one's gain is facilitated by another's loss. Dependency involves a transfer of power as one person comes to act or speak in place of another. This transfer is especially pronounced within nursing relations. The history of professional nursing unequivocally aligns care with femininity as the domestic labour practised by women became increasingly formalized, professionalized, and regulated.[3] In her study of the history of nursing in Canada, Kathryn McPherson explains how Canadian nursing was part of a broader formalization of an emergent occupation: "Once the responsibility of informally trained family, friends, servants, or members of religious orders, nursing was transformed in the late nineteenth century from unpaid care to wage labour. In the industrial societies of Europe and North America the occupation came to be the means of subsistence for many women, usually strangers to the patient but formally trained and certified in the curative practices of scientific medicine" (1). As in Europe and the United States, Canadian "nursing has been defined by particular feminine paradigms, and nursing educators laboured to ensure that new recruits conformed to these codes of gender-specific behaviour" (McPherson 15). Both McPherson and ethics of care critic Peta Bowden draw on the work of Susan Reverby, which demonstrates how the nursing profession grew out of an assumed affinity between women and nurturing, an assumed affinity that obscured the difficult labour involved in nursing care. Nurses were expected to "take on their obligation to care as part of the expression of their natural identities rather than as work chosen and performed by autonomous and self-directed agents" (Bowden 129). As Ellen Knox wrote in her 1919 overview of post-war job opportunities for Canadian women, *The Girl of the New Day*: "Nursing touches the mother instinct, which is alive in every true woman, from the oldest and ugliest spinster driving geese over the common, to the merriest-hearted school girl playing hockey in the field" (qtd. in McPherson 166). The development of professional nursing coincided with the emergence of training that sought to make its disciples more authentically and respectably feminine, the "true" women the profession demanded. After 1900 women were trained via apprenticeships in hospital schools where apprentices were expected to adhere to strict rules of femininity based on an "exaggerated version of Victorian social deference, sexual passivity, disinterest or ignorance, and ladylike gentility" (McPherson 165). By the early 1920s specialized training for nurses was widely available in many provinces, which helped "raise the status of nursing by identifying the nurse as a 'professional' public health worker" (Quiney 95) and allowed "graduate" or "trained" nurses, as they were known, to distinguish themselves from those with minimal or no formal training (Keddy and Dodd 43). In effect, "hospital-based training and work environments aimed to standardize nurses, nursing knowledge, and nursing care, creating the illusion of a universal nurse category while devaluing the vast diversity of persons who did nursing work as well as the many formal and informal settings in which nursing took place" (Elliott, Toman, and Stuart 1–2). The professionalization of nursing drew upon and strengthened gendered class distinction, establishing a hierarchy with elite, "true," feminine graduate nurses at the top and untrained domestic servants at the bottom.[4]

The history of Canadian nursing illustrates the institutionalization of an idealized version of feminine care. Professional nursing has relied on a fantasy of authentically feminine, legitimate, idealized care set against pragmatic, devalued domestic labour. In Munro's stories, this drudgery, the labour of care practised by paid non-professionals is often brought to the fore. Untrained, or partially trained private duty "nurses" appear throughout stories like "Images," "The Love of a Good Woman," "Some Women," and "Friend of My Youth." In these stories and others, women with ambiguous credentials enter, or in Cox's terms, invade and "colonize" the homes of those in need of care, a phenomenon with a historical precedent since, as McPherson explains, nurses in the early twentieth century in Canada fought to assert their professionalism and training, and to "distinguish themselves from domestic servants and from informally trained 'nurses'" (15). But training is deemed unnecessary for many employers in Munro's stories whether they are set in the 1950s, like "Cortes Island," the 1970s, like "Queenie," or later, as in "Floating Bridge," and "Soon." In these stories and others, untrained women, typically young women in need of money, are hired to provide care for disabled or ill dependents. Though training and credentials range, paid caregivers in Munro's stories are consistently employed to do the dependency work that others cannot, or will not, manage. The labour of care is often unpleasant. These stories expose the multiple levels of vulnerability and dependency Bowden associates with nursing, which "both contributes to and aims to overcome patients' objectification and dependency. For as much as it aims at alleviating the patient's subjective experience of distress, nursing is also strongly rooted in the reality of attending bodily functions: dirt, hunger, excreta, breakages and decay, the 'stuff' of the experiential rupture" (115). The intimacy of nursing is fundamental and visceral, yet "distance" is part of nursing protocol and practitioners are "warned about becoming too involved with, and attentive to, patients as individuals" (Bowden 110). Accordingly, the physicality of the body often becomes primary,[5] a dehumanization of afflicted subjects that transforms them into dependent objects and effectively maintains distance between practitioner and patient.

It is significant that the majority of nursing relationships in Munro's fiction occur between women. These female relations, formed around a "problematic," that is, a diseased and/or impaired body, draw attention to the centrality of the corporeal in gender politics. The "thingness" of the female body, identified by Iris Young as a primary barrier to gender equality, is front and centre in stories that revolve around the care and maintenance of female bodies by female caregivers. As Young contends, "for feminine bodily existence the body frequently is both subject and object for itself at the same time and in reference to the same act" (150). As a result, for women "the body is often lived as a thing that is other than it, a thing like the other things in the world. To the extent that a woman lives her body as a thing, she remains rooted in immanence, is inhibited, and retains a distance from her body as transcending movement and from engagement in the world's possibilities" (150). Munro's stories depict women confronting the body as thing, as object of illness and disability, as dependent or depended on, and the shifting power relations that result from such dependency and objectification.

Right Actions, Wrong Feelings: The Politics of Paid Caregiving in "The Love of a Good Woman"

In "The Love of a Good Woman" a nurse adopts an influential role in the family that employs her, gradually usurping the role of the dying wife and mother whom she has been assigned to assist. The story, which approaches novella length and complexity (five sections, spanning seventy-six pages that shift narration, protagonists, and point of view) concerns the suspicious 1951 death of an optometrist, D.M. Willens, which, as we learn in the story's conclusion, was not an accident, as the police have assumed, but murder. Most pertinent for my discussion is the story's portrait of Enid, the practical nurse who provides in-home care for the dying Mrs Quinn, whose connection to Willens gradually becomes clear. Enid, drawn to the nursing profession by her desire to assist and comfort those in need, is disturbed by her own negative reaction to Mrs Quinn and her ailing body. Enid is accustomed to being an unwelcome presence in the households where she works since her patients have often "detested the site of Enid herself, for her sleepless strength and patient hands and the way the juices of life were so admirably balanced and flowing in her" (37). The story suggests there is a significant imbalance in the caregiver/care-receiver relationship, a resentment of the nurse's surfeit of strength, power, and vitality. Indeed, it often seems as if the patient's own seeping life is somehow the inverse consequence of the forceful vitality of the capable nurse, as if Enid's strength is itself enervating. Consequently, as the story progresses, care comes to resemble a battle between giver and receiver, a struggle over the limited resources of life.

Although Enid is familiar with the jealous resentment of her patients, her own negative reaction towards Mrs Quinn surprises and alarms her:

> It was not just that she couldn't supply comfort here. It was that she couldn't want to. She could not conquer her dislike of this doomed, miserable young woman. She disliked this body that she had to wash and powder and placate with ice and alcohol rubs. She understood now what people meant when they said that they hated sickness and sick bodies … She disliked this particular body, all the particular signs of its disease. The smell of it and the discoloration, the malignant-looking little nipples and the pathetic ferretlike teeth. She saw all this as a sign of willed corruption … In spite of being a nurse who knew better, and in spite of its being her job – and surely her nature – to be compassionate. (38)

The use of the "compassionate" recalls Berlant's critique: compassion appears as a morally appropriate response Enid imagines should effectively conceal, if not replace, her disgust. This "natural" compassion that eludes her also recalls the gender assumptions underlying the nursing profession, making Enid's inability to muster positive feelings towards her patient a personal and professional failure. The body, its weakness and ailments, are attributed to Mrs Quinn herself as elements of her identity, marking her as a disturbing and repulsive other that Enid longs to flee. Ironically, it is this furtive, shameful revulsion that shifts the power relation between patient and nurse: "Worse even than the fact that Enid should feel this revulsion was the fact that Mrs Quinn knew it. No patience or gentleness or cheerfulness that Enid could summon would keep Mrs Quinn from knowing. And Mrs Quinn made knowing it her triumph" (38–9). The struggle between Enid and Mrs Quinn becomes overt, a battle for moral superiority that creates a winner and a loser and jettisons the possibility of collaboration or mutual benefits.

Enid's distressing, "inappropriate" reaction to Mrs Quinn's illness and dependency asserts itself in a series of "ugly dreams" of bizarre, grotesque desire:

> In the dreams that came to her now she would be copulating or trying to copulate (sometimes she was prevented by intruders or shifts of circumstances) with utterly forbidden and unthinkable partners. With fat squirmy babies or patients in bandages or her own mother. She would be slick with lust, hollow and groaning with it, and she would set to work with roughness and an attitude of evil pragmatism. "Yes, this will have to do," she would say to herself. "This will do if nothing better comes along." And this coldness of heart, this matter-of-fact depravity, simply drove her lust along. She woke up unrepentant, sweaty and exhausted, and lay like a carcass until her own self, her shame and disbelief, came pouring back into her. The sweat went cold on her skin. She lay there shivering in the warm night, with disgust and humiliation. She did not dare go back to sleep. (51)

Enid's dreams recall the "pagan dreams" experienced by the caregiving protagonist in Munro's "Cortes Island" (145), dreams in which "the safe barrier between the transgressor and the 'normal' self is crossed. The dreamer is no longer a passive witness. She is implicated" (Cox 60). Much like Enid, the narrator's dreams in "Cortes Island" involve sexual transgression. In particular, the young caregiving narrator dreams of sexual acts between her and her elderly, disabled patient.[6] Enid's nightmares involve her violent objectification of the other, transforming the helpless and the vulnerable into sexual objects. In effect, the dreams betray her attitude of contempt towards the dependents (babies, patients) that she regards as mere tools for personal satisfaction, an attitude that is shameful,[7] but undeniable. Enid's dehumanization and degradation of the other forces her to confront alterity, both the other's and, perhaps most distressingly for Enid, her own, in the alarming desires that emerge in sleep. Her "evil pragmatism" and "coldness of heart" cling to her as she wakes, provoking an experience of extreme alienation in which her body is uncannily unfamiliar and she must wait, lying "like a carcass until her own self, shame and disbelief, came pouring back into her." It is only "shame and disbelief" that return her to her waking self. The adjective "cold," repeated twice, echoes an earlier, failed attempt to provide honest care for Mrs Quinn when Enid admits to herself that her offer to fetch a minister was, though "the right thing to ask," made for the wrong reasons: "the spirit in which she asked it was not right – it was cold and faintly malicious" (54). The actions and motivations of Enid's caregiving are not only disparate, but appear in direct opposition to one another; she performs acts of care but feels disdain, even hatred for her dependent.

Enid attempts to "make herself speak compassionately and encouragingly" to her patient (54), but her struggle to feel anything positive towards Mrs Quinn is largely in vain. Enid's effort at compassion, which the narration explicitly associates with pity – Enid typically feels "sorry for" her patients (38) – engages Lauren Berlant's critique of compassion, its potential for, if not creation of, inequality and injustice. Nurses are encouraged, as Bowden makes clear, to engage in compassion, that is, to care from an appropriate distance: "professional behavior entails the avoidance of any personal interactions and the limitation of one's role to the exercise of scientific, technical and managerial capabilities. These injunctions are designed to answer the problems of face-to-face caring relations in the public sphere" (110). Bowden's observations echo Berlant's contention that "training in compassionate action" often coincides with "training in aversion" ("Introduction" 10). Compassion and coldness, attachment and distance, devotion and self-preservation, caregiving floats uneasily between these emotional and behavioural extremes.

In her etymological analysis of "compassion," Marjorie Garber draws attention to a shift in meaning that occurred between the fourteenth and seventeenth centuries. "Compassion" was initially "used to describe both *suffering together with one another*, or 'fellow feeling,' and an emotion felt *on behalf of another who suffers*. In the second sense, compassion was felt not between equals but from a distance – in effect, from high to low: 'shown towards a person in distress by one who is free from it, who is, in this respect, his superior'" (20). As Candace Vogler explains: "of the many species of tenderness directed toward others' troubles, compassion falls squarely in the range of affective orientations with a built-in clean-hands clause" (30). Garber, drawing on the work of Mickey Kaus, draws attention to "three fundamental flaws in compassion": it is "inegalitarian," "sentimental," and "fragile" (24). The condescension and unreliability of compassion discussed by Garber, Berlant, and Vogler shed light on Enid's desire to act compassionately towards her patient. Enid's "hope to be good, and do good" (42) stems from a fantasy of self-satisfying self-sacrifice. Enid's mother hints at this secret purpose when Enid agrees to abandon hospital nursing at her father's request: "Well, I hope that makes you happy," Enid's mother tells her (40). Her mother's use of the second-person pronoun is significant, as the narrator makes clear:

> Not "makes him happy." "Makes *you*." It seemed that her mother had known before Enid did just how tempting this promise [to give up registered nursing] would be. The deathbed promise, the self-denial, the wholesale sacrifice. And the more absurd the better. This was what she had given in to. And not for love of her father, either (her mother implied), but for the thrill of it. Sheer noble perversity. (Emphasis in original 40)

The tension conveyed in the phrase "noble perversity" is at the heart of the story's narrative conflict, a conflict between the desire for personal satisfaction and the desire to be virtuous. Following the implications of this conflict, it is no coincidence that the return of self Enid waits for after her disturbing dreams' "unrepentant" sexual "depravity" involves a flood of "shame and disbelief ... pouring back into her." In "The Love of a Good Woman," Munro imagines the relationship between caregiver and care receiver as distinctly combative. Enid's ministrations often barely conceal her desire for domination. The language of combat recurs throughout the descriptions of their relationship: Mrs Quinn "submit[s]" to having her nightgown removed (35); Mrs Quinn, like all dying people, according to Enid, is "flailing for an enemy" (36); Enid cannot "conquer her dislike" of Mrs Quinn (38); Mrs Quinn's knowledge of Enid's repulsion is her "triumph" (39). The Enid/Mrs Quinn relationship incorporates the dubious, "clean-handed" compassion Vogler describes; Enid attempts to act appropriately, "caringly" in order to maintain moral superiority, despite the sinister fantasies of her dream life and the waking disdain that undermine her belief in her own goodness.

The story's power struggle between caregiver and care receiver demonstrates the potency of knowledge and secrets, since language and stories are the only weapons the dying Mrs Quinn has at her disposal. Her awareness of Enid's dislike empowers her: "Good riddance to bad rubbish," is her self-deprecating articulation of her caregiver's secret thoughts (39), a crude phrasing that haunts Enid with its clairvoyance, its capacity to glean Enid's true feelings for her patient, despite her efforts to conceal them. Enid's inability to convincingly don the mask of concerned, devoted nurse diminishes the only power available to her – the power of devotion, sacrifice, compassion. The Christian overtones of Enid's desire for prostration converge with the story's central revelation, delivered in a deathbed confession. Mrs Quinn confesses to her participation in the cover-up of Mr Willens' murder, perpetrated by her husband in a fit of jealous rage. But the standard power dynamic between penitent and confessor is reversed in the confessional moment. As Sandra Lee Bartky explains, in Foucauldian terms, confession "unfolds within an inegalitarian relationship, for one confesses to another who has authority not only to require the confession but also to determine whether the confession itself reveals a core self that is virtuous or vicious, mature or immature, normal or abnormal" (35). But in "The Love of a Good Woman," the power relationships are not so clearly drawn. Mrs Quinn's deathbed confession suggests an attempt to de-throne both Enid and Mr Quinn, simultaneously exposing her husband's crime and implicating Enid in its concealment. Until now, Enid has been able to perform care work without caring feelings, sidestepping ethical questions of responsibility, justice, and commitment; she does the "right" thing, though not necessarily for the "right" reasons. But Mrs Quinn's confession, delivered in the text as an uninterrupted narrative, introduces Enid to a new kind of ethical responsibility, one with both moral and legal implications.

Initially Enid is distracted and distraught by the morbid tale, wandering the house, wondering "what to do about it" (63), attempting to balance the potential authenticity of Mrs Quinn's story against its demand for justice. Her anxiety is resolved by her realization of the power implied by this new knowledge, and the opportunity it presents: the power to choose who is saved and who is punished. Consequently, she has a happy, buoyant day with the Quinn children as Mrs Quinn dies alone, experiencing a new liberation from responsibility: "She had never absented herself like this before with anybody who was dying" (66–7). Enid now has bigger concerns. She sets about planning the ultimate act of self-sacrifice: she will go see Rupert Quinn, ask him to take her out on the lake in his boat and, after admitting that she cannot swim, confess her new knowledge: "Once he understood his advantage, she would tell him. She would ask, Is it true?" (72). She considers two possible outcomes if Mrs Quinn's tale is true; either he will succumb to her demand for his surrender to police or he will push her into the river where she will drown (72). She anticipates with excitement the possibility of the former scenario and the moral perfection that will result when she devotes herself to him while he is in jail, forming "a bond that is like love but beyond love," a fantasy she finds so intoxicating it verges on "indecent" (73).

But the scene does not unfold according to her plans. When she visits the widowed Mr Quinn, his autonomy and unfamiliarity disarm her, his very scent alerting her to his otherness: "No bodily smell – even the smell of semen – was unfamiliar to her, but there was something new and invasive about the smell of a body so distinctly *not in her power or under her care*" (emphasis added 77). Enid's plan dissolves as the alterity of the other becomes undeniable. In place of the moral superiority and domination she has imagined, she is set adrift by his otherness, invaded by his very smell. So accustomed is she to caring for dependents, a role that has led her to believe in the power of her knowledge and ability, in the transparency and familiarity of other people whom she presumes to understand pathologically, as diseases, symptoms, and disabilities, that she is deeply affected by this new-found mysteriousness.[8] Enid's awakening to the unknown expands to involve the entire setting, the sudden strangeness of the world expressed in narrative questions: "The air was clear in some places, then suddenly you would enter a cloud of tiny bugs. Bugs no bigger than specks of dust that were constantly in motion yet kept themselves together in the shape of a pillar or a cloud. How did they manage to do that? And how did they choose one spot over another to do it in?" (78). Enid is newly perplexed and awed by a world beyond her understanding and control.

The story concludes with a series of paragraphs describing her new vision of the world, her new, detailed attention to landscape. The final lines provide no clear resolution to the story's central mysteries: the cause of Mr Willen's bizarre death, the authenticity of Mrs Quinn's confession, the fate of Enid and of Rupert. Instead, the story ends with secrets and silence as Rupert disappears to fetch the boat's hidden oars: "If she tried to, she could still hear Rupert's movements in the bushes. But if she concentrated on the motion of the boat, a slight and secretive motion, she could feel as if everything for a long way around had gone quiet" (78). Enid's new experience of herself as vulnerable, as unknowing, even unknown, her shifting attention to the world beyond her influence and management, arouses a novel incomprehensibility; it is the first time in the story that Enid can only witness, rather than direct a situation. Prior to her encounter with Rupert Quinn, Enid has wilfully overlooked the otherness of the other, preferring the smug satisfaction of self-sacrifice to actually confronting alterity, the inassimilable mystery of others. Patients have always been objects of care, her attention focused first on symptoms and disease. But in this final scene there is no overt power struggle, no competition, no giving or taking, no devotion, sacrifice, or domination. Instead there is silence and mystery. Enid's nursing career has been based on inequality, self-serving sacrifice that illustrates Kelly Oliver's central argument that "the dichotomy between subject and other or subject and object is itself a result of the pathology of oppression. To see oneself as a subject and to see other people as *the other* or objects not only alienates one from those around him or her but also enables the dehumanization inherent in oppression and domination" (*Witnessing*, emphasis in original 3). Throughout the story, caregiving functions within this structural pathology of subject and object. But the story's final moments evoke the potential for new, ethical relations as Enid pauses to witness the world around her, opening herself to the unknown, the unknowable both within and without. I believe the story's final paragraphs depict a dawning awareness and appreciation of what Oliver calls "the adventure of otherness" (*Witnessing* 20). For Oliver, the appreciation of such otherness is a prerequisite for love, since "love requires a commitment to the advent and nurturing of difference" (20). This kind of commitment is new to Enid, whose version of care has relied on imbalanced, objectifying "compassion." The story's conclusion opens up the possibility of witnessing, of opening the self to the mystery of otherness without resorting to assimilation and domination.

Ironically, it is only after the termination of her professional caregiving duties that Enid awakens to alterity and the respectful witnessing that is necessary for ethical human relations. As Oliver writes, "the otherness of the other, is the greatest joy; and a vulnerability in the face of the other is a sweet surrender, a gift rather than a sacrifice" (*Witnessing* 224).

And yet, Enid's awakening to alterity, her dawning appreciation of silence may be protecting a killer. It may be the company of a murderer that introduces her to otherness and the respectful witnessing it demands. His difference is "welcome" (77), but danger may lurk within this difference. Munro's open-ended conclusion confounds attempts to exonerate or condemn Enid (or Rupert for that matter), in effect extending the experience of baffling, remarkable otherness to the story's reader, who can only quietly witness difference, denied recourse to explanation and clear resolution.

Competitive Care in "Some Women"

The complicated power dynamics of professional caregiving are further explored in Munro's 2009 collection, *Too Much Happiness*. In the story "Some Women" a dying man is surrounded by women who offer him care. The focus of the story's struggle for power is Mr Bruce Crozier, who has developed leukemia after returning from the Second World War. The narrator recalls her time as a hired caregiver, employed by the Crozier women to "look after Young Mr Crozier" while his wife is away teaching summer school at the local college two afternoons a week (164). The narrator's primary responsibilities involve bringing her patient fresh water, adjusting the shades on his window, and moving a fan in and out of the room (164–5). These minimal responsibilities are more than Mr Crozier's stepmother, "Old Mrs Crozier," is able, or willing, to manage. Indeed, Old Mrs Crozier is, from the narrator's perspective, cold and self-absorbed. As the narrator explains, "what Old Mrs Crozier cared about really was her flower garden" (168), where she spends much of her time giving orders to her gardener. This network of care is complicated by the arrival of Mrs Crozier's masseuse, Roxanne, who insists on meeting Mr Crozier and quickly insinuates herself in the Crozier household. Roxanne proclaims her caring intentions and credentials quickly and directly, a style of communication at odds with the Croziers' preference for discretion and decorum. Roxanne assures her adopted patient that she is "not going to pound on [him] like [he] must have heard [her] doing to Dorothy-doodle downstairs" (172). Instead she will employ her expertise: "Before I got my massage training I used to be a nurse. Well, a nurse's aide. One of the ones who do all the work and the nurses come around and boss you. Anyway, I learned how to make people comfortable" (172). To the narrator's surprise, despite Roxanne's crude and abrupt style, the ordinarily staunch Croziers, both old and young, grin in response.

From Roxanne's first appearance, the narrator resentfully derides her as stupid and fake. Unlike Roxanne, Bruce Crozier's wife, Sylvia, is educated and reserved, characteristics admired by the narrator, who longs for knowledge and sophistication, and the opportunity to participate in life beyond her small town. Yet, despite her disdain, the narrator acknowledges Roxanne's attentiveness, her consistent prioritization of her patient's comfort: "She pulled his sheets around, somehow managing not to disturb him" (172); "she was careful never to disturb the patient" (174); "She was dissatisfied with the arrangement of his bedclothes, always, had to put them to rights" (175). She plays games and tells jokes, and "Mr Crozier sat propped up on his pillows and looked for all the world as if he was happy" (177).

As a caregiver, Roxanne is attentive and careful, and at the same time clownish and flirtatious, entertaining her charges with jokes and gossip. She dotes on Mr Crozier, attempting to distract him from his suffering with silly stories and complements, going so far as to lie to him about his appearance: "Nobody sick like you are supposed to be ever looked as good as what you do" (172). The narrator is unimpressed by Roxanne's performance, finding her "flirtatious prattle insulting" (172), and she counters Roxanne's "prattle" with her own bleak vision of Mr Crozier's appearance: "Mr Crozier looked terrible. A tall man whose ribs had shown like those of somebody fresh from a famine when she sponged him, whose head was bald and whose skin looked as if it had the texture of a plucked chicken's, his neck corded like an old man's. Whenever I had waited on him in any way I had avoided looking at him. And this was not really because he was sick and ugly. It was because he was dying" (172–3). The narrator's appraisal, which focuses on signs of disease, marginalizes and dehumanizes Mr Crozier and is, ironically, delivered as a demonstration of respect in its "honest" comparisons of Mr Crozier's body with a chicken carcass. The narrator feels compelled to stigmatize Mr Crozier: "He was the one stricken, marked out from everybody else, and here was Roxanne trespassing on his ground with her jokes and her swagger and notions of entertainment" (173). This dehumanization of Mr Crozier as diseased object, one set apart from vital, living subjects, exposes the narrator's utilitarian understanding of "caregiving" as an action focused exclusively on an objectified body, one marked by its proximity to death. For the narrator, Roxanne's treatment of Mr Crozier as a fully living subject is a transgression that ignores the blight of disease. Roxanne is the "trespasser," daring to blur the distinctions between the living and the dying, subjects and objects that the narrator relies on for her delivery of care. The narrator self-consciously avoids the possibility of witnessing the other in her care, admitting to the reader that she avoids looking at him whenever possible. In Oliver's terms, the narrator's refusal to see the other before her is a denial of subjectivity itself since Oliver claims witnessing to be "the essential dynamic of all subjectivity, its constitutive event and process" (*Witnessing* 7). Witnessing is fundamental for the response-ability that Oliver argues is at the heart of selfhood since "we are selves, subjects, and have subjectivity and agency by virtue of our dialogic relationships with others" (18). But the narrator's reluctance, even refusal to see, to acknowledge and recognize human interconnectivity and responsibility, shifts at the story's climax when her decision to honour a commitment to Mr Crozier dislodges Roxanne from her intimate position within the Crozier family. The narrator's commitment to Mr Crozier causes the dissolution of bonds between Roxanne and the Croziers, suggesting that the ethical obligations of care can require selectivity, a privileging of particular needs and particular others that inevitably marginalizes.

Allegiances shift on the day of Roxanne's final visit. The summer term has ended, and Sylvia will no longer need Roxanne's or the narrator's help caring for her husband. The situation prompts a crisis of loyalty when Mr Crozier asserts his autonomy and marital commitment by asking the narrator to secretly lock his bedroom door before Roxanne's arrival. The narrator complies and Roxanne becomes distraught when she is unable to access her patient. Old Mrs Crozier is less distressed, quickly abandoning the locked door in favour of her beloved garden. Upon discovering her husband's act of rejection, Sylvia is delighted, interpreting his command as confirmation of her status as most valued caregiver. As a result, the narrator comes to regard caregiving as a competition, its participants concerned with "winning and losing" (187). But she is perplexed when she considers the object of this competition: "it was strange to think of the almost openly traded prize, Mr Crozier – and to think that he could have had the will to make a decision, even to deprive himself, so late in his life. The carnality at death's door – or the truelove, for that matter – were things I had to shake off like shivers down my spine" (187). The confluence of life and death, the persistence of desire, emotion, and will despite debilitating illness, unnerve the narrator, upsetting her rigid distinction between living and dying.

The narrator observes triangulated care that focuses on a dying man, that is, a trio of women wishing to give care for the power it affords. Mr Crozier's power within the family is not diminished by his physical weakening, pointing to the centrality of gender in the story's treatment of structures of care and power. Mr Crozier becomes a linchpin for machinations of dominance and subordination among a group of "some women" who, regardless of age, training, or education, remain alienated from roles of authority within public life in the 1950s, resulting in a battle for positions of authority within the private sphere. The narrator resents her subordination as Roxanne's authority increases. She interprets Roxanne's intrusion into the nexus of care as a strategic move, a seized-upon opportunity for mastery, if not over the patient himself, then over his inferior caregivers. Roxanne immediately sets about marking the territory of illness as her space of authority, filling the sick room with donated objects and issuing commands to the narrator, who is relegated to the role of reluctant and resentful assistant. The narrator recognizes Roxanne's strategy of subordination: "She had sized me up, apparently, as somebody who was willing to take orders" (169). Roxanne's authority within the Crozier household is remarkable for its lack of precedent; both stepmother and stepson submit to Roxanne's ministrations with an uncommon docility, even pleasure, a state of being particularly foreign to Old Mrs Crozier, an otherwise intractable matriarch who has refused to rearrange her house to accommodate her stepson's illness and disability. But in Roxanne's presence Old Mrs Crozier appears almost happy, an attitude of positivity and light-heartedness that startles the narrator: "The fact that Old Mrs Crozier snickered [at Roxanne's "smutty" jokes] shocked me as much as the jokes themselves. I thought that she maybe didn't get the point but simply enjoyed listening to whatever Roxanne said. She sat with that chewed-in yet absent-minded smile on her face as if she'd been given a present she knew she would like, even if she hadn't got the wrapping off it yet" (176). The details of the narrator's simile – care as a "present" – grow increasingly significant as the story continues and gifts, both literal and figurative, become pivotal to battles for authority. The story culminates in a series of offerings and rejections that permanently reconfigure the balance of power and responsibility among the story's characters. The gift is a focal point of many discussions of ethics and subjectivity, and philosophers have offered contrasting interpretations of the gift and its implications. For example, Kelly Oliver writes admiringly of Patricia Williams' conviction that gifts can function as models of "asymmetrical reciprocity" able to "[break] out of the economy of exchange" (Oliver, *Witnessing* 55, 57). Nonetheless, Oliver's own philosophy is less optimistic, drawing on Derrida to argue that gifts inevitably initiate obligation, placing giver and receiver in an economy of exchange since receiving a gift necessarily makes one feel obligated to reciprocate (56). Despite the denotative meaning of "gift," which stresses the absence of obligation – a "gift" is given "gratuitously, for nothing"; it is something "transferred to another without the expectation or receipt of an equivalent" ("gift," def. 1) – the gift implies obligation. In fact, etymologically, the term stems from the Old English "*gift*," referring to "payment for a wife" ("gift"), exposing the gift's ethically compromised origins in misogynistic exchange. For Derrida, the gift, much like hospitality or forgiveness, must function outside of an economy of exchange: "For there to be a gift, *it is necessary* [*il faut*] that the donee not give back, amortize, reimburse, acquit himself, enter into a contract, and that he never have contracted a debt" (*Given Time*, emphasis in original 13). Taking this logic even further, Derrida insists that the "donee not *recognize* the gift as gift" since such recognition – "if the present is present to him *as present*" – functions to "annul the gift" (emphasis in original 13). As Derrida explains, "for pure hospitality or a pure gift to occur, however, there must be an absolute surprise" ("Hospitality" 70). Once intelligible as gift, its status as such is negated.

Contrary to conventional usage – gifts as signs of gratitude or appreciation, or fulfilment of debts or obligations – Derrida argues "the gift supposes a break with reciprocity, exchange, economy and circular movement" ("Hospitality" 69). Oliver goes further to explain the ephemeral nature of the "true" gift for Derrida, which "cannot be given out of duty or from expectations; it cannot be given from a position of sovereignty within an economy of exchange. What we usually think of as gifts are 'contaminated' forms of true or pure giving, which cannot even be identified as such without falling into ruin as gifts" (*Animal Lessons* 136). This critique of the gift corresponds to Lauren Berlant's critique of compassion as contaminated by power structures that transform responsibility into gift giving. Suffering is presented as separate from the subject, which "invites the gift of compassion" (Berlant, "Introduction" 9). The pure gift, for Derrida, cannot be calculated: "If the gift is calculated, if you know what you are going to give to whom, if you know what you want to give, for what reason, to whom, in view of what, etc. there is no longer any gift" ("Women in the Beehive" 151). Expanding on Derrida's vision, Oliver argues that "love and joy, like the gift or as forms of gifts, are also beyond any economy of exchange, including symbolic exchange or language" (*Animal Lessons* 137). Such unarticulated, uncalculated gifts are inevitably difficult to locate, and the moments of giving in "Some Women" are no exception.

The economy of exchange governing gift giving in the story becomes explicit when Old Mrs Crozier attempts to mark Roxanne's final day as her stepson's caregiver with a box of macaroons "specially" ordered for the occasion (179). Roxanne steadfastly refuses to accept the gift, claiming if she eats even one confection she will "break out something awful" (179). The macaroons are meant as a "treat … something special" (180), celebratory desserts that anticipate the end of their pleasurable afternoons. As such, the macaroons function as an offering, recompense for the looming loss as well as an attempt at giving pleasure, albeit a very different kind of pleasure than that which Roxanne has afforded the Croziers with her tending, jokes, games, and stories. Roxanne's response to the gift arrests the pattern of exchange that has heretofore marked caring relations in the story, denying Old Mrs Crozier the satisfaction of reciprocity. Roxanne is unable or unwilling to appreciate the symbolic significance of the macaroons, carelessly tossing aside the potent offering: "Don't bother about this stuff, it's not your fault. I know you got it to be nice," she tells Old Mrs Crozier, pinning emotional responsibility for the gift on the giver when she herself should be, according to Mrs Crozier's economy of exchange, grateful and beholden (180). The denial initiates resentment in the rebuffed giver, who turns on her would-be recipient and snaps in response to Roxanne's condescension, repeating Roxanne's words back to her in a "mean mincing voice" (180). Mrs Crozier's imitation of Roxanne is significant, suggesting as it does the larger imitation at work: Mrs Crozier's "gift" imitates Roxanne's giving of care, which has been similarly "contaminated" by power imbalance and pleasure-seeking, given as it is "from a position of sovereignty." In other words, Roxanne's performances of care have been functioning within an affective economy, initiating "narcissistic power plays" between the various givers and receivers (Oliver, *Animal Lessons* 136): Roxanne, Old Mrs Crozier, Sylvia Crozier, and the narrator. The macaroons evoke Derrida and Oliver in their symbolic articulation of Old Mrs Crozier's efforts to regain authority; her gift announces her power – "I am in a position to give this to you" (*Animal Lessons* 136), it says – a symbolic communication similar to the meaning expressed in Roxanne's ministrations.

The narrator remains excluded from this economy: "It occurred to me that they could offer me a golden macaroon out of those sitting in the box, but apparently it did not occur to them" (180). Because the macaroons are not true gifts but symbols of power, they are unavailable to the narrator who is on the margins of the competitive affective economy that surrounds Mr Crozier. But it is her very invisibility within this economy that allows her to initiate the story's narrative climax undetected by the other women: she restricts access to the dying Mr Crozier's room without attracting suspicion from Roxanne or Mrs Crozier because neither woman can fathom her as a rival. It is no coincidence that once the narrator enters the competitive sphere of giving and taking, "winning and losing," by locking the sickroom door, she feels entitled to the macaroons, eating two, "hoping that pleasure would bring back normalcy" (185). Her self-propelled entry into the economy established by the Croziers and Roxanne entitles her to restitution. In other words, her new status endows her with the right to take what she pleases. The narrator's belief in the potential for pleasure to restore "normalcy" is evidence of the primary role pleasure has played throughout the narrative. Assistance, compassion, gifts – these offerings have been "contaminated" by privileging the pleasure of donation over the pleasure of receipt. The economy of exchange that governs the story's caregiving relations reaches its apotheosis with the rebuffed macaroons, bringing to the foreground the competition and calculation that have lurked within performances of care throughout the story. Sylvia's barely concealed glee at the news of Roxanne's rejection provides further evidence of the competitive structure of care: Sylvia basks in "winning" Mr Crozier's loyalty at Roxanne's expense.

Obligation to others in "Some Women" is selective and partial. Throughout Munro's stories one finds these non-idealized depictions of caregiving that expose resentment, sacrifice, loss, even cruelty as aspects of dependency work. Munro's work conjures the insights of ethics of care philosophers who express scepticism towards views of care that emphasize the enriching, rewarding potential of mutual dependence. Ruth Groenhout summarizes these criticisms: "if care for the other is the basic human attitude, then there seems no space left for restricting care, for limiting my responsibilities to others in order to go about my own life in ways that would allow me to flourish" (86). As Bubeck explains in her response to what she sees as the artificial opposition of care and justice, contrary to the belief in strictly positive care, "caring is not mutually beneficial, but is an asymmetrical transaction of material benefit … Hence, unless the carer is remunerated in some way (in kind or paid), or the care she gives is reciprocated, she incurs a material net burden. While caring can be a very empowering and rewarding thing to do, it is nevertheless, and may equally well feel like, a burden" ("Justice" 167). But asymmetry is not necessarily harmful, and many philosophers stress the necessity of moving beyond balanced responsibility. Levinas, Derrida, Oliver, and others suggest that unequal obligation is at the heart of ethical response, most famously articulated in Levinas' insistence that the other's needs are always primary, that the subject is taken "hostage" by his endless obligation to the other (*Otherwise* 117). More moderate is Iris Young's proposed model of "asymmetrical reciprocity" that depends on ethical listening to avoid the risks of assimilating or adopting the other's perspective (Oliver, *Witnessing* 55). Oliver asserts that "for Young, recognition and understanding are mutually constitutive in that the openness of understanding she describes requires recognizing that 'I cannot put myself in her position'" (*Witnessing* 55). In "Some Women" there is a moment of caring that occurs outside of the economy of affection and pleasure, a moment in which the possibility of genuine concern devoid of personal gain or reward appears possible. As Sylvia drives the narrator home for the last time, the narrator glimpses Roxanne once more. She is sitting in her car "at the bottom of Crozier's hill to watch us drive by" (186). The narrator considers the purpose of Roxanne's position, concluding that Roxanne has been waiting to glimpse the Croziers' car and confirm Mr Crozier's safety: "She would notice me. She would know that things must be all right, from the kindly, serious, faintly smiling way that Sylvia was talking to me" (186–7). Roxanne makes no attempt to approach the Crozier house; instead she retreats from the scene, suggesting that the view of Sylvia's car has satisfied her need for reassurance. The silent image of the defeated Roxanne, waiting in her car for a sign of her patient's well-being, suggests a kind of disinterested care previously absent in the story. Much like the moments of ethical action in Munro that Naomi Morgenstern analyses (71), this private demonstration of care suggests a kind of "radical 'gift,'" that is, a gift that "exceeds those conventionally feminine offerings" the characters have hitherto exchanged (in this case, a fleece pad and macaroons, massages and jokes) (75). Roxanne's final act of care requires an acceptance of multiple losses: her status in the Crozier household, the appreciation and satisfaction of those in her care, the affections of Mr Crozier, and the potential for financial remuneration. This private performance of care can offer little satisfaction or comfort, but the act indicates the caregiver's need to confirm the safety of her patient despite her exclusion from the Croziers' affective economy.

"Emotional Housekeeping": Munro's Affective Economies

Munro's stories confront readers with the rarity, if not impossibility of mutually satisfying caregiving relations. Instead, we witness complex, murky affective economies in which characters shrewdly trade affection, assistance, power, and control. These stories demonstrate the repercussions of ethical obligations in which the needs of one eclipse those of another, testing definitions of responsibility, such as Derek Attridge's, that emphasize subjugation: "Responsibility for the other involves assuming the other's needs, being willing to be called to account for the other, surrendering one's goals and desires in deference to the other's" (27). Munro's stories complicate such ethical hypotheses by demonstrating the risks of self-denial and self-sacrifice, particularly in a culture that persistently associates women with "natural" caring and selfless devotion. The impossible demands of ethical response create an unsettling vision of subjectivity and responsibility in which ethical relations debilitate the subject. As Simon Critchley explains, "the subject shapes itself in relation to a demand that it can never meet, which divides and sunders the subject" (40). The violence of this relationship between subject and "sundering" responsibility is explored repeatedly in Munro's stories, which challenge the salubrity of the obligations of care.

Throughout *Too Much Happiness*, Munro confronts the cruel imperfection of interrelational identity and the responsibility it engenders. In the story "Fiction" characters come to recognize in stark terms the affective economies they have unwittingly entered. The story concerns Joyce and her complicated relationship with her ex-husband's stepdaughter, Christie. Joyce first encounters Christie as a child, a student in her music classes, and then again, later, as a grown woman who has published a collection of stories. When Joyce reads the volume, she discovers a story concerning a young girl and her heartbroken music teacher, the familiarity of the narrative provoking an unsettling recognition. In reading Christie's story, Joyce witnesses her own importance in the girl's childhood as mentor and caregiver (the music teacher attends to the girl's scratched knee, takes her out for ice cream, teaches her about the woods, about the wildflowers there, about "purple violets and columbines. Chocolate lilies" [56]). But as Christie's fictional alter ego comes to realize, the music teacher's care conceals ulterior motives: she seeks information about the household from which she has been exiled. The young protagonist of Christie's story comes to recognize her unwitting participation in an affective economy, one in which she is called upon to deliver personal details to feed the jealous curiosity of a rejected lover in exchange for affection and care: "what she can know," Christie writes, "is how little she herself counted for, how her infatuation was manipulated, what a poor little fool she was. And this fills her with bitterness, certainly it does. Bitterness and pride" (58). Joyce, reading the story, expects denouncement: "she really has caught the drift, she can feel the horror coming. The innocent child, the sick and sneaking adult, that seduction. She should have known" (56). But there is a "surprise ending" (58) in which the young woman's perception of her childhood shifts allowing her to recognize her attachment to the manipulative teacher: "She doesn't know how or when, but she realizes that she no longer thinks of that time as a cheat. She thinks of the music she painfully learned to play … The buoyancy of her hopes, the streaks of happiness, the curious and delightful names of the forest flowers that she never got to see" (58). For Joyce, this ending is a revelation, one that confirms the precarious balance of love and dejection at work in the world. She glimpses the possibility of redemption in Christie's writing, the hope that her own suffering may have begotten another's "streaks of happiness," that her treatment of the girl was not exclusively exploitative, despite the fact that at the time her own heartache and resentment blinded her to everything but the source of that pain, namely, the collapse of her marriage. Joyce's interpretation of the story relies upon her detection of a cruel economy that trades in suffering and joy: "Love. She was glad of it. It almost seemed as if there must be some random and of course unfair thrift in the emotional housekeeping of the world, if the great happiness – however temporary, however flimsy – of one person could come out of the great unhappiness of another" (58–9). The language of economic relations, of domestic labour and power imbalances suggests a parsimoniousness underlying affection, implying that care is limited and transferable. The story gestures towards a perverse economy in which an individual's happiness is secured by the suffering of another.

But in typical Munro fashion, this analysis and the faint sense of approval it affords its protagonist – the belief her pain has produced something positive – is quickly reversed. When Joyce nervously waits in line to meet Christie at an author signing she anticipates a happy reunion of teacher and student, but instead she is greeted with cold solicitude. Christie offers her "a smile of polished cordiality, professional disengagement" (60). Joyce's carefully selected gift, a chocolate flower meant to stir private, nostalgic associations, is carelessly received and quickly set aside. In Christie's face Joyce finds "not a scrap of recognition" (60). The language of "scraps" is notable since Joyce herself was a castoff from her own marriage and the ease with which she was dismissed has tortured her for years. Indeed, the story abounds with "scraps," discarded people and histories. Joyce comes to interpret Christie's stories as discarded scraps, "something [Christie] wiggled out of and left on the grass" (60–1). Shedding the skins of the past, skins that obviously still cling to Joyce, appears as the heartless but necessary strategy for preserving oneself from harm. Christie has learned that one must discard dead weight and reorganize oneself to suit ever-changing economies of feeling and attachment.

Up to this point, Joyce has failed to adapt to shifting relations of care, though she has borne the brunt of exchange, being, at the story's opening, swapped for another woman. Yet she persists in offering gifts, expecting reciprocity. In her attempt to give a personal, affecting gift to a character from her past she is upsetting the unspoken terms of the story's economy of care. Christie's refusal to acknowledge the significance of the gift – chocolate tulips meant to recall the chocolate lilies – neutralizes the gift's power, its personal aura, returning it to a simple, edible object. At first, Joyce is shaken by the dismissal, but she begins to recover as she walks away from the bookstore, and discovers she too can transform and neutralize the pain of emotional rejection. Notably, her means are the same as Christie's: she will incorporate the scene into her own narratives, offering up Christie's rejection for public amusement: "This might even turn into a funny story that she would tell one day. She wouldn't be surprised" (61).

In its depiction of painful inversions of care relations, grim "emotional housekeeping," "unfair thrift," and unappreciated, unanswered calls of need, the story evokes an ethics of care that dispenses with the possibility of reciprocity and satisfaction, baldly considering the inequality and suffering that can result from both the desire for, and efforts at, care. The story calls attention to the imbalanced economies of affect and responsibility underpinning the explorations of caregiving in many of Munro's stories: "the great happiness … of one person" comes "out of the great unhappiness of another"; gifts go unappreciated or are rejected completely; assistance conceals resentment and dislike; shame and humiliation are the true inspirations for actions of care. Not only do motivation and action fail to align in a harmonious constellation of "successful" care, but caregiving functions as a shield female characters adopt to conceal transgressive desires for power, domination, elimination, retribution. Care can be a weapon, these stories suggest; self-sacrifice can be a device. For those marginalized by gender, as well as class and age, caregiving is a means to power, an opportunity for "colonization" that proves difficult to resist. In these stories the risks of absolute responsibility emerge: it is not just the obligated subject who may be "sundered" by impossible demands, the source of responsibility, the dependent, "hostage-taking" other may also become an object of self-serving sacrifice, dehumanized and exploited.

Munro's stories consider the impossible position of both caregivers and dependents thrust into relations of care, the resentment and frustration of both being needed and being in need. The discomfort of each position generates systems of exchange in which each (giver and receiver) tries to ease her burden by increasing her power and agency, a competitive arrangement that leads to an affective economy that trades in happiness and suffering, a relational structure Joyce identifies in "Fiction." If ethics of care philosophers often stress absolute commitment and the virtues of care, Munro's stories demonstrate responsibility in action,[9] the unavoidable complications that lurk within performances of care and acts of responsibility. These stories evoke the "impossible demands" (Attridge 30) that define ethics (for Attridge, Critchley, Levinas, and others) and remind readers that these abstract "impossibilities" inevitably collapse into the distinctly possible within particular scenarios of responsibility and particular realms of imperfection, inequality, and inadequacy.

6 Forgetting and the Forgotten: Care at the Margins in David Chariandy's *Soucouyant*

If caregiving is a means to power in Munro's stories, it is quite the opposite in David Chariandy's novel, *Soucouyant*, which explores the many ways difference informs the dynamics of care. In this tale of a family fractured by violence and trauma, the burden of care is one of the many forces that sunder the family, one member after another dying or decamping until the disabled matriarch, Adele, is left alone in her crumbling Scarborough home. Unlike the characters in Munro who struggle to evade, or even reorganize the gender and class discrimination that undermines them, the characters in Chariandy's novel, victimized by racism, are denied opportunities to manipulate power relations.

The novel opens with the narrator's return to his family home two years after leaving his mother to fend for herself. Adele's dementia has worsened since their last meeting, and she has trouble recognizing her youngest child. The narrator convinces his mother of his true identity by guiding her hand to "the walnut-shaped lump of bone at the side of [his] knee" (8), a tangible signal of his familial authenticity, since his grandmother had a similar physical anomaly. Adele identifies her son by his "strange bones" (8), initiating a pattern of tactile recognition in which bodies provide legible traces of identity and history. Once his identity has been established, the narrator moves back in with his mother and the young woman who now resides with her. The narrator assumes this stranger is his mother's nurse, but in fact, the woman, Meera, has assumed the role of caregiver as atonement for the cruel pranks she played on Adele as a child. The cohabitation of the narrator, his mother, and her "nurse" sets the stage for a fragmented, fractured narrative that skips across time and space, positioning stories

and anecdotes from Adele's traumatic childhood past alongside depictions of the strangeness and difficulty of the present. The novel culminates with a collaborative recollection, a memory of racial violence
that is the symbolic origin of Adele's cognitive impairment. Readers
learn that she started a fire that disfigured her mother, a fire fuelled by
solvents tossed at Adele's mother by American soldiers in Trinidad.
The soldiers are outraged when the sexualized, racialized body-object
they have used for their pleasure speaks back, asserting its subjectivity: "It shouts and lays accusations against all those milling about … It
calls men by name and shames them and charges them with stupidity
and cruelty. It shouts out their unfaithfulness, the helplessness of their
bodies, the lies of their manhood" (192). In its placement of incendi-
ary racial, gendered violence suffered in Trinidad alongside the more
insidious discrimination experienced in Canada, Chariandy's novel
evokes a continuum of inequality and injustice spanning generations
and nations. The ordeals of the narrator's family – his father's early,
violent death, his brother's disappearance, the narrator's own isolation and alienation, even Adele's dementia – appear as consequences
of pervasive, if mutable, racism.

Unlike Munro's Joyce, Christie, Enid, and Mrs Quinn, who wield
narrative as shields and weapons in their struggles for power, Chariandy's narrator treats storytelling as a palliative device. In this, *Soucouyant*'s narrator resembles *Scar Tissue*'s unnamed narrator[1] who seeks
redemption in narrative by providing the testimony that his mother
cannot. However, while Ignatieff's narrator delivers his mother's story
as an anodyne for the fractured self, *Soucouyant*'s narrator makes no
therapeutic claims. Instead, his testimony is an attempt to expose the
narrative thread connecting his mother's pathological forgetting and
historical traumas that can make forgetting imperative for survival. In
Soucouyant, dementia appears as a manifestation of traumatic history,
"a symbol of [Adele's] alienation" (Mergeai 90), making caregiving a private demonstration of fidelity that speaks to national and political policies of exclusion and abandonment. As a result, the novel demonstrates
the relevance of ethics of care philosophy to discussions of identity, both
personal and familial, and political and historical.

Multiculturalism, Tolerance, and Care

In *Soucouyant*, the narrator's family is relentlessly marginalized, a pattern
of discrimination unmitigated by Canadian multiculturalism, which

was official policy as of 1971 and became law in 1988 with the passing of the Canadian Multiculturalism Act.[2] Many cultural critics argue that Canadian multiculturalism, which aims to preserve, promote, and protect ethnic diversity (Canadian Multiculturalism Act), in fact reinforces public discourses of accommodation and tolerance that actually reinscribe divisions and inequalities between so-called Canadian Canadians and the nation's "ethnic" populations. Critical analyses of *Soucouyant* by Jennifer Delisle, Kit Dobson, Allison Mackey, and Mathilde Mergeai all draw attention to the novel's self-conscious treatment of the dubious achievements of the Multiculturalism Act. Chariandy's novel demonstrates the impotence of the Act in the face of deep-rooted racial assumptions by depicting a family stricken by the traumatic legacy of a racist history that spans geographies and temporalities, a legacy that amplifies the need for care, and at the same time increases the impediments that make care difficult and daunting.

Though the novel begins with the narrator's return to his Scarborough home, *Soucouyant*'s 2007 trade paperback edition opens with a selection of laudatory reviews, a familiar promotional tactic. However, one excerpt stands out: "This elegant and accomplished book," writes a *Toronto Star* reviewer, "strikes me as Southern in its historical preoccupation with racism, violence, and dispossession, and the impact of these things on contemporary experience." The reviewer's disavowal of Canadian racism, casting it as a topic relevant primarily to writers of the American South, is a jarring response to a novel that represents a surfeit of examples demonstrating *Canada*'s legacy of "racism, violence, and dispossession" that remains, as both the novel and the review make clear, largely overlooked in Canadian public discourse. For Adele, a Trinidadian immigrant who arrives in Toronto in the early 1960s, southern Ontario is rife with racial discrimination. When the young Adele works up her nerve to visit a restaurant and try the tantalizing lemon meringue pie she's been admiring through the window for weeks, she is asked to leave since the establishment, a "family restaurant," doesn't allow "coloureds or prostitutes" (50). After their marriage, Adele and Roger have difficulty finding an apartment. When they make inquiries over the phone they get "evasive answers when their accents are heard" (75), and once they learn to "speak 'Canadian'" they are turned away by landlords who, once they catch sight of the couple, claim the place has just been rented (75). Finally, they locate a landlord who, though "not happy with renting out the place to coloureds," "needs the money" enough to acquiesce (75). However, discrimination escalates into racial violence when Adele and Roger take a Niagara Falls honeymoon: upon their return they find their home ransacked and burgled, "go back" written in shit on the walls (77). Later, when Adele and Roger manage to buy a house in Scarborough, the neighbours exhibit signs of discomfort at the breach of their "good" white neighbourhood that has, so far, remained untouched by the city's "growing ethnic neighbourhoods" (59). As the community's annual "Heritage Day parade" makes clear, the neighbours don't consider Adele and Roger's family true Canadians, but rather tolerated interlopers (60). The parade publicity flyers make an explicit distinction between Canadians and "people of multicultural backgrounds" (60), a hierarchy of legitimacy that suggests a particularly Canadian version of racial prejudice, one that trades explicitly exclusionary policies for superficial inclusion: the "separate but equal" intolerance of the American South reversed to become a "together but unequal" Canadian ethos. In Chariandy's novel difference is clearly a liability for visible-minority Canadians. In school, the narrator's Caribbean pronunciation results in his categorization as a "special needs" student (101), his "different" accent interpreted as a speech impediment. Anecdotes of marginalization and persecution recur throughout the novel as the narrator skips across localities and temporalities, setting present experiences of his mother's dementia alongside stories of distant violations, a pattern that explains his conviction that Adele's dementia is a "creative" forgetting (12, 32), memory loss that signals an escape from histories too painful to recall. Consequently, the novel is not "Southern" in its preoccupation with racial inequality, but distinctly Canadian in its focus on discrimination and alienation.

Soucouyant's depiction of Canadian attitudes towards "people of multicultural backgrounds" calls to mind the work of Canadian cultural critics who argue that the nation's legislated multiculturalism has done little to foster equality or address a national history of racial violence and marginalization. Smaro Kamboureli characterizes multiculturalism as "sedative politics," a policy that recognizes ethnic differences in order to disarm and control them (82). Like the "Heritage Day" celebrations in the narrator's Scarborough neighbourhood, official multiculturalism "pays tribute to diversity and suggests ways of celebrating it, thus responding to the clarion call of ethnic communities for recognition. Yet it does so without disturbing the conventional articulation of the Canadian dominant society" (Kamboureli 82).[3] In her influential analysis of the politics of multiculturalism, Himani Bannerji describes the policy as an "ideological state apparatus" that uses non-white "others" as tools for healing the nation's English-French rift (108). In other words, visible minorities are employed as "pawns" in the production of pluralist unity (96). For Bannerji and Kamboureli, multiculturalism is a superficial panacea that embraces difference without any attention to power relations, failing to address ongoing racism and colonial ethnocentrism. Political philosopher Erin Manning elaborates:

> A discourse entrenched within the vocabulary of the nation, multiculturalism is incapable of delving into the exclusionary practices of racism within a nationalizing regime. Multiculturalism, as a liberal pluralist policy that chooses "culture" over "race," diverts attention from the histories and social effects of racism rather than working as a challenge to politics of race and racial identity within the domain of the nation. (87)

In other words, multiculturalism does little to address difference beyond superficial, often trivializing gestures of inclusivity that fail to unsettle the association between whiteness (whether English or French) and Canadianness: "whatever civil ideals multiculturalism may represent, whiteness still occupies the positions of normalcy and privilege in Canada, and anti-racist activity remains hamstrung until we begin to carry out the historical work that traces genealogy, or 'the ideological lineage of this belief system,' in an effort to combat the national injunction to forget the brutal elements of our racial history" (Coleman 7–8). Chariandy's novel offers a vision of such "historical work," tracing the roots of Adele's cognitive impairments through her experiences of marginalization and violence in Canada and Trinidad. Within this narrative, Canada appears part of a traumatic colonial legacy that makes memory hazardous and forgetting a relief.

"Tolerance" is a term frequently, often contentiously, associated with the purpose and results of multiculturalism, despite the fact that the term fails to appear in the Act itself (Coleman 21; Hutcheon 13; Kamboureli 84–91; E. Mackey; Madison 15–16; C. Taylor 220). In national newspapers and magazines one finds analyses of multiculturalism's "mosaic" that focus on Canadian "tolerance" of difference.[4] However, from an ethics of care perspective, tolerance is an inadequate guiding principal for human interaction. Not only does tolerance fail to address racial or gender inequality, but it is also insufficient for creating and sustaining relational identity. Tolerance allows its practitioners to avoid the kind of reciprocity and engagement that philosophers of care stress as essential for ethical relations. Indeed, tolerance implies an antagonist to be endured since one tolerates what is uncomfortable or unpleasant: illness, pain, strangers. The *OED* confirms such interpretations in its various definitions of "tolerance": in biological terms, it denotes "the ability of an organism to survive or to flourish despite infection with a parasite or an otherwise pathogenic organism" ("tolerance," def. 1d); in physiological terms, it refers to "the power, constitutional or acquired, of enduring large doses of active drugs, or of resisting the action of poison" ("tolerance," def. 1b). To tolerate is "to endure, sustain (pain or hardship)" ("tolerate," def. 1a), literally, "to put up with" ("tolerate," def. 3). In effect, tolerance demands little of the tolerating subject, sanctioning the disengagement that is anathema to the mutuality of care. Rather than foster equality and engagement, "tolerance actually reproduces dominance (of those with the power to tolerate)," according to Eva Mackey, "because asking for 'tolerance' always implies the possibility of intolerance. The power and the choice whether to accept or not accept difference, to tolerate it or not, still lies in the hands of the tolerators" (16). Neil Bissoondath makes a similar point in his appraisal of the term: "tolerance itself may be an overrated quality, a flawed ideal … To tolerate someone is to put up with them; it is to adopt a pose of indifference. Acceptance is far more difficult, for it implies engagement, understanding, an appreciation of the human similarities beneath the obvious differences."[5] Consequently, tolerance appears incompatible with ethical engagement, for how can one engender and support selfhood based on social memory and relational identity in a community, a nation based on indifference and isolation?

The difference between being tolerated by a community and belonging to one is a stark one. Chariandy has written about his own family's experiences of marginalization in Canada, describing his parents' diligent contributions to their adopted homeland, contributions largely overlooked by "privileged people" ("Stranger" 555). Despite being born in Canada, Chariandy describes feeling estranged from his homeland where, as in the United States, "the hierarchies of race are still so plainly evident," so much so that he is surprised to even "occasionally be made to feel welcome or [attain] a sense of belonging" (561). The ideology of multiculturalism encourages tolerance and accommodation, but does little to foster the kind of interconnectedness that facilitates relations of care and a sense of belonging.

Throughout *Soucouyant*, Canada provides few opportunities for care outside of familial and ethnic networks. Vulnerabilities produced by social inequalities, illness, and disability inspire pity at best in Adele's "good" Canadian community. There are no official, trained caregivers; the national health care system remains invisible, unhelpful, unavailable. Only one character, a black neighbour, one of the neighbourhood's only other visible minorities, steps forward to provide care, leaving university to devote herself to the woman whose impairments she had previously mocked. Meera's care suggests an awakening to responsibility, to the relational identity she strove to disavow with prank phone calls and cruel jokes. Despite having a mother with the same ethnic background as Adele, or rather because of this similarity, Meera studiously avoided contact with the narrator and his brother in an attempt to avoid the same ostracism they suffered from their classmates. Indeed, to avoid victimization Meera became the victimizer, mocking the narrator and his family. Meera's initial denial of association and solidarity is an attempt to reject difference and the inequality she regards as its consequence. "She grew up in the shadows cast by this house" (154), remarks the narrator, a looming structure she eventually enters willingly, moving into Adele's "shipwreck of a home" (7) to provide care when all others have fled.

The house is a "shipwreck" in more ways than one. Abandoned and disintegrating, the house is a symbol of Adele's wreckage. Like its residents, the house is isolated and at risk; positioned "alone in a cul-de-sac once used as a dump" on "the weathered edge of the bluffs" (9), the house literalizes the family's peripheral existence. The family home is "old and bracing now for the final assaults of erosion" (9), as if the very landscape refuses the house and its residents, doing its best to eject them. Isolation and marginalization permeate all aspects of the narrator's Canadian life, conjuring a vision of a nation lacking in care. Even the novel's form suggests a marginal, fragmented existence in its frequent ellipses, which represent the lexical equivalent of the home's eroding foundation, the black print dissolving into the margin's white space.

Racial "Epidermalization" and the Caring Touch

Perhaps the novel's most prominent image of margins and marginalization is its titular symbol, which draws attention to the role of skin as a potent signifier of boundaries and their transgression. The soucouyant, a creature from Trinidadian folklore, is a vampirelike being who can slip out of her[6] skin and travel as a glowing ball of flames in order to suck the blood of innocent victims. The soucouyant is not invulnerable, however. Sprinkling salt on her discarded skin so that it will burn her when she attempts to resume her human shape can kill her. Although the soucouyant is a reviled creature according to Caribbean folklore, its transplantation to a Canadian context shifts its connotations. As Claudia Benthien explains, flaying has a curiously ambiguous association in Western representation: "on the one hand, for example, it denotes the most extreme inscription of power in the form of torture and killing; on the other hand, it is understood as an allegory for an act of liberation or (violent) modification. It thus signifies both the loss and the gaining of the self" (94). However, this second, emancipatory potential is distinctly gendered and racialized since

> fantasies of leaving and overcoming one's own skin are positive only in male poets, philosophers, and artists. Female writers and "dark-skinned" authors (both male and female), by contrast, tend to speak of a passive captivity in one's own skin, which is often experienced as stigmatized. Fantasies of overcoming and modifying the body surface by the protagonists in these works are marked by violence, pain, and anxieties over identity. (237)

Chariandy's recruitment of the skin-shedding soucouyant as a central symbol provocatively engages both positive and negative representational connotations of flaying.

As the primary marker of difference and the literal boundary of the subject, skin engages both subjectivity and objectification. It is the tissue that lies between the subject and the world, between the subjectivity of the embodied self and the body as another's object. In her monograph on the subject, Benthien elegantly summarizes skin's "peculiar place within figurative speech" (23):

> As perhaps no other part of the human body, it serves both as a representation of the whole and as that which conceals it. On the one hand, skin, in the idioms, sayings, and metaphors … is a stand-in for "person," "spirit," "body," or "life"; that is to say, it is a synecdoche for the human being. Yet at the same time, and this is what makes it so singular, skin functions as the other of the self, by representing its cover, its prison or mask, its medium of communication with the world. (23–4)

This second connotation, skin as "prison or mask," is particularly significant in *Soucouyant* since, for the narrator and his family, skin is a marker of racial difference that threatens to overdetermine, even erase subjectivity. The soucouyant's estrangement from her epidermis resonates with Franz Fanon's theorization of racialized embodiment. In a famous moment from *Black Skin, White Masks* (1967), Fanon conjures a scene of racial interpolation in which a young boy identifies him according to the colour of his skin. The boy's cry of "Mama, see the Negro! I'm frightened!" (112), initiates the transformation of human subject into racial object, a hollow epidermis: "the corporeal schema crumbled, its place taken by a racial epidermal schema" (112). Fanon's skin colour obliterates his subjectivity: "I am given no chance. I am overdetermined from without. I am the slave not of the 'idea' that others have of me but of my own appearance" (116). For Fanon, racial discrimination explodes the self, which is then reconstituted, fractured, and alienated: "I burst apart. Now the fragments have been put together again by another self" (109). This process anticipates Adele's degeneration and her family's disintegration, suggesting Adele's cognitive disorder is as much a historical phenomenon as a biological one. Adele's dementia appears as a form of post-traumatic stress disorder; overwhelmed by racial violence, Adele detaches from reality. Dementia implies a kind of dissolution of the ego, or at least a weakening, a process of alienation that is very like the destruction Fanon describes.

Kelly Oliver interprets Fanon's racialized objectification as an inversion of Lacan's mirror stage: "In the reversed mirror stage, racism, through epidermalization, reduces the ego to skin, not even a fragmented body. Rather than create or maintain the illusion of agency and wholeness that supports the ego, the subject is deflated to a flattened sense of self as nothing but skin" (*Witnessing* 33). In other words, the subject becomes a hollow receptacle of predetermined "ethnic characteristics" that "[batter]" subjectivity: "cannibalism, intellectual deficiency, fetichism [*sic*], racial defects" overtake the subject, shackling him to a racialized body which can never be his own (Fanon 112). Within this racist, "epidermalizing" framework, the prospect of shedding one's skin takes on heightened, potentially positive significance, a fantasy of emancipation from the burden of blackness within racist culture. According to such an interpretation, the soucouyant's attempt to slip into her salted skin is a scorching return to "epidermalization," a return to blackness amid, in Fanon's words, "All this whiteness that burns me" (114).

Adele's history includes terrible epidermal violence: her mother's skin has been reviled, exploited, and attacked by white American soldiers in Trinidad. By igniting the fire that results in her mother's dis-figurement, Adele punishes the stigmatized black skin, transforming it into a monstrous "mask" of scar tissue (Chariandy, *Soucouyant* 115). Adele's violence takes epidermalization to the limit, transforming the epidermis into its own disguise. The burns cause scarring that lends a "plastic look to the old woman's face" where her "skin has buck-led with heat and then set into something hard and senseless" (115). The narrator's grandmother is transformed into "a monster. Some-one with a hide, red-cracked eyes, and blistered hands" (116). Like Fanon, like the soucouyant, she wears, rather than inhabits her own skin, her plasticized "hide." Adele also bears the traces of the fire, but her scars are more discreet, easily hidden beneath a wig. However, as her dementia worsens, or as the narrator puts it, she "forget[s] to forget" (32), her efforts at concealment relax and the narrator gains a view of his mother's scars: "I look upon her skull as if for the first time. The glistening pink skin infected with purple and brown. The corrugations and whorls like an organ exposed to air. A brain obscenely naked and pulsing with life" (122). For Adele, outside and inside have converged, the skin resembling the brain it conceals. Or perhaps her skin is as good as gone, the scarring effecting a symbolic flaying, the permanent separation of epidermis and self that is the result of her racial trauma. Adele's scars are historical traces that she reads with her fingers.[7] When she touches her scorched scalp she begins to weep, a moment of tactile interpretation in which the objective and subjective elements of skin are combined: she is both reader and read, toucher and touched.

So how can one care for and with bodies scarred by historical trau-mas? The narrator, terrified by his "monstrous," scarred grandmother, squirms as she attempts to bless him. Throughout the novel, physi-cal and psychological scars like the grandmother's, traces of histori-cal violence and stigmatization, diminish, even destroy, the ability to give and receive care. Vulnerability prompts withdrawal, abandon-ment: "We each left Mother in our own ways," explains the narrator (25). His father dies in a suspicious industrial accident in the factory that has exploited his labour for years. His brother, enraged by every-day prejudice, becomes "increasingly quiet and withdrawn, his body toughening around him like a carapace" (28), racial discrimination transforming his body into a shell, a mask like the grandmother's. When Adele fails to recognize the narrator he packs his things and leaves, taking pains to make arrangements, "provisions" (30), with his mother's bank and her friend Mrs Christopher in order to assure her care in his absence.

Philosopher of care Maurice Hamington insists that it is our shared embodiment that makes care possible, perhaps inevitable. According to his model,

> when the flesh confronts other bodies as objects in the world, its reversibility allows for an ambiguous, limited understanding of the other body. The other body that I perceive is also subject and object. I recognize its form (a body) and movement (its habits), and immediately I have a level of shared knowledge that is both tacit and explicit. When my body confronts another, even if it is a foreign body attired and socially constructed differently from my own, there is still a fundamental connection and understanding in the flesh that Merleau-Ponty refers to as the "propagation" of bodily experience. If a knife accidentally cuts that other body, I do not have to ask whether pain was felt. (54)

Hamington's theory provides a compelling case for embodied empathy as a human inevitability. Although he is somewhat flippant in his dismissal of difference, the powerful obstacle to empathy that race and gender can, and do, become within cultures structured by inequality, his theory can help explain how the "epidermalization" of the subject would inhibit intrinsic embodied care. In disassociating from one's own skin, the capacity for caring, empathic touch would be obstructed. Consequently there is a destructive tension between the universality of sensation and the visual difference of skin. Touch may be a powerful means to care, comfort, and connection; however, skin is a sign of difference that, within racist cultures, precipitates the denial, even destruction of subjectivity, a process of devastation that is the very opposite of care.

So how does one theorize care in societies like Canada's, structured by racial inequality and marginalization? As much as the body, both haptically and visually, can provide the reciprocal connections that philosophers of care recommend for ethical relations, Chariandy's novel stresses another, essential form of commitment that establishes and fortifies relational identity. In *Soucouyant*, witnessing and testimony become the primary acts of care.[8] As the narrator explains, his storytelling is not merely an attempt to document his mother's illness, but an effort to creatively narrativize in a way that honours and protects his mother: "I wanted to imagine her growing, not diminishing. I wanted to portray her awakening to something that we wouldn't have guessed at otherwise. The freedom of meaning, the wild magic of existence …" (ellipses in original 194). In other words, the narrator's representation is not a fixed portrait, but an attempt to approximate living testimony, to communicate something beyond historical documentation. In this sense, the narrator is self-consciously transitioning from *"eyewitness* testimony" to *"bearing* witness to something beyond recognition that can't be seen" (Oliver, *Witnessing*, emphasis in original 16). The narrator seeks to deliver a narrative that is open to revision and imagination, testifying to his mother's traumatic history and at the same time acknowledging omissions and elisions. The novel's recurring ellipses at once indicate and refuse to represent the unknown, the forgotten, that which is beyond representation, the existence of that which is "beyond recognition."

Conclusion: Creative Forgetting and Creolized Care

In her theory of hybridity, Anjali Prabhu rehearses the consequences of diasporic solidarity, which preserves discrete ethnic identities via a preoccupation with past traumas (Prabhu 14). According to its critics, Canada's multiculturalism encourages this kind of backward-looking solidarity by promoting discrete, ossified ethnic communities whose members are designated by hyphenated identities, "Canadian" always preceded by some "other," primary affiliation. According to Prabhu, unlike diasporic solidarity, creolization shrugs off antiquated solidarity with its forward-looking animus; its hybridized subjects direct "energies toward interaction and connections to the present" (5). In a sense, creolization is "post-diaspora" since it describes efforts to move beyond a preoccupation with past traumas, and identities, in order to engage with blended identities in the present (9). A difficult prescription no doubt, but, as Prabhu suggests, postcolonial discourses typically depend on "balancing the two tendencies" (14). Canadian multiculturalism's exclusive focus on diasporic solidarity, on the preservation and enhancement of ethnic categories, overlooks the productive potential of creolization, of interaction and blending. Instead of feeling rooted and at home, Chariandy's characters struggle with ethnic visibility, with community boundaries that separate and isolate. According to Prabhu, "it is the memory of shared trauma that assures diasporic cohesion in the present" (10). The narrator's initial flight from his mother suggests an attempt to escape the oppressive legacy of his diasporic identity, an attempt to engage with the present, to refuse the burden of past traumas, a burden Marianne Hirsch explores in her theory of "postmemory." Both Delisle and Allison Mackey draw on Hirsch's idea of "postmemory," those second-generation, second-hand memories of ancestral traumas that haunt the children of Holocaust survivors and other victims of persecution, to theorize the narrator's relationship to his mother and a broader diasporic history. By providing care for Adele, the narrator risks contracting her trauma, her disability, becoming overdetermined by diasporic history. Consequently, the novel suggests an ethical dilemma for its narrator, a choice between diasporic intimacy, postmemory's absorption of trauma, and devoted caregiving, on the one hand, and creolization, refusal of victimhood, and familial abandonment on the other. However, in the novel's final section, the narrator manages to blend both approaches, testifying to historical traumas and at the same time allowing space for revision and new perspectives. By the novel's conclusion the narrator has found a way to incorporate the present into tales of the past, to avoid ossification, to blend synchronic and diachronic perspectives.

The novel's central tension between remembering and forgetting, its exploration of the creativity of forgetting (and, I would argue, remembering), produces a hybrid, one might say, creolized text, one that incorporates telling and silence, history and imagination, past and present,[9] in ways that challenge multiculturalism's privileging of historical, static identities. *Soucouyant* demonstrates dementia theorist and activist Anne Basting's reminder that forgetting is both "a necessary and positive feature of our humanity" (19).[10]

This productive view of forgetting and fragmentation is a provocative one that counters the tendency to regard dementia and its losses within gothic scripts of ghosts, zombies, terror, and pathos (J. Taylor 321). Though the novel contains ominous moments of unnerving strangeness, it also incorporates the creativity, regeneration, and humour that can be a part of relations of care between victims of dementia and their caregivers. In an interview, Chariandy described his desire to engage a new, productive perspective of memory loss: "I'm indeed dabbling with casting forgetting in more creative and at least not-wholly-pejorative terms – a desire motivated both by my sympathies towards people with dementia, and a critical take on what you might call nostalgic or naïve recuperative agendas" (Chariandy, "Spirits of Elsewhere Past" 813). Nostalgic, recuperative agendas cannot incorporate the kind of instability and transformation that is involved in both creolization and dementia. In Chariandy's novel, the anxiety produced by the unavoidable forgetting of dementia converges with diasporic communities' anxiety about losing cultural and familial history. As he explains, "dementia … enabled me to explore the fragility and endurance of cultural memory, and, most particularly, the challenge of cultural memory for a second-generation immigrant. Obviously, because Adele is now forgetting her past in Trinidad, the burden of memory is thrust upon her Canadian-born and -raised son" ("Spirits" 812–13). This "burden of memory," one common to members of diasporas, overlaps with the burden of care: for the novel's narrator, remembering and testifying are essential to his caregiving. But the novel transforms such "burdens" into a mutually beneficial creative process that blends history and mythology, storytelling and listening, creating a collaborative methodology in which mother and son simultaneously recollect and fabricate formative narratives. As a result, the novel manages to represent both remembering and forgetting, history and fiction, and, perhaps most significantly, their inextricability. This creolization of memory and mythology allows for creative, collaborative recollection, reinforcing Basting's assertion that "*memory is social, that the 'self' is relational*" (emphasis in original 161). *Soucouyant* shows its readers the mutuality of care, a mutuality rarely seen in the literature considered throughout *Imagining Care*. Chariandy's novel explores collaboration and care, the narrator's efforts to move beyond a nihilistic response to racism, a response that has claimed the narrator's brother. According to Cornel West, such "nihilism is not overcome by arguments or analyses; it is tamed by love and care" (19). In *Soucouyant*, readers discover the narrator's first, tentative steps towards a new relational politics, a politics of care that is distinctly *Canadian* in its preoccupation with racism, trauma, and the restorative potential of creative remembering *and* forgetting.

Conclusion:
Imagining the Future of Care

Imagining Care is motivated by a desire to bring various discourses – philosophical, literary, pragmatic – into dialogue by exploring care in fiction and memoirs by contemporary Canadian writers, including Margaret Atwood, Ian Brown, David Chariandy, Michael Ignatieff, and Alice Munro, alongside ethics of care philosophy and its discontents. Throughout *Imagining Care* I have sought to demonstrate how Canadian literature imagines and, in a sense, theorizes relations of care, and how its representations interact with the claims made by ethical philosophers and feminist theorists. These selections from Canadian literature offer ethical situations, which, unlike instrumental narratives, like the Heinz dilemma, include the multiple details, contexts, and everyday particularities that obviate the possibility of clear, conclusively "right" actions and answers to the complicated questions care poses.

These Canadian texts expose the fallacy of Canada as a caring nation characterized primarily by equality and compassion. The ambiguity and complexity of caregiving scenarios depicted in literature by Atwood, Brown, Chariandy, Ignatieff, Munro, and others – aesthetically constructed scenarios complicated by the human desires for power, for attention, for affection – provide compelling territory to investigate both the satisfaction and connection, along with the ambivalence and unease, produced by caregiving relations. As I have argued in the preceding chapters, Canadian literary narratives imagine care as necessary and desirable, but also precarious and perilous. Narratives of caregiving grapple with the enigmatic ethics of care, the entanglement of love and labour so complicated by the inscrutability of human motivation and intentionality, the porous boundaries between responsibility and dependence. The power politics of care, its occasion for, and manifestation of inequality demands attention and vigilance from both participants and observers. *Imagining Care* attends primarily to contemporary caregiving relationships between human subjects. I want to conclude with a consideration of recent technological interventions (both actual and speculated) that conjure a future dominated by posthuman care. Literary speculations about the future of care, read in tandem with the rising prominence of actual robotic caregivers, foretell a future in which human interaction is no longer an inevitable feature of care relations.

The Future of Care: Literary Speculation Then and Now

Chapter 2 examines Margaret Atwood's short story collection *Moral Disorder*, interpreting it as a polemic that interrogates the responsibilities of care. In particular, the chapter explores how and why caregiving is so often unsuccessful in Atwood's collection, harming as often as helping both the giver and the receiver. In *Moral Disorder* harmonious compromise is impossible, I argue, because in these stories pain, trauma, and obligation cannot be extinguished, only reassigned, making suffering unavoidable, but transferable. As in many of the texts studied throughout *Imagining Care*, care in Atwood's work is rarely a constructive combination of "right" feeling and "right" action. In *Moral Disorder* the reader follows the protagonist from her childhood in the mid-twentieth century to her twenty-first-century later life, demonstrating the limitations experienced by women in recent Canadian history, the various forces that encourage women to live lives devoted to domestic labour, to caretaking.

However, Atwood along with other Canadian women writers, including Larissa Lai and Nalo Hopkinson, has also produced fiction that conjures fascinating, often alarming future societies in which relations of care are no longer inevitable, and sometimes even prohibited. Atwood has published four speculative novels that envision dystopic future societies: *The Handmaid's Tale* (1985), *Oryx and Crake* (2003), *Year of the Flood* (2009), and *MaddAddam* (2013).[1] Like Lai and Hopkinson, Atwood creates future scenarios in which the meaning and power of national identity have crumbled. In these texts, relationships become increasingly, or entirely mediated by science and technology, by cyborgs, genetically engineered species, robots, and ubiquitous Web surveillance, making humans increasingly dependent not on one another, but on non-human entities. It is telling that none of Atwood's speculative fictions, nor Hopkinson's *Midnight Robber*, are set in a future Canada, though the territory may be formerly Canadian. In *The Handmaid's Tale*, one finds an exaggerated, satirical projection of the future based on a 1980s present dominated by fundamentalist Christianity, anti-feminist backlash, and neoliberal capitalist culture. But this too is distinctly *non*-Canadian in its formulation. Atwood has explained that such an extremist state is unimaginable in Canada. According to Atwood critic and biographer Rosemary Sullivan, Atwood found the idea of setting a "futuristic nightmare" in Canada "problematic" due to the nation's "genius for compromise" (851).[2]

Even Atwood, whose literary criticism emphasizes the extreme inhospitality of the Canadian environment, deems Canada an unlikely setting for dystopia. However, Canada's "genius for compromise" is a mixed blessing since, in *Moral Disorder* and other Canadian fiction, compromise often involves the persistence of inequality and sacrifice, the elimination of opportunities for reciprocal, affirming care. Though "compromise" and "care" are clearly not interchangeable, there is an impulse, as I explore in chapter 6, to imagine slippages between the two, to imagine "tolerance," and compromise, however unequal, as markers of a caring, compassionate national identity. But Atwood, Hopkinson, and Lai's fiction implies that such mythologies will become increasingly irrelevant as we move into the globalized future where corporate, rather than national citizenship will determine identity.

The centrality of capitalistic power, so prominent in *Oryx and Crake* and *The Year of the Flood*, is already apparent in *The Handmaid's Tale*, which, argues Pamela Cooper, draws together "feminist film theory and Foucault's discourses on power, [and] mobilizes sexuality and gender as crucial factors in the power-knowledge nexus of capitalist culture" (51). *The Handmaid's Tale* imagines a totalitarian, fundamentalist future in which the sterile elite engage "handmaids" to bear their children. Handmaids are reproductive slaves, walking wombs forced into surrogacy (the alternative is exile and hard labour handling the radioactive waste created by nuclear accidents). The patriarchal regime determines who may and may not give and receive care: though handmaids may bear children, they are prohibited from raising them; such labour is performed by other indentured workers, and occasionally by the elite parents themselves. Raising children is a privilege afforded the rich and powerful, while pregnancy is work done by marginalized women. In Gilead, the division of affect and labour is stark, intimacy and affection divorced from the labour of reproduction. The severing of feeling and work is taken to its limit, where the two become mutually exclusive: handmaids are prohibited from intimate relationships and conscripted into unemotional, procreative sexual intercourse with their commanders and banal scripted conversations with their walking companions. As such, *The Handmaid's Tale* imagines a limit-case of the tension between the emotions and practices of care, an exaggeration of the friction between love and labour that one often finds in Alice Munro's stories.

The prohibition of affective opportunities effects a powerful subjugation that threatens the handmaid's subjectivity. Indeed, though the protagonist, Offred, retains the "inner witness" discussed in chapter 2 by testifying to her struggle and survival, other handmaids are not so lucky, their selfhood broken by the denial of the "address-ability" and "response-ability" Kelly Oliver insists are integral for subjectivity. Offred remarks on her status as a "two-legged womb" (Atwood, *The Handmaid's Tale* 171), recognizing that her reproductive corporeality obliterates her subject status in the eyes of the regime. Coral Ann Howells elaborates the implications of Offred's perverse synecdoche, this image of grotesque fusion in which an ambulatory womb replaces a person: "As a Handmaid deprived of her own name and identity, she has no rights as an individual but instead has been conscripted into sexual service to the state, reduced by its doctrine of biological essentialism to her female role as a child breeder" ("Margaret Atwood's Dystopian Visions" 165). In this scenario, biology is destiny, a utilitarian ethic that provides scarce opportunity for care. Citizens, particularly women, are tools of the state. Stephanie Hammer argues that "one of the most striking features" of the novel is its lack of futuristic tools, of "technological trappings – be they gismos, robots, or outlandish scientific theories, advances, or practices" (44). Unlike other speculative novels, such as, "*1984, Brave New World, A Clockwork Orange*, or even *Fahrenheit 451*[, which] all present worlds which are techno-nightmares – systems which dehumanize their citizens, forcing them to operate like machinery, rather than like individuals," Atwood's novel conjures the future as a "a reactionary step backwards in time" (Hammer 44–5). However, despite the striking absence of "technological trappings," *The Handmaid's Tale* explores the same territory as its futurist predecessors. There may be few actual machines in *The Handmaid's Tale* (antiquated computers, mechanized prayer printers), but animated objects are

prominent nonetheless. In *The Handmaid's Tale* one discovers a haunting depiction of the human-as-machine, a radical objectification of the
female body conceived of as reproductive machine without the needs,
vulnerabilities, or ethical demands of a sentient human being.

In the new millennium Atwood has returned to the genre of speculative fiction. Coral Ann Howells summarizes the differences between
the 1985 publication and Atwood's more recent futurist novels:

> *The Handmaid's Tale*, centered on human rights abuses and particularly the
> oppression of women under a fundamentalist regime, is entirely social
> and political in its agenda, whereas *Oryx and Crake* projects a world defa-
> miliarized not through military or state power but through the abuse of
> scientific knowledge, where genetic engineering has created transgenic
> monsters and humanoid creatures in a post-apocalyptic scenario much
> closer to conventional science fiction. ("Margaret Atwood's Dystopian
> Visions" 163)

Oryx and Crake, which, Howells argues, can be read as a sequel to *The
Handmaid's Tale* (161), depicts a future in which global warming and an
engineered virus have caused massive species annihilation, leaving only
a few humans alive. These few survivors share the transformed environment with a genetically engineered humanlike species, designed
by the "mad scientist" figure, Crake, to exclude the human flaws that
have been the species' downfall. For much of *Oryx and Crake*, the sole
surviving human seems to be "Snowman," formerly Jimmy, whose
life has been spared by Crake himself. Jimmy is preserved, "leaving
him the protector and guide of the Crakers, the result of Crake's grand
project to bioengineer a new, non-predatory, non-territorial hominid,
one adapted to, and not in competition with, the natural environment"
(Bouson, "It's Game Over" 149). "Care" for the planet, according to
Crake's plan, is manifested perversely through genocide. In order to
save the planet he attempts to exterminate earth's destructive human
inhabitants. Critics describe Crake as a "scientist-imperialist" (Bouson,
"It's Game Over" 141), a "hero-villain" (Howells, "Margaret Atwood's
Dystopian Visions" 162), and a "boy-genius-cum-mad-scientist-cum-
ecoterrorist" (Hoogheem 67), but Atwood has remarked that, "from a
certain perspective, Crake is the most altruistic person around" (qtd. in
Bouson, "It's Game Over" 149) in his efforts to engineer a posthuman
future in which his engineered species exists in harmony with the natural
environment, rather than at its expense.

In this darkly satirical vision of the future, caring relations, ethical reciprocity, dependency work, the dynamics of witnessing, along with multitudes of species have become endangered by the capitulation of social institutions to corporate control. The sinister CorpSeCorps has usurped the role of government, embodying neoliberalism and globalization gone wild. Atwood conjures a "bleak future in which science and global capitalism have displaced any sense of moral agency in daily life" (Bosco 159). *Oryx and Crake*'s narrator, Jimmy, is the bereft, alienated subject who has survived this new world order and its fallout, at least long enough to deliver his narration. The society Crake has destroyed was one devoid of care. As the reader discovers, "Jimmy [has grown] up in a dystopian world devoid of any moral framework, a world of rampant consumerism, pervasive violence, and impoverished humanity" (166). The absence of care and interrelationality in Jimmy's life produces a profound estrangement: "Jimmy lacks ... community. He sees himself not as an integral member of a cosmos in which he can live in harmony, but as the conscripted caretaker of beings fundamentally different from himself ... [H]e interprets his life as a series of abandonments" (Hoogheem 65). In *Oryx and Crake*, "conscripted caretak[ing]" has replaced any opportunities for voluntary, sustaining, reciprocal caregiving. In this harrowing vision of the future, biotechnology, global capitalism, and corporate culture have eliminated all possibilities for a human ethics of care. The potential of the Crakers, engineered to collaborate, to care, in an eerily automaton fashion, remains to be seen.

The sequels to *Oryx and Crake* call into question its gloomy prospects. In *The Year of the Flood*, the reader meets the "God's Gardeners," a religious cult whose members espouse and embody a commitment to radical interdependency, a religious devotion to ecological harmony that privileges ecosystems over individuals. Theirs is a revolutionary decentering of the human that blends Christian theology with environmentalism to produce a spiritual practice that reveres all life and eschews ecologically destructive practices. After the "waterless flood," the term used by the God's Gardeners to describe the genocidal bioform engineered to eliminate the human race, the few survivors who remain are largely God's Gardeners since their environmental theology has provided them with the training and tools to avoid infection and survive in a decimated landscape. As Andrew Hoogheem explains, though Jimmy and the Gardeners survive Crake's bioterrorism with equal access to limited resources, "as *The Year of the Flood* draws to a close, the surviving Gardeners have forged a functioning community and are planning their next moves while Jimmy is angry, confused, alone, malnourished, and, in the novel's final pages, incoherent with fever" (65). Separation and isolation are incompatible with well-being, both psychological and physiological. *The Year of the Flood* evokes a future in which community, caring, collaboration, and interdependency persist amid the dissolution of neoliberal global capitalism. Without interdependence, survival in Atwood's dystopia is impossible, an image of the future that reflects ethics of care philosophy's insistence on interrelationality as fundamental for survival, subjectivity, and identity. Atwood's speculative fiction recalls the point, made by Held and others, that no one survives infancy without substantial care; however, in Atwood, the boundaries of responsibility have been extended to acknowledge ecological dependency, exposing the degree to which human life is sustained by non-human life forms. Consequently, Atwood's speculations function as a provocation to ethics of care philosophers who would limit their attention to human relations. Interdependence, Atwood implies, extends far beyond the human to the ecological. What, Atwood's fictions seem to ask, might be the future of care? A posthuman interdependency that looks beyond species boundaries to acknowledge the responsibilities demanded by human dependence on and, more to the point, exploitation of non-human animals and the diverse ecological systems that sustain life on earth.[3]

One finds attention to ecological dependencies and the impact of technological intervention in other contemporary Canadian speculative fiction. Hopkinson's *Midnight Robber* (2000), for example, concerns Tan-Tan, a young woman cast into exile when her father commits murder on their utopic home planet, Toussaint. Father and daughter end up in the dangerous wilderness of New-Half-Tree, a dystopic mirror of Toussaint's civilized, technologically monitored utopia. *Midnight Robber*'s narrator explains the relationship of these two realms: "New Half-Way Tree is how Toussaint planet did look before the Marryshow Corporation sink them Earth Engine Number 127 down into it like God entering he woman; plunging into the womb of soil to impregnate the planet with the seed of Granny Nanny" (2). The seemingly benevolent Marryshow Corporation has sown the planet with the artificial intelligence of "the Grande Nanotech Sentient Interface: Granny Nansi's Web," which keeps "the Nation Worlds protected" (10). However, this protection comes with a price: "a Marryshevite couldn't even self take a piss without the toilet analyzing the chemical composition of the urine and logging the data in the health records" (10). As Giselle Anatol

explains, in Toussaint "there is no 'privacy' per se, but more importantly, no individual risks a potentially destructive isolation. Nanny's
presence protects the safety of All instead of the privacy rights of One"
("Maternal Discourses" 113). At birth the population is "seeded with
nanomites" (10), which develop into receivers that allow lifelong connection to the Grande Nanotech Sentient Interface, but this technological cohabitation of the human body lacks the sinister exploitation of
bodies one finds in Atwood's fiction. Indeed, in an interview Hopkinson remarked on Granny Nanny's benevolence: "Rather than being a
'Big Brother' paradigm it's an affectionate ... sense of love, care and
duty" (qtd. in Anatol 114).[4] Granny Nanny's name "invokes that of
Nanny of the Maroons, a historical resistance leader of pre-Emancipa-
tion Jamaica whose name and story often take on mythic proportions"
(Anatol 113). Jillana Enteen argues that "like the legendary fighter,
Nanny uses her knowledge to ensure harmony, security, health, and
freedom from outside oppression for the planet's occupants" (271). Not
all critics celebrate the novel's surveilling technologies. Erin Feshkens
is circumspect in her appraisal:

> Hopkinson's Nanny web ... lull[s] Toussaint's populace into a leisurely
> freedom from physical harm, stress, or change at the expense of privacy.
> Nanny's nanomites blast the fiction of an inviolable human subject or
> body to shreds. At the intersection of Nanny's benevolent mothering and
> insidious smothering, Hopkinson launches a critique of globalization's
> promises by creating tension between the immanent and laboring body
> and the transcendent, pleasure-seeking self. (139)

Even for those sympathetic to the virtues of collectivism, and antagonistic towards neoliberalism, the dark shadows of Granny Nanny reveal
the central ambiguity at the heart of the idealized communal sense of
interdependence promoted by ethics of care philosophers.

Hopkinson's creation of a planet free from the care of the Nanotech
Sentient Interface demonstrates the loss that accompanies this "freedom." As Feshkens argues, "New Half-Way Tree quickly reveals itself
to be a planet free of Nanny, but also free of leisure, confirming the
link between this networked power and liberation from embodiment.
Its criminal inhabitants must labour for food, shelter and clothing, and
their bodies are variously, physically marked by this punitive dispensa-
tion" (144–5). Tan-Tan mourns the loss of her Toussaint life, the care and
comfort she enjoyed as the mayor's daughter. However, the care Tan-Tan

enjoyed on Toussaint was not provided by parents or relatives, but by robots, computers, and employees, challenging humanistic discourses of care that overlook or distrust the efficacy of non-human interventions. In fact, there is very little caregiving between humans in Hopkinson's vision of the future. Humans prove unreliable, self-centred, cruel, whereas the non-human world of animals, plants, and machines provides more consistent, selfless care. When, on her sixteenth birthday, Tan-Tan is sexually and physically abused by her father, and exiled yet again, this time by her New Half-Tree community, she finds solace and sustenance in the non-human world of the planet's birdlike indigenous population, its native flora and fauna.

In the novel's conclusion, the reader discovers that the narrator is in fact non-human. It is the "house eshu," Tan-Tan's personal connection to the Granny Nanny interface, who tells her story, who has, in fact been witnessing her throughout her struggles on New Half-Tree and seeking a means to reverse her undeserved exile. When the novel ends Tan-Tan has just given birth to her son, Tubman, whose in utero development has included the growth of "nanomites" in his very blood, making him "literally a living bridge between humans and Nanny" (Feshkens 153). This cyborg child evokes a posthuman future in which cybernetics will be indivisible from the human body. Yet this is not a nightmarish scenario of invasion and infiltration, but a utopic vision of caring interdependence. The future of care, in *Midnight Robber*, involves a fortifying convergence in which the myth of independence is obsolete since the "I" is always already a technologically inflected "we."

Consider the Robot

The preponderance of engineered, sentient entities in speculative fiction reflects the ubiquity of technological intervention in everyday human life. While machines are becoming more like humans in their abilities and functions, the discovery of DNA and its determining forces can lead to the proscriptive perception of humans as genetically programmed machines. In *Oryx and Crake* Crake describes humans as ("faulty") "hormone robots" (203), a perspective that makes him immune to human suffering and leads, ultimately, to his genocidal attempt to save the planet. His attitude towards human life is an uncanny echo of Nobel Prize–winning geneticist Herman J. Muller, who writes: "Man is a giant robot created by DNA to make more DNA" (qtd. in Holler 88). If humans are simply DNA, or hormonal robots, why not replace the species with a superior model, such as the carefully engineered Crakers? The Crakers are like organic robots, meticulously constructed rather than haphazardly evolved. Both Atwood and Hopkinson create fiction that grapples with the increasingly fraught distinction between humans and machines in the late twentieth and early twenty-first centuries as technological advancement facilitates posthuman entities and complicates relations of care.

In Canada there has been a relative reticence in embracing technological care, but in Japan, Denmark, Norway, the Netherlands, Sweden, and Germany robots currently perform a variety of caregiving tasks, including providing companionship and comfort for sufferers of dementia. The number of "social robots" available worldwide is significant: over one hundred models were on the market as of 2012 (Ito). This "family" of robots "includes machines that can act as nursemaids and housekeepers, provide companionship, talk patients through physical rehabilitation, and act as surrogate pets" (Ito). Japan is a leader in the development of caregiving robotics. In a nation where low birth rates have resulted in a growing elderly population and a shrinking workforce (Lin 6), technologies of care have become a significant business opportunity. Journalist Olivia Solo estimates that "by 2015 some 5.69 million people in Japan will be in need of nursing care" (Solo), while the "Japan Robot Association, an industry trade group, predicts today's $5-billion-a-year market for social robots will top $50 billion a year by 2025" (Ito). As Jason Borenstein and Yvette Pearson explain, whereas in the past it was "customary for robots and humans to work separately from one another," robots are becoming increasingly integrated into everyday life: "the cordoning off of humans from robots is becoming a thing of the past. For instance, South Korea plans to have a robot in each home by 2020" ("Robot Caregivers: Harbingers" 277). This enthusiasm for technological care has yet to be felt in Canada or the Untied States, but some critics see it as inevitable since the growing demand for care and the paucity of available human caregivers create a compelling argument in favour of adopting robotic caregivers (Aronson). Current trends in robotics suggest a future in which robots play a significant role in a variety of human activities, including caregiving, a prospect that raises a number of questions. In particular, what are the political implications of future caregiving relations in which human agency is replaced by the kinds of cyborgian and robotic interventions anticipated by speculative fiction like Atwood's and Hopkinson's? Though humans may not yet be bearers of Granny

Nanny's nanomites, posthuman interventions in care do exist in a nascent form.

"Robots," writes David Lin, "are often tasked to perform the 'three Ds,' that is, jobs that are dull, dirty, or dangerous" (4). The etymology of the term confirms these negative connotations. First appearing in Karel Čapek's 1920 play *R.U.R.: Rossum's Universal Robots*, "robot" comes from the Czech word *robota*, which translates to 'drudgery' or 'forced labor'" (Petersen 283). In addition, robots are often designed to complete tasks beyond human ability, making up for "human frailties and limitations" (Lin 4). In other words, robots are typically designed to absent humans from those activities that we can't, won't, or don't want to do. Those made vulnerable by aging and impairment require both the labour and affect of care, and robotics have been developed and produced to respond to the demands of both requirements. According to Lin, the creation of caregiving robots speaks to the human desire to avoid caregiving, both its labour and affect. As the caregivers depicted in contemporary Canadian literature imply, there are notable psychological and physical risks involved in care. It is not only the strenuous labour of care, such as wheelchair transfers, that robots can undertake. A number of "companion" robots have been developed to provide emotional support for their users.

Despite the high demand for both affective and utilitarian robotic care, there are few models designed to provide both (Shaw-Garlock 258; Broekens, Heerink and Rosendal 94).[5] More commonly, one finds robots designed to assist with daily functioning, mobility, and monitoring,[6] on the one hand, or psychological well-being, on the other. Robots have been designed to perform utilitarian, "dangerous" work (one of Lin's "three Ds"), including transfers, which typically involve lifting patients in and out of beds and wheelchairs. For example, the RIBA (Robot for Interactive Body Assistance) uses "very strong human-like arms," as described on its promotional website, to move users in and out of beds or wheelchairs ("World's First").[7] Other utilitarian caregiving robots eschew human or animal design. "My Spoon," designed by Secom of Japan, looks much like what it is, an elaborate, automated feeding device[8] that allows users with disabilities to eat, as the website puts it, "with only minimal help from a caregiver." A similarly nonhuman assistance device is Panasonic's hair-washing robot, which appeared on the market in 2010. Though it may have sixteen robotic "fingers" that work to wash, condition, and dry the user's hair, like My Spoon, the hair-washing robot has a mechanistic look that belies any affective or animal associations. As with most caregiving robotics producers, Panasonic stresses the therapeutic benefits of its integrated wheelchair and hair-washing robot, which, it claims, is "designed to help support safe and comfortable living of the elderly and people with limited mobility while reducing the burden of caregivers" (Ricker), reinforcing associations between care and toil, implying that caregiving is obligated labour, drudgery to be avoided whenever possible. As well, the commentary reduces caregiving to physical tasks, excluding the affective dimension of care.

At the other end of the spectrum from utilitarian, mechanistic care tools, such as My Spoon and Panasonics' hair-washing wheelchair, one finds the remarkable and popular Japanese creation, Paro. Visually and aurally patterned on a baby seal, Paro is a white and fuzzy robotic doll designed to elicit affection and good will from its users. Unlike other caregiving robots, Paro simulates animalistic vitality and vulnerability in order to create intimacy and care between user and robot.[9] Robots like Paro make the posthuman care provided by pet therapy appear antiquated. The vitality of the companion animal supplying pet therapy can be replicated and its unpredictability and fallibility remedied through the technology of robotics.[10] Indeed, Robert Ito reports that "in one study, a few people in two nursing homes seemed to believe that the Paro was a real animal; others spoke to it, and were convinced that the Paro, who can only squeak and purr, was speaking back to them." In the case of Paro, there is a kind of robotic sleight of hand in which the caregiving robot delivers care by eliciting it from its users. As Sherry Turkle explains, "We are psychologically programmed not only to nurture what we love but to love what we nurture" (*Alone* 11), a predisposition that, she argues, makes us vulnerable to technological attachment. Paro's appealing design makes it particularly effective at eliciting affection from its users, an effectiveness that, for Turkle, is cause for concern. Turkle is wary of the "simulations of love" offered by "sociable robots" (*Alone* 10), arguing that at the "robotic moment" – when people are emotionally and philosophically "read[y]" to connect with robots as friends and companions – "We don't seem to care what these artificial intelligences 'know' or 'understand' of the human moments we might 'share' with them. At the robotic moment, the performance of connection seems connection enough. We are poised to attach to the inanimate without prejudice. The phrase 'technological promiscuity' comes to mind" (*Alone* 9–10). Turkle's phrasing implies that there is something indecent or immoral, even perverse about relationships between humans and non-human care providers.[11] Why, for Turkle and others, does the prospect of robotic companionship inspire such unease?

Although companion robots like Paro appeal to the desire for reciprocity in caregiving, fabricating a relationship in which users are able to simultaneously receive and *give* care, the artificiality of the relationship troubles critics like Turkle. Paro's ability to usurp the otherwise distinctly human prerogatives of caregiving – affection, intimacy, even love – unsettles some care practitioners. In the United States, even caregiving professionals who welcome the benefits of robots "are wary of entirely non-human care," insisting on the importance of a "good balance of technology and heart ... Our seniors are more and more interested in technology in general, but nobody wants to lose the personal touch" (Ahern). Underlying such responses to robotic care is the assumption that good care requires emotional motivation; in other words, good care is human care.[12] Both "heart" and labour are essential for care. However, as the various depictions of care examined throughout *Imagining Care* suggest, achieving a balance of love and labour is difficult in day-to-day caregiving experiences in a pre-posthuman care context. It is promising that professional caregivers maintain "personal touch" as indispensible to care, but the pervasiveness of begrudging, frustrated, coerced, or marginalizing care reframes the question of posthuman care. Robots lack heart and spleen in equal measure.

As much as robots might alleviate the burdens and strain of caregiving, and thereby reduce the risk of deficient, even dangerous caregiving, there is an equal risk that such assistive technologies will "cure" human caregiving altogether, reducing, even eliminating human contact in vulnerable populations, particularly the elderly and impaired. The prospect of robots at once "curing" and causing harm, recalls the concept of the *pharmakon*, which Derrida adopts from Plato's *Phaedrus*. As Grayson Cooke explains, "The term *pharmakon* ... can mean medicine, remedy, drug, charm, philtre, recipe, colour, pigment, and, most importantly, both poison *and* cure" (emphasis in original 112). Like the *pharmakon*, the caregiving robot is a site of contestation with its simultaneous potential for assistance and harm. As many of the texts examined in *Imagining Care* suggest, this tension is not so different from human care, which tends to help and hinder in equal measure.

In addition to the risks robotic care poses for receivers, companion robots like Paro could produce a division of labour that consigns human caregivers to the role of caretaker, responsible for maintaining property rather than relationships. In other words, confining human intervention to *either* emotional assistance *or* physical labour, to the realm of affect or effect, would hinder care and the relationality it both engenders and is engendered by.[13] Due to their necessarily task-oriented design, caregiving robots, whether utilitarian or social, threaten to divide caregiving into labour and affect, a bifurcation at odds with the ethics of care. As Kittay reminds us in her analysis of the vulnerability of dependency workers, "care of dependents – dependency work – is most commonly assigned to those in a society with the least status and power" (*Love's Labour* 6). The robotic bifurcation of affect and labour risks exaggerating the marginalization of care workers, transforming them from caregivers into caretakers.

The Future of Care: Posthuman Relations

As Carey Wolfe explains, "posthumanism" has very different functions according to its disciplinary context. For ecofeminists, ecocritics, and animal studies theorists, the term often describes a radical "decentering of the human in relation to either evolutionary, ecological, or technological coordinates" (Wolfe xvi). Posthumanism

> forces us to rethink our taken-for-granted modes of human experience, including the normal perceptual modes and affective states of *Homo sapiens* itself, by recontextualizing them in terms of the entire sensorium of other living beings and their own autopoetic ways of 'bringing forth a world' – ways that are, since we ourselves are human *animals*, part of the evolutionary history and behavioural and psychological repertoire of the human itself. (xxv)

However, for some involved in the study of robots, cyborgs, and other technological interventions into the category of "human," "posthuman" can imply what Wolfe prefers to call "transhumanism": the notion that "the human is achieved by escaping or repressing its animal origins in nature, the biological, and the evolutionary, but more generally by transcending the bonds of materiality and embodiment altogether" (Wolfe xv). In imagining a future of care, both usages are relevant. On the one hand, Atwood's fictional speculations conjure a post-Enlightenment future in which anthropocentrism could be reoriented towards an ecocritical perspective that acknowledges, whether by choice or by force, the impossibility of disconnected, autonomous human existence. On the other hand, the posthuman future is evoked by recent developments in assistive technologies, as well as Hopkinson's fiction, in which human caregiving is no longer inevitable, necessary, or perhaps even desirable.

Robots evoke a vision of the future in which humans can no longer expect a privileged position in a hierarchy of caregiving relations, positing instead a continuum of care, in which the human and non-human could coexist, even collaborate in responding to human dependency. Might hybridity be the future of care? Like the cyborgian Tubman whose blood contains the nanomites that will assist and protect him, we might dream of a blended, "creolized" care reminiscent of Chariandy's *Soucouyant*. In Hopkinson's novel, assistive technologies remind users of their corporeal vulnerability: like "Nanny's nanomites [that] blast the fiction of an inviolable human subject or body to shreds" (Feshkens 139), caregiving robots threaten to unseat the human from a privileged position by drawing attention to the human body's animalism and dependencies. Hopkinson finds not loss in this unseating, but a potential for collaboration between different entities, biological and technological, that could liberate humans from the contingencies of species-specific caregiving.[14]

Fictional speculations, robotics, cybernetics, and posthuman perspectives summon a possible future in which human embodiment, vulnerability, interdependence, that is, our animality, our ecological interconnectedness becomes increasingly assertive as ecological systems become exhausted and collapse, and technological beings enter our homes, institutions, even our bodies. Ecological disaster awakens us to our environmental dependence, just as robotic interaction alerts us to our haptic dependence, our unease at the prospect of care without human "heart" or touch. The disappearance of human caregiving relations might alert us to their integrity. In other words, the future of care might help cultivate a posthumanist awareness of the fiction of autonomy, a confirmation of Wolfe's argument that "posthumanism ... isn't posthuman at all – in the sense of being 'after' our embodiment has been transcended – but is only posthuman*ist*, in the sense that it opposes the fantasies of disembodiment and autonomy, inherited from humanism itself" (emphasis added, xv). In their shared scepticism towards the "fictive creation" that is the "independent individual" (Kittay, *Love's Labor* 17), posthumanism and ethics of care philosophy converge to advocate a cultural shift away from illusions of independence produced by structural inequalities towards an acknowledgment of interdependencies, human, animal, ecological, and even technological. When we imagine such a posthuman future, utopic and dystopic speculations seem beside the point. Whatever scientific innovations and interventions may come, caregiving is likely to remain confoundingly human: at once difficult and unpredictable, messy and improvisational, gruelling and gratifying.

Notes

Introduction

1 Sally Chivers offers a similar reading of Polley's film adaptation, arguing that it "offer[s] up Grant as the sacrificial spouse willing to endure any fantasy that provides care to his ailing wife and, eventually, to cheat again in order to try to get Fiona what she needs" (90).

2 There are, of course, exceptions to the rule, such as Eva Kittay's moving account of her relationship with her disabled daughter, Sesha. See "Not *My* Way, Sesha, *Your* Way, Slowly."

3 An exception to this focus on the familiar is the inclusion of Alice Munro's story "The Love of a Good Woman," which involves a paid, in-home nurse. I make this story relevant to my project by drawing attention to the character's minimal training and her operation outside of any regulated system of care. She is a private employee of the families that hire her to attend to their ailing loved ones. As I explain further in chapter 5, the introduction of remuneration into relations of care has significant consequences for the dynamics of power and responsibility. Though Munro's character, Enid, may have trained to be a nurse, her training remains incomplete, and she is not beholden to any code of ethics (medical or otherwise) beyond her own, an ethical latitude that leads to a significant crisis for the character. Munro's work recurs throughout *Imagining Care* because of its remarkably insightful depictions of illness, impairment, and the caregiving that results. In Munro's stories, the particularities of care, whether manifested as affect or action, expose the undertones of what can, superficially, appear as "good" or "successful" care.

4 For a detailed description of these levels and their various stages, see Detlef (39–46), Gilligan (27, 73), and Kohlberg (*Philosophy* 17–20).

5 Gilligan holds cultural rather than biological forces responsible for women's "ethics of care" (1–2). As she explains, her goal is to recognize and validate women's moral development, "to expand the understanding of human development by using the group left out in the construction of theory to call attention to what is missing in its account" (4). However, many feminist critics have read Gilligan's thesis as essentialist, as reinforcing patriarchal scripts of femininity characterized by maternal-based affect. Claudia Card regards care as an inadequate guiding principle for ethical relations since "care ethics threatens to exacerbate the position of women and other caregivers in a sexist or otherwise oppressive society" (73). As I discuss in further detail below, the history of care responsibilities as imposed and highly gendered has been an obstacle for those promoting care as an egalitarian ethical model.

6 The foundational opposition between care and justice is common to ethics of care philosophy (see, e.g., Gilligan, Held), which is perhaps predictable for a philosophy with its roots in the assertion that a "different" perspective has value. As a result, there are a number of oppositions at the heart of ethics of care: care as opposed to justice, female as opposed to male, contextual as opposed to abstract.

7 In her response to the Kohlberg-Gilligan debate, Seyla Benhabib goes so far as to claim that morality based on abstraction and universality is actually self-defeating since "ignoring the standpoint of the concrete other leads to epistemic incoherence in universalistic moral theories. The problem can be stated as follows: according to Kohlberg and Rawls, moral reciprocity involves the capacity to take the standpoint of the other, to put oneself imaginatively in the place of the other, but under conditions of the 'veil of ignorance,' the *other as different from the self* disappears. Unlike in previous contract theories, in this case the other is not constituted through projection, but as a consequence of total abstraction from his or her identity. Differences are not denied; they become irrelevant" (emphasis in original 165). This erasure of otherness, or absorption of the other into the self, constitutes a denial of difference that prominent ethical philosophers, including Emmanuel Levinas, have decried as incompatible with ethical relations.

8 Hamington adopts a similar view, characterizing care as metaethical (34).

9 For a discussion of the significance of context and specificity within the philosophy of care, see Seyla Benhabib and Peta Bowden.

10 In an effort to circumvent such political ramifications, Clare Ungerson seeks to distinguish between "tending" and "caring," aligning the former

with "caring *for*," the latter with "caring *about*" (31). Kari Waerness has a similar approach, differentiating between "personal services" and "care":

> *"In principle*, caring for healthy adults might be based on equal give-and-take relationships between people who have personal ties to each other … However, as caring first and foremost tends to be associated with women, *much* of the caring women do for their husbands, older children, and other adult members of the family does not imply this kind of reciprocity and should therefore, in terms of activities be defined rather as *personal services* … When providing help and services to persons who cannot perform these activities themselves – young children, the ill, the disabled, the frail elderly – the situation is different. In such relations, the receiver of care is the subordinate in relation to the caregiver. These groups are dependent on some people who feel an obligation or desire to *care for others*" (emphases in original 234–5).

11 This critical anxiety over the "burden" of care is consistent with more general fears associated with dependency. For example, in Anne Basting's investigation of attitudes toward dementia, "by far, the fear of being a burden was the most common response" (7). As Basting explains, respondents saw "shame" in dependency, in "enslaving those you love to your care" (8). As she points out, caregiving exclusively conjured visions of encumbrance and suffering: "No one imagined the caregiving experience had the potential to be reciprocal. Instead, all the responses about being a burden assumed that the person with dementia takes while the caregiver gives and gives and gives" (8).

12 Groenhout's misgivings recall Judith Butler's description of her initial reaction to Levinas' ethical theory: "When I first encountered this position, I ran in the opposite direction, understanding it as a valorization of self-sacrifice" ("Ethical Ambivalence" 19).

13 See, e.g., Taras; Madison.

14 In 2010 US President Barack Obama signed the Patient Protection and Affordable Care Act, often referred to as "Obamacare," into law. The Act involves a number of provisions aimed at removing barriers to "affordable" health care and ensuring all citizens are covered by private health insurance. In other words, the Act is focused on creating universal access to private health care, thereby maintaining the opposition between Canadian (public) and American (private) systems of care.

15 As I will discuss in chapter 6, this kind of magnanimous assessment of Canadian multiculturalism, which recurs frequently in public and political debate, is not without its critics. As Neil Bissoondath, Daniel Coleman, Smaro Kamboureli, Eva Mackey, and others have pointed out, the discourse of tolerance is problematic for its implicit adherence to hierarchies of belonging

in which certain populations are commended for tolerating others. Canadian multiculturalism has been exposed as a tool of national solidarity that relies on internal others remaining separate and different from the dominant population, others in need of and grateful for the "tolerance" they receive from white, so-called, Canadian Canadians (Mackey 16, 20). In her groundbreaking essay, "On the Dark Side of the Nation: Politics of Multiculturalism and the State of 'Canada,'" Himani Bannerji describes multiculturalism as a "central pillar" of Canada's "ideological state apparatus" that deals with Canada's English-French division by effectively shifting attention onto non-white "others" (108). These others must remain different to be effective. In other words, the presence of "visible minorities" is necessary for the production of pluralist unity. According to Bannerji, multiculturalism embraces difference without any attention to power relations, and as a result, fails to address racism and colonial ethnocentrism. Consequently, "at the same moment that difference is ideologically evoked it is also neutralized" (96). Rather than creating conditions for "relational practices that foster mutual recognition and realization," in other words, for interrelationality and care, multiculturalism maintains boundaries and distinctions.

16   The rhetorical invocation of dependency's universality is a common strategy employed by both disability scholars and ethics of care philosophers. For example, in their introduction to their disability studies reader, Sharon Snyder, Brenda Jo Brueggermann, and Rosemarie Garland-Thomson propose "the fact that many of us will become disabled if we live long enough" as "perhaps the fundamental aspect of human embodiment" (Introduction 1–2). Tobin Siebers makes the point that able-bodiedness is the exception that we imagine to be the rule: "Most people do not want to consider that life's passage will lead them from ability to disability. The prospect is too frightening, the disabled body, too disturbing. In fact, even this picture is overly optimistic. The cycle of life runs in actuality from disability to temporary ability back to disability, and that only if you are among a most fortunate, among those who do not fall ill or suffer a severe accident ("Disability in Theory" 176). In her book *Illness*, Havi Carel asserts that "inability and limitation are part and parcel of human life, just as ability and freedom are" (69). See also, Tom Shakespeare's "The Social Model of Disability" and Lennard Davis' "The End of Identity Politics and the Beginning of Dismodernism: On Disability as an Unstable Category."

17   For arguments promoting care as integral to moral theory see, Held's *The Ethics of Care*; Kittay's *Love's Labor: Essays on Women, Equality, and Dependency*; *The Subject of Care*, edited by Kittay and Feder; *An Ethic of Care*, edited by Mary Jeanne Larrabee.

1 Embedded and Embodied

1 The terminology associated with life writing is extensive and nuanced. As Joanne Saul explains, "the range of new terms for the various manifestations of life writing (including 'autofiction,' 'autobiographics,' 'autography,' 'biofiction,' 'self-portraiture,' 'life narrative,' 'autographie,' and ... 'biotext') also points to the different strategies that writers (and their critics) are making use of in the field of writing and theorizing life writing" (5). To Saul's list, I would add Couser's "somatography" and "autosomatography."

2 The cultural value of life writing is very clearly linked to the truth claims made by its authors. The significance of veracity becomes clear when one considers the powerful *de*valuing of auto/biographies that are exposed as fabrications. Eakin demonstrates the consequences of breaking the rules of life writing in his analysis of James Frey's *A Million Little Pieces*, a highly successful memoir that sparked outrage when its author admitted to the inclusion of invention and embellishment. Such transgression can do more than ruin a writer's cultural capital: "Breaking trust with the readers of your memoir ... proves to be a potentially actionable offense: in September of 2006, Frey and his publisher apparently agreed to recompense readers who filed lawsuits claiming they had been defrauded when they bought *A Million Little Pieces*" (*Living Autobiographically* 21–2).

3 As a result, Couser terms such narratives "auto/biography" (*Vulnerable Subjects* 56).

4 Couser describes disabled children as "doubly vulnerable subjects – triply so if their impairment compromises their competence or diminishes their autonomy" (*Vulnerable Subjects* 57). This amplified vulnerability results from the formidable authority and intimacy of parents, whose memoirs are typically "unauthorized or *self*-authorized, insofar as parents assume rather than request the right to write their children's lives" (57). As a result, parental memoirs are "inherently, literally, paternalistic, particularly when they are undertaken before the subject has reached the age of consent" (57). I would argue that similar ethical complications arise in familial memoirs written by adult children whose parent has developed dementia. As we shall see, questions of authority, intimacy, and consent trouble the ethical valence of memoirs of dementia and disability by both parents and adult children.

5 In her treatment of women's collaborative writing Lorraine York works to develop a perspective balanced between essentialist idealization, and the equally problematic dismissal of collaborative writing as "textual

miscegenation" (*Rethinking* 12). As York demonstrates, there are significant connections between the idealization of women's collaboration and ethics of care theory since the "tendency to celebrate women's collaborations unproblematically and idealistically" takes its cue from feminist theories developed by Nancy Chodorow and Carol Gilligan, which conceive of women as "more other-directed and caring, and thus more given to relational ethics and collaborative problem-solving" (*Rethinking* 6).

6 Other "unrequitable tasks" include "speaking to and for the dead," and reconciling the need to reveal and uphold family secrets (Gilmore 72–3).

7 For further discussion of how assumptions of autonomy and independence affect life-writing criticism, see Saul 20; Gilmore 2, 12–13; Mason.

8 Disability theory typically differentiates between disability and impairment. While "'impairment' refers to the specific physical or cognitive deficiency that leads to a reduced capacity to fully actualize all aspects of one's life," "disability" refers "to the socially regulated parameters that exacerbate the effect of the impairment" (Quayson 3). However, as Ato Quayson explains, such distinctions are difficult to maintain: "in practice, it is almost impossible to keep the two separate, since 'impairment' is automatically placed within a social discourse that interprets it and 'disability' is produced by the interaction of impairment and spectrum of social discourses on normality that serve to stipulate what counts as disability in the first place" (4).

9 David Mitchell and Sharon Snyder's landmark contribution to disability studies, *Narrative Prosthesis*, proposes disability as a ubiquitous literary device with a long history as a stand-in for multiple meanings and effects that fails to represent disability as a lived experience: "disability pervades literary narrative, first, as a stock feature of characterization and, second, as an opportunistic metaphoric device. Sharon Snyder and I have termed the perpetual discursive dependency on disability in the first instance *narrative prosthesis*. Disability lends a distinctive idiosyncrasy to any characters that differentiate themselves from the anonymous background of the norm" ("Narrative Prosthesis" 15–16).

10 In *Extraordinary Bodies: Figuring Disability in American Literature and Culture*, author Rosemarie Garland-Thomson employs the titular term to describe "corporeal otherness we think of variously as 'monstrosity,' 'mutilation,' 'deformation,' 'crippledness,' or 'physical disability'" (5). Garland-Thomson seeks to add disability to critical conversations around difference: "I intend to introduce such figures as the cripple, the invalid, and the freak into the critical conversations we devote to deconstructing figures like the mulatto, the primitive, the queer, and the

lady" (5). Garland-Thomson's argument exposes disability as a "cultural interpretation" (6) constructed via representation, particularly literature.

11 Lennard Davis has explored the evolution of the notion of "normal" bodies in his groundbreaking book, *Enforcing Normality*, which argues that the concept of "normalcy," and therefore, of the abnormal, is a relatively recent phenomenon. The development of statistics and the concept of the bell curve in the early nineteenth century resulted in the "idea of a norm" ("Bodies of Difference" 101), which replaced the prior "concept of the ideal" (100), an impossible standard that left all human beings existing "in varying degrees of imperfection" (100). As a result of this paradigm shift, "people in the past 150 years have been encouraged to strive to be normal, to huddle under the main part of the [bell] curve" (101).

12 The ethical implications of disability representation extend to the genre of life writing. Indeed, life writing raises particular ethical questions regarding the "responsibilities of the 'normal' to those with apparently damaged identities" (Eakin, "Introduction" 6). As a result, Eakin considers ethics the "deep subject of autobiographical discourse" (6).

13 Using Damasio's neurobiological research, Eakin suggests that "instead of a teller, there is only – and persistently – what we might call a teller-effect, a self that emerges and lives its life only within the narrative matrix of consciousness. For Damasio, self and narrative are so intimately linked that to speak of the one is reciprocally to speak of the other" (Eakin, "What Are We Reading …?" 128–9).

14 Edelson's experience as a graduate student introduces her to ethics of care philosophy, which fuels her critique of health care, the problematic short-sightedness of medical care that saves the lives of vulnerable subjects, but provides few resources for the long-term assistance necessary for their quality of life, or even survival. Edelson demands that a belief in the "quality of life" be balanced with a belief in the "sanctity of life" (153). She invokes the ethics of care tenant that "human interdependency is fundamental" (151) to argue in favour of social and health policy transformation in her province of residence, Ontario. In particular, she seeks changes to "the Child and Family Service Act to fully mandate the extended care of medically fragile children. There must be a commitment to help these babies live well and with dignity until they die" (152). Edelson's laudable political activism, documented throughout *My Journey with Jake*, provides an outlet for her frustration with the limited support offered to familial caregivers and the artificial division between care that extends life and care that improves it.

15 Brown's book is not without its critics. In particular, disability scholars have expressed concern over the book's perpetuation of the association between cognitive ability and "what counts as valuable human existence" (Watt 88), a criticism I explore further below. However, such critical responses remain peripheral to the largely celebratory treatment the book received in the popular press, which, in tandem with its various awards and nominations implicitly endorses its representation of disability and care.

16 The role of the gaze is important here, since, as cultural theory has made clear, looking inevitably engages and often inscribes power imbalances between the subject and the object of his or her look. The power dynamics involved in looking have been explored to great effect in feminist film theory, most famously in Laura Mulvey's "Visual Pleasure and Narrative Cinema." According to Mulvey and others, the gaze involves gendered subordination and objectification. However, in *Staring: How We Look*, Garland-Thomson differentiates between the gaze and the stare, outlining a variety of stares, including "the blank stare, the baroque stare, the separated stare, and the engaged stare," in order to dismantle common interpretations of staring and "[lay] bare staring's generative potential" (10).

17 All of the authors included are women, which reflects Canadian caregiving statistics. According to Statistics Canada, 57% of those providing elder care in 2007 were women (Cranswick and Dosman 49). As well, government analysis of 2002 statistics draws attention to the gender gap in care provided by members of the "sandwich generation," that is, men and women "sandwiched" between child care and elder care: "About 25% of 45- to 64-year-old men with children at home provided elder care compared with 32% of women in similar circumstances" (C. Williams 18). Not only do more women provide care, they provide more of it, with working women spending an average of 29 hours per month providing elder care compared with the 13 hours spent by their male counterparts (18). In addition, women are both more likely to give *and* receive care: 30% of women studied received care "because of a long-term health problem" compared with "fewer than 20% of men" (12).

18 Nancy K. Miller draws attention to the benefits and pitfalls of representations of mother-daughter relationship in contemporary memoirs: "the mother-daughter relation, central to a great deal of women's writing, and notably to the contemporary autobiographical tradition, has been good for literature – that is, aesthetically productive – and at the same time, politically bad, by which I mean divisive, as a model (or metaphor) for the relations between women involved in feminist transmission" (14).

19 This same allusion to Jacob wrestling the angel is central to Margaret
   Laurence's iconic Canadian novel, *The Stone Angel*, which tells the story of
   a woman, Hagar, who resists the dependence and vulnerability of late life.
20 Couser draws attention to the important questions Booth raises in his
   study of fiction, including, "What Are the Author's Responsibilities to
   Those Whose Lives Are Used as 'Material'?" (Booth 130). As Couser points
   out, these ethical concerns "are perhaps even more compelling for life
   writing than for fiction" (Couser, "Making" 209).

2 Moral Obligation, Disordered Care

1 A number of the stories collected in *Moral Disorder* first appeared in
   magazines. "The Bad News" appeared in the *Guardian* in 2005 and in
   Playboy in 2006. "The Art of Cooking and Serving" was published in
   Toronto Life and the *New Statesman* in 2005. "The Entities" first appeared in
   Toronto Life in 2006. A slightly different version of "The Labrador Fiasco"
   was published as "A Bloomsbury Quid" in 1996 and "The Boys at the Lab"
   appeared in *Zoetrope: All-Story* in 2006.
2 Seyla Benhabib's oft-cited essay, "The Generalized and the Concrete
   Other," argues against impartiality in moral theory by suggesting that
   attention to individual particularity is essential for moral reasoning. This
   is perhaps the best example of this preference for the "concrete" over the
   abstract within ethics of care.
3 This allusion to Atwood's previous work is just one of many in the
   collection, as Ellen McWilliams points out. "*Moral Disorder*," she argues,
   "seems to look back on the body of work that came before and reshape it,
   presenting the reader with a retrospective of a different kind to Atwood's
   other female Bildungsromane" (McWilliams 128).
4 The Demeter-Persephone myth is a common allusion for feminist
   perspectives on female power. Indeed, Carol Gilligan employs it
   in her recommendation of women's "different" moral voice: "The
   elusive mystery of women's development lies in its recognition of
   the continuing importance of attachment in the human life cycle.
   Woman's place in man's life cycle is to protect this recognition while the
   developmental litany intoned the celebration of separation, autonomy,
   individuation, and natural rights. The myth of Persephone speaks
   directly to the distortion of this view by reminding us that narcissism
   leads to death, that the fertility of the earth is in some mysterious way
   tied to the continuation of the mother-daughter relationship, and that the
   life cycle itself arises from an alternation between the world of women

and that of men" (23). Atwood's allusion invokes such interpretations, but at the same time challenges them by emphasizing the myth's darker implications.

5 This is not the first time Atwood has employed an allusion to this myth. Sherrill Grace discusses *Surfacing* as a retelling of the Demeter story, sharing its themes of "silencing, and loss" (37).

6 Hamington comments on the "messiness" of care: "Care is not easy. It is messy and has many entanglements, but it is also imaginative and responsive, and this is its strength as a constellation of morality" (36).

7 Many critics have analysed Atwood's engagement with the Gothic tradition, particularly in *Lady Oracle*, which self-consciously reworks and parodies Gothic conventions. See, e.g., Bouson (*Brutal Choreographies* 63–86) and Davis (65–70). Gothic tropes are also central to *Alias Grace* (see Blackford, DeFalco, Goldman), *Bodily Harm*, *Cat's Eye*, and others. The Gothic, argues Fiona Tolan, "is, in itself, a contradictory genre; it is both empowering and imprisoning to the female character" (74), a contradiction that parallels the conflicting urges to engage and escape that I regard as central to *Moral Disorder's* ethical impact. For a comprehensive treatment of the Gothic in Atwood's fiction, see Howells ("Margaret Atwood").

8 In Atwood's *Negotiating with the Dead: A Writer on Writing*, the reader is roped into this voyeurism. The reader is "a spy, a trespasser, someone in the habit of reading other people's letters and diaries" (126).

9 For detailed analyses of the interrelation of subjectivity and care, see Held, Kittay, and Oliver ("Subjectivity as Responsivity" and *Witnessing*).

3 Caring for Relative Others

1 Ignatieff has published three novels: *Asya* (1991), *Scar Tissue* (1993), and *Charlie Johnson in the Flames* (2003). *Scar Tissue* was shortlisted for the Booker prize.

2 Hawkins defines "pathography" as "a form of autobiography or biography that describes personal experiences of illness, treatment, and sometimes death" (1).

3 My analysis of "blindness" in the novel is a response to the novel's own preoccupation with this admittedly problematic extended metaphor. The novel's employment of blindness as a sign of various occlusions, most frequently of understanding or insight, operates within a literary tradition that, as Mitchell and Snyder, Quayson, and others have made clear, regards disability as an "opportunistic metaphorical device" (Mitchell and Snyder, "Narrative Prosthesis" 205).

4 Here I am relying on Levinas' vision of alterity and its attendant claims
   on the self. Though I do not adopt the absolutism of Levinas' theory
   of infinite indebtedness, his claim that subjectivity is a consequence of
   responsibility is at the heart of much of my analysis. See Levinas, *Otherwise
   than Being or Beyond Essence.*

5 The "hollowness" of the witness is even more pronounced in Felman's
   idiosyncratic translation of this passage: "'The witness ... testifies to what
   has been said *through* him. Because the witness has said "here I am" before
   the other.' By virtue of the fact that the testimony is *addressed* to others,
   the witness, from within the solitude of his own stance is the vehicle of an
   occurrence, a reality, a stance or a dimension *beyond himself*" (Felman and
   Laub, emphasis in original 3).

6 Here Marlene Goldman is drawing on Jane Adamson's article, "Against
   Tidiness: Literature and/versus Moral Philosophy," which examines the
   tension between literature's embrace of ambiguity and moral philosophy's
   reliance on "intellectual control" (108).

7 This perspective is important to many ethics of care philosophers,
   including Maurice Hamington, Virginia Held, Eva Kittay, and others.

8 This preoccupation with *King Lear* appears in Ignatieff's non-fiction
   writing as well. In his exploration of individual obligation and state
   responsibility, *The Needs of Strangers*, he refers to the play as "probably
   the most profound examination of need as a human obligation" (20).
   He emphasizes blindness as well, interpreting the play's central trope
   as a comment on "our blindness to our own needs. What we need, Lear
   discovers, we can barely admit; we learn what we need by suffering ...
   Our education in need is a tragic passage from blindness to sight" (20).
   For Ignatieff, the play's ontological questions, its queries into equality
   and difference are answered with a caustic vision of humanity that
   corresponds to his own bleak perspective: in suffering alone are we
   equal and the same (43).

9 The narrator's preoccupation with ancestry and inheritance mimics
   Ignatieff's own obsession with family legacy, which has manifested itself in
   two family memoirs. *The Russian Album* (1987) conjures the experiences of
   his father's family during their move from Russia to Canada. More recently,
   he has explored his mother's heritage in the seemingly politically inspired
   True Patriot Love (2009), which chronicles four generations of the Grants.

10 Stan van Hooft stresses the self-oriented aspects of prioritizing
   others, going so far as to construct caring as a "self-project," that is,
   a demonstration of self: "my faithfulness to what I care about, my
   commitment to it, is an expression of my deep care ... And deep care

provides the internal motivational strength so to act. When one acts caringly, one implicates oneself in what one does, and that is why it matters" (47).

4 "Parodies of Love"

1 As Beverly Rasporich explains, "In its most comprehensive sense ... Munro's work is that of collective female mind and experience, of a cultural enclave that is largely domestic and traditionally treated as folk by both sociologists and literary critics alike" (100). Magdalene Redekop interprets Munro's strategic attention to the domestic as a "radical" rejection of the "defamiliarizing techniques common to many contemporary writers" (12). See Howells (*Alice Munro*) and York (*The Other Side of Dailiness*) for further explorations of the connections between the everyday and gender identity in Munro's fiction.

2 As Munro herself has explained in reference to her story "The Ottawa Valley": "I'm looking at all this material, I'm looking at real lives, and then I not only have to look at the inadequacy of the way I represent them but my right to represent them at all. And I think any writer who deals with personal material comes up against this" (qtd. in Ware, "Tricks" 127).

3 Many critics have seized upon the implications of Munro's metafictional style. See, in particular, Carrington, Heble, McGill, McIntyre, Redekop, Rhys.

4 In stories such as "The Bear Came over the Mountain," "Post and Beam," and "Queenie" new attachments have serious consequences for caregivers and dependents alike.

5 My investigation into the meanings and consequences of dependency in Munro's fiction builds on my work in *Uncanny Subjects*, which analyses the relationship between fiction and aging. In this book I consider the various ways Munro's stories convey the uncanny identity produced by aging that disrupts narrative ability and exposes the illusion of consistent selfhood. For further discussion of aging in Munro, see also the illuminating critiques provided by Sally Chivers, who considers the "relationships among autonomy, monogamy, and institutional care" in Munro's "The Bear Came over the Mountain" and its film adaptation, *Away from Her* (*Silvering Screen* 84) and Sara Jamieson ("The Fiction of Agelessness"), who focuses on Munro's implicit critique of the problematic "postmodern culture of positive aging" that overvalues independence and marginalizes vulnerability and dependence (117).

6 Jamieson's analysis of the story "Pictures of the Ice," draws attention to the gendered marginalization of aging, which effectively "feminizes" the older masculine body by associating it with supposedly feminine qualities of weakness, passivity, and dependency (120).

7 Alice Munro has referred to "The Peace of Utrecht" as "the first story I absolutely had to write and wasn't writing to see if I could write that kind of story" (qtd. in Howells 14).

8 The preponderance of beleaguered caregivers in Munro's fiction has a significant biographical antecedent. In 1943, when Munro was twelve years old, her mother, Anne Laidlaw, began exhibiting troubling symptoms that would lead to the diagnosis of Parkinson's disease. As the eldest daughter, with her nearest sister five years behind, Munro was her mother's primary caregiver, responsible for the domestic duties that Anne could no longer manage, duties that often kept Munro home from school (Thacker 57). The impact of this period on Munro's fiction has been considerable and persistent since "the onset of Anne's Parkinson's disease came just as Munro had reached puberty and was realizing her vocation as a writer" (73). Her time spent managing the household provided the opportunity to "think my thoughts," as she has put it (qtd. in Thacker 57), and the labour of care produced the simultaneous resentment and empowerment reflected in many of her stories depicting caregiving. As Munro has confessed in interview, "The material about my mother is my central material in life" ("The Art").

9 Coral Ann Howells uses similar terms to discuss the stories "The Peace of Utrecht" and "The Ottawa Valley," describing them as Munro's "first attempts to represent the scandal of a mother's debilitating illness and death" (15).

10 Munro's language here recalls Lauren Berlant's suggestion of "compassion and coldness as perhaps not opposite at all but … two sides of a bargain that the subjects of modernity have struck with structural inequality" ("Introduction" 10). Berlant's provocative critique of compassion has further parallels with Munro's treatment of care, which I discuss in further detail in chapter 5.

11 Disability studies has done much to correct this misidentification of independent, able-bodied subject as "normal." See, e.g., Mairian Corker and Sally French's *Disability Discourse*, Ato Quayson's *Aesthetic Nervousness: Disability and the Crisis of Representation*, and Rosemarie Garland-Thomson's *Freakery: Cultural Spectacles of the Extraordinary Body*.

12 Critical assessments of empathy counter the common perception that literature's ability to inspire empathy in its readers is one of its primary

ethical possibilities. In particular, Keen is responding to the work of Martha Nussbaum and Steven Pinker's claim that "storytelling has made the human species nicer" (Keen 25). For further discussion of the relationship between empathy and literature, see Kathleen Lundeen's "Who Has the Right to Feel? The Ethics of Literary Empathy" and James Mensch's *Ethics and Selfhood: Alterity and the Phenomenology of Obligation* (particularly chapter 2, "Empathy and Self-Presence").

13 Compassion fatigue is a widely recognized "secondary traumatic stress disorder" that commonly affects caregivers. The "Compassion Fatigue Awareness Project" website describes the disorder's most common symptoms, "apathy, isolation, bottled up emotions and substance abuse," which can result "when caregivers focus on others without practicing self-care" ("Compassion Fatigue"). According to the CFAP, the risks of caregiving are real and dangerous and the website's home page opens with this arresting warning: "Caring too much can hurt."

14 In her inquiry into the aesthetics of "ugly feelings," Sianne Ngai finds disgust to be the most extreme of the affective states she investigates, suggesting that it draws her work "closer to the domain of political theory, perhaps even of political commitment, then these others" (354), namely, "animatedness, irritation, envy, anxiety, stuplimity [sic], and paranoia" (353). Ngai's analysis suggests that the "intense and ambivalent negativity" marked by disgust "prepar[es] us for more instrumental or politically efficacious emotions. It therefore brings us to the edge of this project on the aesthetics of minor affects, marking the furthest it can go" (354).

5 Caregiving and Caretaking

1 My usage here echoes Sara Ahmed's in her article "Affective Economies." In it, Ahmed stresses the tangible impacts of emotions, which, she argues, "do things" (119). Munro's work is particularly sensitive to to what emotions do, and "how they work, in concrete and particular ways, to mediate the relationship between the psychic and the social, and between the individual and the collective" (Ahmed 119).

2 In her treatment of the ethics of home health care, Jennifer Parks prefers the term "caretaking" over "caregiving," arguing that the former reminds readers that "care should not be viewed as merely a 'gift' to be given by women but that it is, indeed, work" (7). The association between care and gift giving is one I return to later in the chapter.

3 The process of professionalization was slow and gradual. Though the first nurse training program appeared in 1874 at the General and Marine

Hospital in St Catharines, Ontario (S. Richardson 20), "Not until 1922 did all nine provincial nurses' associations have some form of nurse registration legislation on which to base nursing education standards" (23). As a result, "In the early twentieth century 'trained' nurses struggled to distinguish themselves not only from untrained competition but also from those women who boasted some training, however limited. The term 'graduate' nurse thus emerged to categorize those practitioners who had successfully completed a three-year apprenticeship" (McPherson 20)

4 Barbara Keddy and Dianne Dodd further elaborate the late nineteenth-century professionalization of nursing: "As graduates of [hospital] schools came onto the labour market, they helped change the concept of the nurse from that of a domestic worker, who could be any woman with nurturing skills, to a trained 'professional.' At this time, nursing leaders were working to dissociate the profession of nursing from untrained domestic labour that passed for nursing in former times" (43). As Keddy and Dodd explain, though the current hierarchical designation, RN ("registered nurse"), did not become widespread until the 1940s, "early nurses called themselves 'trained' or 'graduate' nurses in order to distinguish themselves from the untrained women who also hired themselves out as nurses" (43).

5 Historically, the nurse's familiarity with the human body has posed a risk to the profession's respectability. As McPherson explains, "nurses had to desexualize themselves in order to distance themselves from the only other group of women with intimate knowledge of strangers' bodies – prostitutes" (16). Furthermore, in the Canadian context McPherson describes, the desire to reify nursing and disassociate it from the carnal manifested in racist practices and policies: "Because nursing relied on an image of feminine respectability to legitimate nurses' presence in the health-care system and their knowledge of the body, respectability was constructed in a racial and national context. Nurses' respectability and definition of gentility were European in origin. White, native-born Canadian women were expected to bring their superior sense of sexual and social behaviour to the bedside, either to act appropriately while caring for their social 'equals' or 'superiors' in private care or to serve as role models for their social 'inferiors,' such as immigrants and non-Whites. Visible minorities were not trusted to attend the needs of ailing White Canadians, and until the post–World War II years administrators remained convinced that the very presence of non-White attendants might exacerbate the health problems of White patients" (17).

6 Naomi Morgenstern, in response to another story, comments on the unusual role played by dreams in Munro's fiction: "While dreams are usually

taken to be the 'royal road' to the individual's unconscious, in Munro's narratives ... dreams pleasingly register the other's otherness" (72).

7 The influence of shame in the story recalls the determining influence of the feeling in the story "Heirs of the Living Body" and others, as discussed in chapter 4.

8 The story's second section opens with Enid recording Mrs Quinn's disease, "glomerulonephritis," in her notebook. The reader's introduction to Mrs Quinn is via Enid's fascinated account of her diseased state and we first know her as a series of symptoms and ailments, a medical novelty: hers is the "first case [Enid] had ever seen" (31). Mrs Quinn, the person, is obscured in Enid's mind by the novelty of her illness.

9 Naomi Morgenstern's insightful exploration of ethics and femininity in Munro's fiction also draws attention to the ways "specific obligations" and "concrete situations" in her stories evoke the "risks of the ethical" (69). Morgenstern's argument demonstrates how these "risks" are necessary to reach "the ethical insight – that the other exists beyond the self" (71). Her inquiry is primarily concerned with the ethical theories of Levinas and others who insist on the impossibility and necessity of ethical responsibility rather than on the ethics of care. All in all, Morgenstern has a somewhat more optimistic reading of the vision of responsibility that runs through Munro's stories, regarding the ethical crises in stories such as "Post and Beam" and "Meneseteung" as moments when characters awaken, albeit often painfully, to the otherness of the other.

6 Forgetting and the Forgotten

1 Like the narrator of Ignatieff's novel, *Soucouyant*'s narrator remains unnamed. In *Scar Tissue*, few characters have proper names; instead, they are known by their relation to the narrator: brother, mother, father, wife, etc. *Soucouyant* reverses this potentially solipsistic arrangement in which the identities of others are determined by their association with the self. In Chariandy's novel it is the narrator's identity that is relational, determined by Adele, Meera, his father, Roger, his friend, Miss Cameron, and others.

2 The novel's narrator draws attention to the fact that the Multiculturalism Act has been passed one year before the novel's present tense, implying that multiculturalist policy has done little to reverse his exclusion from white Canadian culture (33).

3 Delisle makes a similar observation, regarding the novel's depiction of Heritage Day "as an indictment of official multiculturalism" (13). The

fact that both of us, writing about the novel at roughly the same time, employed the same quotation to discuss this particular scene in the novel highlight the pertinence of Kamboureli's remarks.

4 For example, see the *Economist*'s headline, "One nation or many? Canadians continue to believe in diversity and tolerance. But it is becoming harder." The *Globe and Mail*'s "Multiculturalism Debate" series from 2010 offers further examples, such as "Part 3: Are We Too Tolerant?" In her analysis of popular discourses surrounding Canadian multiculturalism, Kamboureli provides an astute critique of "media discourse that attempts to define, and to show the erosion suffered by, the dominant tradition following the advent of multiculturalism" (82).

5 Chelva Kanaganayakam makes a similar point: "the myth of multiculturalism ensures the significance of citizenship and nationality [in Canada]. But that is a far cry from belonging, from an ethos that paves the way for a sense of rootedness" (145).

6 The soucouyant is distinctly female, adding an element of taboo sexuality to her crimes since she often chooses "careless travelers usually men who are attracted to her" for her victims (Gadsby 67). Giselle Anatol ("Transforming") and Meredith Gadsby regard this destruction as part of the soucouyant's significance as "a symbol of female sexual identity and independence [who is] is constantly punished (via the poisoning of her skin with salt or pepper) for challenging patriarchal control of women's bodies" (Gadsby 66). Gadsby suggests that just as the soucouyant "has been used in folklore as a cautionary tale for women who disobey men, she can also be read as a woman who refuses to sacrifice her sexual or emotional independence for middle-class domestic stability. The price she pays for this is extreme violence" (70).

7 In this image of epidermal literacy, Adele's skin is the site of legible historical traces. Paul Ricoeur proposes "three sorts of traces: the written trace, which has become the documentary trace on the plane of the historiographical operation; the psychical trace, which can be termed impression rather than imprint, impression in the sense of an affection left in us by a marking – or as we say, striking – event; finally, the cerebral, cortical trace which the neurosciences deal with" (415). The scarred flesh collapses the distinctions between these imprints, uniting the documentary, psychical, and cerebral trace since Adele's body, psyche, and cognition bear the traces of history.

8 Delisle interprets the novel's witnessing within a larger practice of cultural memory in which "the second generation participates in an active construction of the past that does not preserve racial difference but

witnesses and memorializes its wounds, and provides rich alternative memories to whitewashed versions of Canada" (18).

9 Kit Dobson's summary of the novel points to the important interaction of memory and care: "The protagonist is driven away from home by the gruelling challenges of caring for someone with dementia, but also by the lurking truths about his mother's past, and he himself embarks on a project of forgetting during his travels before returning home to confront his mother and his own unresolved past" (in Chariandy, "Spirits" 812).

10 Dobson picks up on the novel's revisionist perspective, remarking on its representation of "cultural dislocation" as potentially positive, "as both a loss and as possibility, as an ancestry that is productively fragmented, and not as a pure or unquestionably 'true' past" (in Chariandy, "Spirits" 811).

Conclusion

1 Her fifth contribution to the genre, *The Heart Goes Last*, was published just as *Imaging Care* went to press. Like the *MaddAddam* trilogy, this novel at once stokes and satirizes anxieties about the future of human care in posthuman societies dominated by artificial intelligence and biotechnology.

2 Instead, Atwood chose an Americanized future. In her investigation into the novel's genesis, Sullivan explains Atwood's reasoning: "if you are writing a futuristic nightmare, the setting becomes problematic. She thought of Montreal and Toronto, but concluded that the idea would not fly in Canada. Canada, with its genius for compromise, did not veer towards extremes. Then she thought of Cambridge, Massachusetts, where she had spent four years as a graduate student. She decided the mind-set of her fictional Gilead would be close to that of the seventeenth-century Puritans whom she had studied and who in fact were her own ancestors" (851). However, as I explore in the previous chapter, Chariandy's novel casts doubt on the Canadian "genius for compromise," exposing the underlying marginalization and prejudice suffered by many visible minority Canadians.

3 Atwood's perspective intersects with ecofeminist theory, which "insist[s] that the oppression of women, the oppression of the environment, and the oppressive treatment of non-human animals are deeply linked. As one kind of feminism it can emphasize that personhood is embodied, and that through the food which becomes our bodies we are engaged in food practices that reflect who we are" (Curtin 100).

4 In Lai's *Salt Fish Girl*, surveillance adheres to the "Big Brother paradigm" that Hopkinson subverts. Instead of "Granny Nanny," there is the "Guardian Angel" device used by corporations to "keep track of" their cloned sweatshop workers. As Evie, an escapee from a shoe factory explains, "The GA looks after us, monitors our body temperature, notes the presence of disease, helps rescuers find us if we get lost" (159). To gain her freedom Evie has ripped the monitoring device from her back and shoulders. But freedom from slave labour means the loss of her community, her fellow clones and co-workers, her duplicates and family. Like Atwood's speculative fiction, Lai's novel imagines the sinister potential of biotechnology, particularly the possibility that genetic manipulation could be exploited by corporations to evade human rights legislation. Genetically modified clones – Evie's "genes are point zero three percent *Cyprinus carpio* – freshwater carp" (158) – raise the spectre of perverse biological hybridity that exceeds and challenges moral and legislative boundaries based on species specificity and individual rights.

5 Aibo, for example, is a rare exception: a dog-shaped robot developed and produced by Sony with functionalities related to both service and companionship (Broekens et al. 95). Aibo, which was designed to interact with humans, as well as to move autonomously and find its own power supply, is no longer in production (96–7).

6 For example, assistive technologies, such as The Companion, CareBot, and Hospi-Rimo, maintain connections between users and their human care providers. Often these devices, including The Companion, designed by researchers at Brunel University, and the CareBot, involve a degree of surveillance, allowing caregivers to monitor their charges offsite. These robots seek to increase communication and alleviate the risks of isolation, functioning as intermediaries in human care relations that involve both labour and feeling. Unlike the mechanistic My Spoon, or the animalistic RIBA, these technologies are designed to support human care, rather than obviate human toil.

7 The RIBA's developers, the RIKEN-TRI Collaboration Centre for Human-Interactive Robot Research (RTC), in collaboration with Tokai Rubber Industries, de-emphasize the robotic aspects of the machine to evoke a cyborgian creation that is not merely a machine. The images of RIBA on the RTC website show a smiling, bearlike face, a young woman carried in its outstretched arms. The woman held in the robot's "human-like arms," smiles up at the bear face. The smile of the care receiver imputes an affective dimension to the robotic care, lending emotionality to a relation that is, in essence, brute-strength labour. The robot's physique is clearly gendered male with its broad shoulders, narrow waist, and barrel chest; however, its head

is teddy-bear like, featuring oversized circular eyes and a vaguely smiling mouth, topped by prominent rounded ears. At once authoritative and non-threatening, beefy and cute, angular and cuddly, the RIBA at once protects care workers from the injuries associated with lifting, and seeks to comfort and reassure those transferred in its capable, "human-like" embrace.

8 The robot recalls the disturbingly overzealous feeding machine from Chaplin's *Modern Times* (1936), a film that expresses anxieties similar to Turkle's (discussed below) regarding the prospect of an automated, posthuman future dominated by technology.

9 There is evidence that caregiving robots provide great benefits to their users. In their 2009 literature review, Joost Broekens, Marcel Heerink, and Henk Rosendal found notable positive outcomes related to assistive social robots used for elderly care. Their review of forty-three citations demonstrates that caregiving robots lead to improvements in mood and immune system response and the diminishment of loneliness and stress, with some studies also attributing a decrease in symptoms of dementia to robot interaction (98–100). Robot ethicists also delineate hypothetical benefits for human caregivers, suggesting that robot caregivers might diminish the strain of care work for their human counterparts, a respite that could mitigate the inferior caregiving that can result from overwork or incompetence (Borenstein and Pearson; Sharkey and Sharkey; Sparrow and Sparrow).

10 Robotics engineer Kjerstin Williams equates the impact of losing a robot with the death of a companion animal: "you grieve and move on, and you try to reengage with the next animal, or the next set of robots" (Ito). Borenstein and Pearson make a similar comparison: "In some sense, a robot that is viewed as being 'kind' to people could bring out laudable traits in us similar to the way pets can" ("Robot Caregivers: Ethical Issues" 257).

11 The spectre of robotic hybridity challenges species boundaries; not only is Paro a machine able to effect human affect, it is a distinctly *animal*-inflected machine.

12 Even those ethicists who acknowledge the potential advantages of robot care express concern and warnings about deleterious effects. For example, Jason Borenstein and Yvonne Pearson suggest that although caregiving robots could help abolish obligatory, possibly begrudging care and provide relief for overworked and exhausted caregivers ("Robot Caregivers: Ethical Issues" 257–8), they insist that, "at least for the foreseeable future, it is crucial to emphasize that no matter what benefits the technology is perceived to have, a robot should be viewed as a complement to human caregivers, and not as a replacement for them" (256). As Linda and Robert Sparrow point out, "it is naive to think that the development of robots to

take over tasks currently performed by humans in caring roles would not lead to a reduction of human contact for those people being cared for" (152).

13 An article appearing in the *Wall Street Journal*, describes the controversy Paro inspires and the opposition some American doctors have mounted to the use of robots for affective care. The article quotes Dr Bill Thomas to explain health care providers' misgivings: "If you give me a robot that helps perform mundane tasks associated with caregiving, such as vacuuming or doing the dishes, I'm all for that … But if we wind up with nursing homes full of baby-seal robots, the robots will be trying to fulfill the relationship piece of caregiving, while the humans are running around changing the beds and cooking the food" (in Rooney).

14 Hopkinson's novel seems to embrace Donna Haraway's endorsement of cyborg technologies as potentially liberating transgressive instruments. For Haraway, "the cyborg is a creature of a post-gender world" that breaks down artificial gender and species binaries (316). Her "essay is an argument for *pleasure* in the confusion of boundaries and for *responsibility* in their construction" (emphasis in original 316). Hopkinson's novel dramatizes both the potential pleasure and responsibility associated with blended, cyborgian beings.

References

Abramson, Alexis, and Mary Anne Dunkin. *The Caregiver's Survival Handbook: How to Care for Your Aging Parent without Losing Yourself.* New York: Berkeley Publishing Group, 2004.

Adamson, Jane. "Against Tidiness: Literature and/versus Moral Philosophy." *Negotiating Ethics in Literature, Philosophy, and Theory.* Ed. Jane Adamson, Richard Freadman, and David Parker. Cambridge: University of Cambridge Press, 1998. 84–110.

"Aging at Home Strategy Expands." Ontario. Ministry of Health and Long-Term Care, 31 Aug. 2010. Web. 10 Feb. 2012.

Ahern, Patti. "Caregiving Robots on the Way." *Chicago Tribune*, 2 Sept. 2009. Web. 1 Nov. 2012.

Ahmed, Sara. "Affective Economies." *Social Text* 22.2 (2004): 117–139.

Anatol, Giselle Liza. "Maternal Discourses in Nalo Hopkinson's *Midnight Robber.*" *African American Review* 40.1 (2006): 111–24.

– "Transforming the Skin-Shedding Soucouyant: Using Folklore to Reclaim Female Agency in the Caribbean." *Small Axe* 7 (Mar. 2000): 44–59.

Anderson, Linda. *Autobiography.* London: Routledge, 2001.

Angus, Ian. *Identity and Justice.* Toronto: University of Toronto Press, 2008.

Aronson, Louise. "The Future of Robot Caregivers." *New York Times*, 19 July 2014. Web. 2 Aug. 2014.

Attridge, Derek. "Innovation, Literature, Ethics: Relating to the Other." *PMLA* 114 (1999): 20–31.

Atwood, Margaret. *Bodily Harm.* Toronto: McClelland and Stewart, 1998 [1981].

– *Good Bones and Simple Murders.* New York: Doubleday, 1994 [1992].

– *The Handmaid's Tale.* Toronto: McClelland and Stewart, 1985.

– *The Heart Goes Last.* Toronto: McClelland and Stewart, 2015.

– *MaddAddam*. Toronto: Random House, 2013.
– *Moral Disorder*. Toronto: McClelland and Stewart, 2006.
– *Oryx and Crake*. New York: Seal, 2003.
– *Second Words: Selected Critical Prose*. Toronto: Anansi, 1982.
– *Surfacing*. Toronto: McClelland and Stewart, 1972.
– "Survival." *A Passion for Identity: An Introduction to Canadian Studies*. 2nd
  ed. Ed. Eli Mandel, David Taras, and Beverly Rasporich. Scarborough, ON:
  Nelson, 1993. 258–67.
– *True Stories*. Toronto: Oxford University Press, 1981.
– *The Year of the Flood*. Toronto: McClelland and Stewart, 2009.
Away from Her. Dir. Sarah Polley. Perf. Julie Christie, Gordon Pinsent. Capri
  Films, 2006.
Bannerji, Himani. *The Dark Side of the Nation: Essays on Multiculturalism,
  Nationalism and Gender*. Toronto: Canadian Scholars' Press, 2000.
Barthes, Roland. *Camera Lucida: Reflections on Photography*. Trans. Richard
  Howard. New York: Hill and Wang, 1981.
Bartky, Sandra Lee. *"Sympathy and Solidarity" and Other Essays*. New York:
  Rowman and Littlefield, 2002.
Basting, Anne Davis. *Forget Memory: Creating Better Lives for People with
  Dementia*. Baltimore, MD: Johns Hopkins University Press, 2009.
Benhabib, Seyla. "The Generalized and the Concrete Other: The Kohlberg-
  Gilligan Controversy and Moral Theory." *Women and Moral Theory*. Ed. Eva
  Feder Kittay and Diana T. Meyers. Savage, MD: Rowman and Littlefield,
  1987. 154–77.
Benner, Patricia, Suzanne Gordon, and Nel Noddings. Introduction.
  Caregiving: Readings in Knowledge, Ethics, Practice and Politics. Ed. Patricia
  Benner, Suzanne Gordon, and Nel Noddings. Philadelphia, PA: University
  of Philadelphia Press, 1996. vii–xvi.
Benner, Patricia, and Suzanne Gordon. "Caring Practice." *Caregiving: Readings
  in Knowledge, Ethics, Practice and Politics*. Ed. Patricia Benner, Suzanne
  Gordon, and Nel Noddings. Philadelphia, PA: University of Philadelphia
  Press, 1996. 40–55.
Benthien, Claudia. *Skin: On the Cultural Border between Self and the World*.
  Trans. Thomas Dunlap. New York: Columbia University Press, 2002.
Berlant, Lauren, ed. *Compassion: The Culture and Politics of an Emotion*. New
  York: Routledge, 2004.
– "Introduction: Compassion (and Withholding)." *Compassion: The Culture and
  Politics of an Emotion*. Ed. Lauren Berlant. New York: Routledge, 2004. 1–13.
Berman, Claire. *Caring for Yourself While Caring for Your Aging Parents: How to
  Help, How to Survive*. 2nd ed. New York: Henry Holt, 2001.

Bissoondath, Neil. "Multiculturalism." *New Internationalist Magazine*, 5 Sept. 1998. Web. 10 June 2012.

Blackford, Holly. "Haunted Housekeeping: Fatal Attractions of Servant and Mistress in Twentieth-Century Female Gothic Literature." *LIT: Literature Interpretation Theory* 16.2 (2005): 233–61.

Blanchot, Maurice. *The Writing of Disaster*. Trans. Ann Smock. Lincoln, NE: University of Nebraska Press, 1995.

Booth, Wayne. *The Company We Keep: An Ethics of Fiction*. Berkeley, CA: University of California Press, 1988.

Borenstein, Jason, and Yvette Pearson. "Robot Caregivers: Ethical Issues across the Human Lifespan." *Robot Ethics: The Ethical and Social Implications of Robotics*. Ed. Patrick Lin, Keith Abney, and George Bekey. Cambridge, MA: MIT Press, 2012. 251–65.

– "Robot Caregivers: Harbingers of Expanded Freedom for All?" *Ethics and Information Technology* 12.3 (2010): 277–88.

Bosco, Mark "The Apocalyptic Imagination in Margaret Atwood's *Oryx and Crake*." *Margaret Atwood: The Robber Bride, The Blind Assassin, Oryx and Crake*. Ed. J. Brooks Bouson. New York: Continuum, 2010. 156–71.

Bouson, J. Brooks. *Brutal Choreographies: Oppositional Strategies and Narrative Design in the Novels of Margaret Atwood*. Amherst, MA: University of Massachusetts Press, 1993.

– "'It's Game Over Forever': Atwood's Satiric Vision of a Bioengineered Posthuman Future in *Oryx and Crake*." *Journal of Commonwealth Literature* 39.3 (2004): 139–56.

Bowden, Peta. *Caring: Gender-Sensitive Ethics*. London and New York: Routledge, 1997.

Brabeck, Mary. "Moral Judgment: Theory and Research on Differences between Males and Females." *An Ethic of Care*. Ed. Mary Jeanne Larrabee. New York: Routledge, Chapman and Hall, 1993. 33–48.

Brady, Mary Pat. *Extinct Lands, Temporal Geographies: Chicana Literature and the Urgency of Space*. Durham, NC: Duke University Press, 2002.

Broekens, Joost, Marcel Heerink, and Henk Rosendal. "Assistive Social Robots in Elderly Care: A Review." *Gerontechnology* 8.2 (2009): 94–103.

Brown, Ian. *The Boy in the Moon: A Father's Search for His Disabled Son*. Toronto: Random House, 2009.

Bubeck, Diemut. *Care, Gender and Justice*. Oxford: Clarendon, 1995.

– "Justice and the Labor of Care." *The Subject of Care: Feminist Perspectives on Dependency*. Ed. Eva Feder Kittay and Ellen K. Feder. New York: Rowman and Littlefield, 2002. 160–85.

Butler, Judith. *The Psychic Life of Power: Theories in Subjection*. Stanford, CA: Stanford University Press, 1997.

– "Ethical Ambivalence." *The Turn to Ethics*. Ed. Marjorie Garber, Beatrice Hanssen, and Rebecca L. Walkowitz. New York: Routledge, 2000. 15–28.

Canadian Multiculturalism Act. *Revised Statutes of Canada*, c. 24. (4th Supp). Department of Justice. 1985. *Department of Justice*. Web. 5 Jan. 2013.

Card, Claudia. *The Unnatural Lottery: Character and Moral Luck*. Philadelphia, PA: Temple University Press, 1996.

"Care." *OED* (*Oxford English Dictionary*), 2013. Web. 10 Aug. 2013.

"Caregiver." *OED*. 2013. Web. 5 Jan. 2013.

"Caregiving." *OED*. 2013. Web. 5 Jan. 2013.

Carel, Havi. *Illness*. Stocksfield: Acumen, 2008.

"Caretake." *OED*. 2013. Web. 5 Jan. 2013.

"Caretaker." *OED*. 2013. Web. 5 Jan. 2013.

Carrington, Ildikó de Papp. *Controlling the Uncontrollable: The Fiction of Munro*. DeKalb, IL: Northern Illinois University Press, 1989.

Carse, Alisa. "Facing Up to Moral Perils: The Virtues of Care in Bioethics." *Caregiving: Readings in Knowledge, Ethics, Practice and Politics*. Ed. Patricia Benner, Suzanne Gordon, and Nel Noddings. Philadelphia, PA: University of Philadelphia Press, 1996. 83–110.

Caruth, Cathy. "Trauma and Experience: Introduction." *Trauma: Explorations in Memory*. Ed. Cathy Caruth. Baltimore, MD: Johns Hopkins University Press, 1995. 3–12.

– *Unclaimed Experience: Trauma, Narrative, and History*. Baltimore: Johns Hopkins University Press, 1996.

Cassel, Christine K. Foreword. *Ethical Foundations of Palliative Care for Alzheimer Disease*. Ed. Ruth B. Purtilo. Baltimore: Johns Hopkins University Press, 2004. ix–xi.

Chariandy, David. *Soucouyant*. Toronto: Arsenal Pulp Press, 2007.

– "Spirits of Elsewhere Past: A Dialogue on *Soucouyant*." Interview with Kit Dobson. *Callaloo* 30.3 (2007): 808–17.

– "Stranger in the Quarter." *Callaloo* 32.2 (2009): 555–61.

Cheadle, Bruce. "Universal Health Care Much Loved among Canadians, Monarchy Less Important: Poll." *Globe and Mail*, 25 Nov. 2012. Web. 18 Oct. 2013.

Chivers, Sally. *The Silvering Screen: Old Age and Disability in Cinema*. Toronto: University of Toronto Press, 2011.

Chodorow, Nancy. *The Reproduction of Mothering*. Berkeley, CA: University of California Press, 1978.

Clement, Grace. *Care, Autonomy, and Justice: Feminism and the Ethic of Care.* Boulder, CO: Westview, 1996.

Coleman, Daniel. *White Civility: The Literary Project of English Canada.* Toronto: University of Toronto Press, 2006.

"Compassion Fatigue Awareness Project." N.p. 2012. Web. 11 May 2012.

Cooke, Grayson. "Technics and the Human at Zero-Hour: Margaret Atwood's *Oryx and Crake.*" *Studies in Canadian Literature* 31.2 (2006): 105–25.

Cooke, Maeve. "Questioning Autonomy: The Feminist Challenge and the Challenge to Feminism." *Questioning Ethics: Contemporary Debates in Philosophy.* Ed. Richard Kearney and Mark Dooley. London: Routledge, 1999. 258–82.

Cooper, Pamela. "Sexual Surveillance and Medical Authority in Two Versions of *The Handmaid's Tale.*" *Journal of Popular Culture* 28.4 (1995): 49–66.

Corker, Mairian, and Sally French, eds. *Disability Discourse.* Buckingham: Open University Press, 1999.

Couser, G. Thomas. "Making, Taking, and Faking Lives: Ethical Problems in Collaborative Life Writing." *Mapping the Ethical Turn: A Reader in Ethics, Culture, and Literary Theory.* Ed. Todd F. Davis and Kenneth Womack. Charlottesville, VA: University Press of Virginia, 2001. 209–26.

– *Vulnerable Subjects: Ethics and Life Writing.* Ithaca, NY: Cornell University Press, 2004.

– *Signifying Bodies: Disability in Contemporary Life Writing.* Ann Arbor, MI: University of Michigan Press, 2009.

Cox, Ailsa. *Alice Munro.* Devon: Northcote House, 2004.

Cranswick, Kelly, and Donna Dosman. Statistics Canada. "Eldercare: What We Know Today." *Canadian Social Trends* (Oct. 2008): 48–56.

Critchley, Simon. *Infinitely Demanding: Ethics of Commitment, Politics of Resistance.* London: Verso, 2007.

Curtin, Deane. "Toward an Ecological Ethic of Care." *The Feminist Care Tradition in Animal Ethics.* Ed. Josephine Donovan and Carol J. Adams. New York: Columbia University Press, 2007. 87–104.

Davies, Madeleine. "Margaret Atwood's Female Bodies." *The Cambridge Companion to Margaret Atwood.* Ed. Coral Ann Howells. Cambridge: Cambridge University Press, 2006. 58–71.

Davis, Lennard J. "Bodies of Difference: Politics, Disability, and Representation." *Disability Studies: Enabling the Humanities.* Ed. Sharon L Snyder, Brenda Jo Brueggermann, and Rosemarie Garland-Thomson. New York: Modern Language Association of America, 2002. 100–6.

– "The End of Identity Politics and the Beginning of Dismodernism: On Disability as an Unstable Category." *The Disability Studies Reader.* Ed. Lennard J. Davis. New York: Routledge, 2006. 231–42.

Davis, Todd F., and Kenneth Womack, ed. *Mapping the Ethical Turn: A Reader in Ethics, Culture, and Literary Theory*. Charlottesville, VA: University Press of Virginia, 2001.

DeFalco, Amelia. "Haunting Physicality: Corpses, Cannibalism, and Carnality in Margaret Atwood's *Alias Grace*." *University of Toronto Quarterly* 75.2 (2006): 771–83.

– *Uncanny Subjects: Aging in Contemporary Narrative*. Columbus: Ohio State University Press, 2010.

Delisle, Jennifer Bowering. "'A Bruise Still Tender': David Chariandy's *Soucouyant* and Cultural Memory." *ARIEL: A Review of International English Literature* 41.2 (2011): 1–21.

Derrida, Jacques. *Given Time*, vol. 1, *Counterfeit Money*. Trans. Peggy Kamuf. Chicago, IL: University of Chicago Press, 1992.

– "Hospitality, Responsibility and Justice: A Dialogue with Jacques Derrida." *Questioning Ethics: Contemporary Debates in Philosophy*. Ed. Richard Kearney and Mark Dooley. London: Routledge, 1999. 65–83.

– "Women in the Beehive: A Seminar with Jacques Derrida." *Differences: A Journal of Feminist Cultural Studies* 16.3 (2005): 139–57.

Detlef, Garz. *Lawrence Kohlberg: An Introduction*. Farmington Hills, MI: Barbara Budrich, 2009.

Duffy, Dennis. "Too Little Geography; Too Much History: Writing the Balance in 'Meneseteung.'" *National Plots: Historical Fiction and Changing Ideas of Canada*. Ed. Andrea Cabajsky and Brett Josef Grubisic. Waterloo, ON: Wilfrid Laurier University Press, 2010. 197–213.

Eakin, Paul John. "Relational Selves, Relational Lives: The Story of the Story." *True Relations: Essays on Autobiography and the Postmodern*. Ed. G. Thomas Couser and Joseph Fichtelberg. London: Greenwood, 1998. 63–81.

– *How Our Lives Become Stories: Making Selves*. Ithaca, NY: Cornell University Press, 1999.

– "Introduction: Mapping the Ethics of Life Writing." *The Ethics of Life Writing*. Ed. Paul John Eakin. Ithaca, NY: Cornell University Press, 2004. 1–16.

– "What Are We Reading When We Read Autobiography?" *Narrative* 12.2 (2004): 121–32.

– *Living Autobiographically: How We Create Identity in Narrative*. Ithaca, NY: Cornell University Press, 2010.

Edelson, Miriam. *My Journey with Jake: A Memoir of Parenting and Disability*. Toronto: Between the Lines, 2000.

Edwards, Caterina. *Finding Rosa: A Mother with Alzheimer's, a Daughter in Search of the Past*. Vancouver: Greystone, 2008.

Eliott, Jayne, Cynthia Toman, and Meryn Stuart. Introduction. *Place and Practice in Canadian Nursing History*. Ed. Jayne Elliott, Cynthia Toman, and Meryn Stuart. Vancouver: UBC Press, 2008. 1–7.

"Engross." *OED*. 2013. Web. 5 Jan. 2013.

Enteen, Jillana. "'On the Receiving End of the Colonization': Nalo Hopkinson's 'Nansi Web.'" *Science Fiction Studies* 34.2 (2007): 262–82.

Evans, Robert G. "Two Systems of Restraint: Contrasting Experiences with Cost Control in the 1990s." *Canada and the United States: Differences that Count*. Ed. David M. Thomas. Peterborough, ON: Broadview, 2000. 21–51.

Fairfield, Paul. "The Bearers of Rights: Individuals or Collectives?" *Is There a Canadian Philosophy? Reflections on the Canadian Identity*. Ed. Paul Fairfield, Ingrid Harris, and G.B. Madison. Ottawa: University of Ottawa Press, 2000. 117–38.

Fairfield, Paul, Ingrid Harris, and G.B. Madison. Introduction. *Is There a Canadian Philosophy? Reflections on the Canadian Identity*. Ed. Paul Fairfield, Ingrid Harris, and G.B. Madison. Ottawa: University of Ottawa Press, 2000. 1–7.

Fanon, Franz. *Black Skin, White Masks*. Trans. Charles Lam Marmann. New York: Grove Weidenfeld, 1967.

Federico, Meg. *Welcome to the Departure Lounge: Adventures in Mothering Mother*. New York: Random House, 2009.

Felman, Shoshana, and Dori Laub. *Testimony: Crises of Witnessing in Literature, Psychoanalysis, and History*. New York: Routledge, 1992.

Feshkens, Erin M. "The Matter of Bodies: Materiality on Nalo Hopkinson's Cybernetic Planet." *Global South* 4.2 (2010): 136–56.

Finch, Janet. "Community Care: Developing Non-Sexist Alternatives." *Critical Social Policy* 9 (1984): 16–18.

Finch, Janet, and Dulcie Groves, eds. *A Labour of Love: Women, Work and Caring*. London: Routledge and Kegan Paul, 1983.

Fineman, Martha L.A. "Masking Dependency: The Political Role of Family Rhetoric." *The Subject of Care: Feminist Perspectives on Dependency*. Ed. Eva Feder Kittay and Ellen K. Feder. New York: Rowman and Littlefield, 2002. 215–44.

– *The Autonomy Myth: A Theory of Dependency*. New York: New Press, 2004.

Fisher, Berenice, and Joan Tronto. "Toward a Feminist Theory of Caring." *Circles of Care: Work and Identity in Women's Lives*. Ed. Emily K. Abel and Margaret K. Nelson. Albany, NY: State University of New York Press, 1990. 35–62.

Foucault, Michel. *The Birth of the Clinic*. Trans. A.M. Sheridan. New York: Routledge, 2003.

Frank, Arthur. "Moral Non-Fiction: Life Writing and Children's Disability." *Ethics of Life Writing*. Ed. Paul John Eakin. Ithaca, NY: Cornell University Press, 2004. 174–94.

Friesen, Joe. "Stephen Harper's Census and His Vision for Canada." *Globe and Mail*, 4 Feb. 2012. Web. 10 Feb. 2012.

Frye, Northrop. "Sharing the Continent." *A Passion for Identity: An Introduction to Canadian Studies*. 2nd ed. Ed. Eli Mandel, David Taras, and Beverly Rasporich. Scarborough, ON: Nelson, 1993. 249–57.

Gadsby, Meredith. *Sucking Salt: Caribbean Women Writers, Migration, and Survival*. Columbia, MO: University of Missouri Press, 2006.

Garber, Marjorie. "Compassion." *Compassion: The Culture and Politics of an Emotion*. Ed. Lauren Berlant. New York: Routledge, 2004. 15–27.

Garland-Thomson, Rosemarie. "Introduction: From Wonder to Error – A Genealogy of Freak Discourse in Modernity." *Freakery: Cultural Spectacles of the Extraordinary Body*. Ed. Rosemarie Garland-Thomson. New York: New York University Press, 1996. 1–22.

– *Extraordinary Bodies: Figuring Disability in American Literature and Culture*. New York: Columbia University Press, 1997.

– "The Politics of Staring: Visual Rhetorics of Disability in Popular Photograph." *Disability Studies: Enabling the Humanities*. Ed. Sharon L. Snyder, Brenda Jo Brueggermann, and Rosemarie Garland-Thomson. New York: Modern Language Association of America, 2002. 56–75.

– "Integrating Disability, Transforming Feminist Theory." *The Disability Studies Reader*. Ed. Lennard J. Davis. New York: Routledge, 2006. 257–73.

– *Staring: How We Look*. Oxford: Oxford University Press, 2009.

"Gift." *OED*. 2013. Web. 5 Jan. 2013.

Gilligan, Carol. *In a Different Voice: Psychological Theory and Women's Development*. Cambridge, MA: Harvard University Press, 1982.

Gilmore, Leigh. *The Limits of Autobiography: Trauma and Testimony*. Ithaca, NY: Cornell University Press, 2001.

Goldman, Marlene. "Introduction: Literature, Imagination, Ethics." *University of Toronto Quarterly* 76.3 (2007): 809–20.

– *DisPossession: Haunting in Canadian Fiction*. Montreal: McGill-Queen's University Press, 2012.

Grace, Sherrill E. "In Search of Demeter: The Lost, Silent Mother in *Surfacing*." *Margaret Atwood: Visions and Forms*. Ed. Kathryn Van Spanckeren and Jan Garden Castro. Carbondale, IL: Southern Illinois University Press, 1988. 35–47.

Graham, Hillary. "Caring: A Labour of Love." *A Labour of Love: Women, Work and Caring*. Ed. Janet Finch and Dulcie Groves. London: Routledge and Kegan Paul, 1983. 13–30.

Groenhout, Ruth. *Connected Lives: Human Nature and the Ethics of Care*. New York: Rowman and Littlefield, 2004.

Guberman, Nancy. "Designing Home and Community Care for the Future: Who Needs Care?" *Caring For/Caring About: Women, Home Care, and Unpaid Caregiving*. Aurora: Garamond, 2004.75–87.

Gwyn, Richard. *Nationalism without Walls: The Unbearable Lightness of Being Canadian*. Toronto: McClelland and Stewart, 1995.

Halwani, Raja. *Virtuous Liaison: Care, Love, Sex, and Virtue Ethics*. Chicago, IL: Open Court, 2003.

Hamington, Maurice. *Embodied Care: Jane Addams, Maurice Merleau-Ponty, and Feminist Ethics*. Chicago, IL: University of Illinois Press, 2004.

Hammer, Stephanie Barbé. "The World as It Will Be? Female Satire and the Technology of Power in *The Handmaid's Tale*." *Modern Language Studies* 20.2 (1990): 39–49.

Haraway, Donna. "A Cyborg Manifesto." *The Cultural Studies Reader*. Ed. Simon During. London: Routledge, 2007. 314–34.

Hargrave, Terry. *Strength and Courage for Caregivers: 30 Hope-Filled Morning and Evening Reflections*. Grand Rapids, MI: Zondervan, 2008.

Hawkins, Anne. *Reconstructing Illness: Studies in Pathography*. 2nd ed. West Lafayette IN: Purdue University Press, 1999.

Heble, Ajay. *The Tumble of Reason: Alice Munro's Discourse of Absence*. Toronto: University of Toronto Press, 1994.

Held, Virginia. *The Ethics of Care*. Oxford: Oxford University Press, 2006.

Hirsch, Marianne. *Family Frames: Photography, Narration, and Postmemory*. Cambridge, MA: Harvard University Press, 1997.

Hoagland, Sarah. "Some Thoughts about 'Caring.'" *Feminist Ethics*. Ed. Claudia Card. Lawrence, KS: University Press of Kansas, 1991. 246–63.

Holler, Linda. *Erotic Morality: The Role of Touch in Moral Agency*. New Brunswick, NJ: Rutgers University Press, 2002.

Hollis, Hilda. "Between the Scylla of Essentialism and the Charybdis of Deconstruction: Margaret Atwood's *True Stories*." *Various Atwoods*. Ed. Lorraine York. Concord, ON: Anansi, 1995. 117–45.

Hoogheem, Andrew. "Secular Apocalypses: Darwinian Criticism and Atwoodian Floods." *Mosaic: A Journal for the Interdisciplinary Study of Literature* 45.2 (2012): 55–71.

Hopkinson, Nalo. *Midnight Robber*. New York: Grand Central Publishing, 2000.

Howells, Coral Ann. *Alice Munro*. Manchester: Manchester University Press, 1998.

– "Margaret Atwood: Twenty-Five Years of Gothic Tales." *Littcrit* 28.1 (2002): 10–27.

– "Margaret Atwood's Dystopian Visions: *The Handmaid's Tale* and *Oryx and Crake*. *The Cambridge Companion to Margaret Atwood*. Ed. Coral Ann Howells. Cambridge: Cambridge University Press, 2006. 161–75.

Hutcheon, Linda. Introduction. *Other Solitudes: Canadian Multicultural Fictions*. Ed. Linda Hutcheon and Marion Richmond. Oxford: Oxford University Press, 1990.

Ignatieff.me. Conservative Party of Canada, 2009. Web. 5 June 2009.

Ignatieff, Michael. *Asya*. Toronto: Viking, 1991.

– *Charlie Johnson in Flames*. Toronto: Viking, 2003.

– *The Needs of Strangers*. London: Chatto and Windus, 1984.

– *The Russian Album*. New York: Penguin, 1987.

– *Scar Tissue*. Toronto: Penguin, 1993.

– *True Patriot Love: Four Generations in Search of Canada*. Toronto: Penguin, 2009.

Ito, Robert. "The Love Bot." *Pacific Standard*, 30 Oct. 2012. Web. 1 Nov. 2012.

Jamieson, Sara. "The Fiction of Agelessness: Work, Leisure, and Aging in Alice Munro's 'Pictures of the Ice.'" *Studies in Canadian Literature/Etudes en littérature canadienne* 29.1 (2004): 106–26.

Jefferes, David, "Responsibility, Nostalgia, and the Mythology of Canada as Peacekeeper." *University of Toronto Quarterly* 78.2 (2009): 709–27.

Kamboureli, Smaro. *Scandalous Bodies: Diasporic Literature in English Canada*. Waterloo, ON: Wilfrid Laurier University Press, 2009.

Kanaganayakam, Chelva. "Cool Dots and a Hybrid Scarborough: Multiculturalism as Canadian Myth." *Is Canada Postcolonial? Unsettling Canadian Literature*. Ed. Laura Frances Errington Moss. Waterloo, ON: Wilfrid Laurier University Press, 2003. 140–8.

Karafilly, Irena F. *The Stranger in the Plumed Hat: A Memoir*. Toronto: Viking, 2000.

Karr, Katherine. *Taking Time for Me: How Caregivers Can Effectively Deal with Stress*. Buffalo, NY: Prometheus, 1992.

Katz, Stephen. *Cultural Aging: Life Course, Lifestyle, and Senior Worlds*. Peterborough, ON: Broadview, 2005.

Keddy, Barbara, and Dianne Dodd. "The Trained Nurse: Private Duty and VON Home Nursing (Late 1800s to 1940s)." *On All Frontiers: Four Centuries of Canadian Nursing*. Ed. Christina Bates, Dianne Elizabeth Dodd, and Nicole Rousseau. Ottawa: University of Ottawa Press, 2005. 43–56.

Keen, Suzanne. *Empathy and the Novel*. New York: Oxford University Press, 2007.

Kittay, Eva Feder. "When Caring Is Just and Justice Is Caring: Justice and Mental Retardation." *Caregiving: Readings in Knowledge, Ethics, Practice and Politics.* Ed. Patricia Benner, Suzanne Gordon, and Nel Noddings. Philadelphia, PA: University of Philadelphia Press, 1996. 257–76.

– *Love's Labor: Essays on Women, Equality, and Dependency.* London: Routledge, 1999.

– "Not *My* Way, Sesha, *Your* Way, Slowly: 'Maternal Thinking' in the Raising of a Child with Profound Intellectual Disabilities." *Mother Troubles: Rethinking Contemporary Maternal Dilemmas.* Ed. Julia E. Hanigsberg and Sara Ruddick. Boston: Beacon, 1999. 3–27.

Kittay, Eva Feder, and Diana T. Meyers. Introduction. *Women and Moral Theory.* Ed. Eva Feder Kittay and Diana T. Meyers. Totowa, NJ: Rowman and Littlefield, 1987. 3–16.

– eds. *Women and Moral Theory.* Totowa, NJ: Rowman and Littlefield, 1987.

Kittay, Eva Feder, and Ellen K. Feder. Introduction. *The Subject of Care: Feminist Perspectives on Dependency.* Ed. Eva Feder Kittay and Ellen K. Feder. New York: Rowman and Littlefield, 2002. 1–12.

– eds. *The Subject of Care: Feminist Perspectives on Dependency.* Lanham, MD: Rowman and Littlefield, 2002.

Kohlberg, Lawrence. *The Philosophy of Moral Development: Moral Stages and the Idea of Justice.* San Francisco, CA: Harper and Row, 1981.

Konigsberg, Eric. "Running on Book Sense and Charm." *New York Times*, 1 Feb. 2009. Web. 6 Mar. 2009.

Lai, Larissa. *Salt Fish Girl.* Toronto: Thomas Allen, 2002.

Larrabee, Mary Jeanne, ed. *An Ethic of Care.* New York: Routledge, Chapman and Hall, 1993.

Laub, Dori "Truth and Testimony: The Process and the Struggle." *Trauma: Explorations in Memory.* Ed. Cathy Caruth. Baltimore, MD: Johns Hopkins University Press, 1995. 61–75.

Laurence, Margaret. *The Stone Angel.* Toronto: McClelland and Stewart, 1968.

Leavitt, Sarah. *Tangles: A Story about Alzheimer's, My Mother, and Me.* Calgary: Freehand, 2010.

Levinas, Emmanuel. *Ethics and Infinity: Conversations with Philippe Nemo.* Trans. Richard A. Cohen. Pittsburgh, PA: Duquesne University Press, 1985.

– *Otherwise than Being or Beyond Essence.* Trans. Alphonso Lingis. Dordrecht: Kluwer, 1991.

Levinas, Emmanuel, and Richard Kearney. "Dialogue with Emmanuel Levinas." *Face to Face with Levinas.* Ed. Richard A. Cohen. Albany, NY: State University of New York Press, 1986. 3–34.

Lin, Patrick. "Introduction to Robot Ethics." *Robot Ethics: The Ethical and Social Implications of Robotics.* Ed. Patrick Lin, Keith Abney, and George A. Bekey. Cambridge, MA: MIT Press, 2012. 3–15.

Lipset, Seymour Martin. *Continental Divide: The Values and Institutions of the United States and Canada.* Toronto: C.D. Howe Institute and National Planning Association, 1989.

– "Revolution and Counterrevolution: The United States and Canada." *A Passion for Identity: An Introduction to Canadian Studies.* 2nd ed. Ed. Eli Mandel, David Taras, and Beverly Rasporich. Scarborough, ON: Nelson, 1993. 150–61.

Lundeen, Kathleen. "Who Has the Right to Feel? The Ethics of Literary Empathy." *Mapping the Ethical Turn: A Reader in Ethics, Culture, and Literary Theory.* Ed. Todd F. Davis and Kenneth Womack. Charlottesville, VA: University Press of Virginia, 2001. 83–92.

Mackey, Allison. "Postnational Coming of Age in Contemporary Anglo-Canadian Fiction." *English Studies in Canada* 38.3–4 (2012): 227–53.

Mackey, Eva. *The House of Difference: Cultural Politics and National Identity in Canada.* London: Routledge, 1999.

Madison, G.B. "Nationality and Universality." *Is There a Canadian Philosophy? Reflections on the Canadian Identity.* Ed. Paul Fairfield, Ingrid Harris, and G.B. Madison. Ottawa: University of Ottawa Press, 2000. 9–88.

Madore, Odette. "The *Canada Health Act*: Overview and Options." *Parliament of Canada.* 2nd ed. Parliament of Canada, 16 May 2005. Web. 10 Feb. 2012.

Manfredi, Christopher P. "Rights and the Judicialization of Politics in Canada and the United States." *Canada and the United States: Differences that Count.* Ed. David M. Thomas. Peterborough, ON: Broadview, 2000. 301–18.

Manning, Erin. *Ephemeral Territories: Representing Nation, Home, and Identity in Canada.* Minneapolis, MN: University of Minnesota Press, 2003.

Mason, Mary G. "The Other Voice: Autobiographies of Women Writers." *Autobiography: Essays Theoretical and Critical.* Ed. James Olney. Princeton, NJ: Princeton University Press, 1980. 207–35.

McGill, Robert. "'Daringly Out in the Public Eye': Alice Munro and the Ethics of Writing Back." *University of Toronto Quarterly* 76.3 (2007): 874–89.

– "No Nation but Adaptation: "The Bear Came over the Mountain,' *Away from Her,* and What it Means to Be Faithful." *Canadian Literature* 197 (2008): 98–113.

McIntyre, Tim. "'The Way the Stars Really Do Come Out at Night': The Trick of Representation in Alice Munro's 'The Moons of Jupiter.'" *Canadian Literature* 200 (2009): 73–90.

McLeod, Beth Witrogen, ed. *And Thou Shalt Honor: The Caregiver's Companion.* Emmaus, PA: Rodale, 2002.

McPherson, Kathryn. *Bedside Matters: The Transformation of Canadian Nursing, 1900–1990.* Toronto: University of Toronto Press, 2003.

McWilliams, Ellen. *Margaret Atwood and the Female Bildungsroman*. Surrey: Ashgate, 2009.

Meffan, James, and Kim L. Worthington. "Ethics before Politics." *Mapping the Ethical Turn: A Reader in Ethics, Culture, and Literary Theory*. Ed. Todd F. Davis and Kenneth Womack. Charlottesville: University Press of Virginia, 2001. 131–50.

Mensch, James. *Ethics and Selfhood: Alterity and the Phenomenology of Obligation*. Albany, NY: State University of New York Press, 2003.

Menzies, Heather. *Enter Mourning: A Memoir on Death, Dementia, and Coming Home*. Toronto: Key Porter, 2009.

Mergeai, Mathilde. "Towards a New Canadianness: Re(-)Membering Canada in Lawrence Hill's *Any Known Blood* (1997) and David Chariandy's *Soucouyant* (2007)." *Canada and Beyond: A Journal of Canadian Literary and Cultural Studies* 1.1–2 (2011): 83–103.

Merivale, Patricia. "From 'Bad News' to 'Good Bones': Margaret Atwood's Gendering of Art and Elegy." *Various Atwoods*. Ed. Lorraine York. Concord, ON: Anansi, 1995. 253–70.

Miller, Nancy K. "Out of the Family: Generations of Women in Marjane Satrapi's *Persepolis*." *Life Writing* 4.1 (2007): 13–29.

Miller, Sarah Clark. "Need, Care and Obligation." *The Philosophy of Need*. Ed. Soran Reader. Cambridge: Cambridge University Press, 2005. 137–60.

Mindszenthy, Bart, and Michael Gorden. *Parenting Your Parents: Support Strategies for Meeting the Challenge of Aging in the Family*. Toronto: Dundurn, 2002.

Mitchell, David. "Narrative Prosthesis and the Materiality of Metaphor." *Disability Studies: Enabling the Humanities*. Ed. Sharon L Snyder, Brenda Jo Brueggermann, and Rosemarie Garland-Thomson. New York: Modern Language Association of America, 2002. 15–30.

Mitchell, David, and Sharon Snyder. *Narrative Prosthesis: Disability and the Dependencies of Discourse*. Ann Arbor, MI: University of Michigan Press, 2000.

– "Narrative Prosthesis and the Materiality of Metaphor." *The Disability Studies Reader*. Ed. Lennard J. Davis. New York: Routledge, 2006. 205–16.

Morgenstern, Naomi. "The Baby or the Violin? Ethics and Femininity in the Fiction of Alice Munro." *LIT: Literature Interpretation Theory* 14.2 (2003): 69–97.

Mulvey, Laura. "Visual Pleasure and Narrative Cinema." *Issues in Feminist Film Criticism*. Ed. Patricia Erens. Bloomington, IN: Indiana University Press, 1990. 28–40.

Munro, Alice. "The Art of Fiction No. 137." Interview with Jeanne McCulloch and Mona Simpson. *Paris Review* 131 (Summer 1994). Web. 10 June 2011.

– "The Bear Came over the Mountain." *Hateship, Friendship, Courtship, Loveship, Marriage*. Toronto: McClelland and Stewart, 2001. 274–322.

– "Cortes Island." *The Love of a Good Woman*. Toronto: McClelland and Stewart, 1998. 117–45.
– *Dance of the Happy Shades*. Toronto: Penguin, 1997 [1968].
– "Day of the Butterfly." *Dance of the Happy Shades*. Toronto: Penguin, 1997 [1968]. 101–12.
– "Fiction." *Too Much Happiness*. Toronto: McClelland and Stewart, 2009. 32–61.
– "Floating Bridge." *Hateship, Friendship, Courtship, Loveship, Marriage*. Toronto: McClelland and Stewart, 2001. 53–83.
– *Friend of My Youth*. Toronto: Penguin, 2007 [1990].
– "Friend of My Youth." *Friend of My Youth*. Toronto: Penguin, 2007 [1990]. 3–24.
– "Goodness and Mercy." *Friend of My Youth*. Toronto: Penguin, 2007 [1990]. 139–59.
– "Heirs of the Living Body." *Lives of Girls and Women*. Toronto: Penguin, 1997 [1971]. 31–69.
– *Hateship, Friendship, Courtship, Loveship, Marriage*. Toronto: McClelland and Stewart, 2001.
– "Hired Girl." *The View from Castle Rock*. Toronto: McClelland and Stewart, 2006. 227–54.
– "Images." *Dance of the Happy Shades*. Toronto: Penguin, 1997 [1968]. 30–43.
– "Jesse and Meribeth." *The Progress of Love*. New York: Penguin, 1987 [1986]. 3–31.
– *Lives of Girls and Women*. Toronto: Penguin, 1997 [1971].
– *The Love of a Good Woman*. Toronto: McClelland and Stewart, 1998.
– "The Love of a Good Woman." *The Love of a Good Woman*. Toronto: McClelland and Stewart, 1998. 3–78.
– "Memorial." *Something I've Been Meaning to Tell You*. Toronto: Penguin, 1990 [1974]. 24–44.
– "Meneseteung." *Friend of My Youth*. Toronto: Penguin, 2007 [1990]. 45–66.
– "Monsieur, les Deux Chapeaux." *The Progress of Love*. New York: Penguin, 1987 [1986]. 56–83.
– *The Moons of Jupiter*. Toronto: Penguin, 2006 [1982].
– "Mrs Cross and Mrs Kidd." *The Moons of Jupiter*. Toronto: Penguin, 2006 [1982]. 160–80.
– "My Mother's Dream." *The Love of a Good Woman*. Toronto: McClelland and Stewart, 1998. 293–340.
– *Open Secrets*. Toronto: Penguin, 1994.
– "Open Secrets." *Open Secrets*. Toronto: Penguin, 1994. 150–86.
– "Post and Beam." *Hateship, Friendship, Courtship, Loveship, Marriage*. Toronto: McClelland and Stewart, 2001.186–216.

– "The Ottawa Valley." *Something I've Been Meaning to Tell You*. Toronto: Penguin, 1990 [1974]. 227–46.
– "The Peace of Utrecht." *Dance of the Happy Shades*. Toronto: Penguin, 1997 [1968]. 192–213.
– *The Progress of Love*. New York: Penguin, 1987 [1986].
– "Queenie." *Hateship, Friendship, Courtship, Loveship, Marriage*. Toronto: McClelland and Stewart, 2001. 242–73.
– "A Queer Streak." *The Progress of Love*. New York: Penguin, 1987 [1986]. 208–53.
– *Runaway*. Toronto: McClelland and Stewart, 2004.
– "Runaway." *Runaway*. Toronto: McClelland and Stewart, 2004. 3–47.
– "Some Women." *Too Much Happiness*. Toronto: McClelland and Stewart, 2009. 164–87.
– *Something I've Been Meaning to Tell You*. Toronto: Penguin, 1990 [1974].
– "Soon." *Runaway*. Toronto: McClelland and Stewart, 2004. 87–125.
– "Spelling." *Who Do You Think You Are?* Toronto: Penguin, 1996 [1978]. 216–33.
– *Too Much Happiness*. Toronto: McClelland and Stewart, 2009.
– *The View from Castle Rock*. Toronto: McClelland and Stewart, 2006.
– *Who Do You Think You Are?* Toronto: Penguin, 1996 [1978].
– "Winter Wind." *Something I've Been Meaning to Tell You*. Toronto: Penguin, 1990 [1974]. 192–206.
Ngai, Sianne. *Ugly Feelings*. Cambridge, MA: Harvard University Press, 2005.
Noddings, Nel. *Caring: A Feminine Approach to Ethics and Moral Education*. Berkeley, CA: University of California Press, 1984.
– "The Cared-For." *Caregiving: Readings in Knowledge, Ethics, Practice and Politics*. Ed. Patricia Benner, Suzanne Gordon, and Nel Noddings. Philadelphia, PA: University of Philadelphia Press, 1996. 21–39.
Nussbaum, Martha Craven. *Cultivating Humanity: A Classical Defense of Reform in Liberal Education*. 6th ed. Cambridge, MA: Harvard University Press, 1997.
Oliver, Kelly. *Witnessing: Beyond Recognition*. Minneapolis, MN: University of Minnesota Press, 2001.
– "Subjectivity as Responsivity: The Ethical Implications of Dependency." *The Subject of Care: Feminist Perspectives on Dependency*. Ed. Eva Feder Kittay and Ellen K. Feder. New York: Rowman and Littlefield, 2002. 322–33.
– *Animal Lessons: How They Teach Us to Be Human*. New York: Columbia University Press, 2009.
"One Nation or Many?" *Economist*, 16 Nov. 2006. Web. 11 June 2011.
"Ontario's Aging at Home Strategy." Ontario Ministry of Health and Long-Term Care. 2007.
– Ontario Ministry of Health and Long-Term Care, *n.d.* Web. 10 Feb. 2012.

Parks, Jennifer A. *No Place Like Home? Feminist Ethics and Home Health Care.*
Bloomington, IN: Indiana University Press, 2003.

"Part 3: Are We Too Tolerant?" *Globe and Mail,* 7 Oct. 2010. Web. 11 June 2012.

Petersen, Steve. "Designing People to Serve" *Robot Ethics: The Ethical and Social
Implications of Robotics.* Ed. Patrick Lin, Keith Abney, and George Bekey.
Cambridge, MA: MIT Press, 2012. 283–98.

Prabhu, Anjali. *Hybridity: Limits, Transformations, Prospects.* Albany, NY: State
University of New York Press, 2007.

Quayson, Ato. *Aesthetic Nervousness: Disability and the Crisis of Representation.*
New York: Columbia University Press, 2007.

Quiney, Linda. "'Suitable Young Women': Red Cross Nursing Pioneers and
the Crusade for Healthy Living in Manitoba, 1920–30." *Place and Practice
in Canadian Nursing History.* Ed. Jayne Elliott, Meryn Stuart, and Cynthia
Toman. Vancouver: UBC Press, 2008. 91–110.

Rasporich, Beverly. *Dance of the Sexes: Art and Gender in the Fiction of Alice Munro.*
Edmonton: University of Alberta Press, 1990.

Reader, Soran. Introduction. *The Philosophy of Need.* Ed. Soran Reader. Cambridge:
Cambridge University Press, 2005. 1–24.

Reader, Soran, ed. *The Philosophy of Need.* Cambridge: Cambridge University
Press, 2005.

Redekop, Magdalene. *Mothers and Other Clowns: The Stories of Alice Munro.*
New York: Routledge, 1992.

Reverby, Susan. *Ordered to Care: The Dilemma of American Nursing.* New York:
Cambridge University Press, 1987.

Rhys, John C. Van. "Fictional Violations in Alice Munro's Narratives." *Through
a Glass Darkly: Suffering, the Sacred, and the Sublime in Literature and Theory.*
Ed. Holly Faith Nelson and Lynn Szabo. Waterloo, ON: Wilfrid Laurier
University Press, 2010. 269–85.

Richardson, Brian. Introduction. *Narrative Dynamics: Essays on Time, Plot,
Closure, and Frames.* Ed. Brian Richardson. Columbus, OH: Ohio University
Press, 2002. 1–7.

Richardson, Sharon. "The Historical Relationship of Nursing Program
Accreditation and Public Policy in Canada." *Nursing History Review: Official
Journal of the American Association for the History of Nursing* 4 (1996): 19–41.

Ricker, Thomas. "Panasonic's Hair-Washing Robot: Rinse, Kill, Repeat."
Engadget. AOL Tech, 24 Sept 2010. Web. 1 Nov. 2012.

Ricoeur, Paul. *Memory, History, Forgetting.* Trans. Kathleen Blamey and David
Pellauer. Chicago, IL: University of Chicago Press, 2006.

Rooney, Ben. "The Robot That Helps Dementia Patients." *Wall Street Journal,*
15 Mar. 2012. Web. 27 June 2012.

Roy, Wendy. "'The Word Is Colander': Language Loss and Narrative Voice in Fictional Canadian Alzheimer's Narratives." *Canadian Literature* 203 (Winter 2009): 41–61.

Ruddick, Sara. "Maternal Thinking." *Feminist Studies* 6.2 (1980): 342–57.

– "Remarks on the Sexual Politics of Reason." *Women and Moral Theory*. Ed. Eva Feder Kittay and Diana T. Meyers. Totowa, NJ: Rowman and Littlefield, 1987. 237–60.

– *Maternal Thinking: Toward a Politics of Peace*. Boston: Beacon, 1995.

– "Care as Labor and Relationship." *Norms and Values: Essays on the Work of Virginia Held*. Ed. Joram C. Haber and Mark S. Halfon. Lanham, MD: Rowman and Littlefield, 1998. 3–26.

Saul, Joanne. *Writing the Roaming Subject: The Biotext in Canadian Literature*. Toronto: University of Toronto Press, 2006.

Sawicki, Jana. *Disciplining Foucault: Feminism, Power, and the Body*. New York and London: Routledge, 1991.

Shakespeare, Tom. "The Social Model of Disability." *Disability Studies Reader*. Ed. Lennard J. Davis. New York: Routledge, 2006. 197–204.

Sharkey, Noel, and Amanda Sharkey. "The Rights and Wrongs of Robot Care." *Robot Ethics: The Ethical and Social Implications of Robotics*. Ed. Patrick Lin, Keith Abney, and George Bekey. Cambridge, MA: MIT Press, 2012. 267–82.

Shaw-Garlock, Glenda. "Looking Forward to Sociable Robots." *International Journal of Social Robotics* 1.3 (2009): 249–60.

Shuman, Amy. *Other People's Stories: Entitlement Claims and the Critique of Empathy*. Urbana, IL: University of Illinois Press, 2005.

Siebers, Tobin. *The Subject and Other Subjects: On Ethical, Aesthetic and Political Identity*. Ann Arbor, MI: University of Michigan Press, 1998.

– "Disability in Theory: From Social Constructionism to the New Realism of the Body." *The Disability Studies Reader*. Ed. Lennard J. Davis. New York: Routledge, 2006. 173–83.

Snyder, Sharon L., Brenda Jo Brueggermann, and Rosemarie Garland-Thomson. "Introduction: Integrating Disability into Teaching and Scholarship." *Disability Studies: Enabling the Humanities*. Ed. Sharon L. Snyder, Brenda Jo Brueggermann, and Rosemarie Garland-Thomson. New York: Modern Language Association of America, 2002. 1–12.

Solo, Olivia. "Robo-Teddy Bear RIBA II Can Lift You Off the Floor." *Wired*, 3 Aug. 2011. Web. 27 July 2012.

Somacarrera, Pilar. "Power Politics: Power and Identity." *The Cambridge Companion to Margaret Atwood*. Ed. Coral Ann Howells. Cambridge: Cambridge University Press, 2006. 43–57.

Sparrow, Robert, and Linda Sparrow. "In the Hands of Machines? The Future of Aged Care." *Minds and Machines* 16.2 (2006): 141–61.

Splint, Sarah Field. *The Art of Cooking and Serving.* Cincinnati, OH: Procter and Gamble, 1926.

Staines, David. "Margaret Atwood in Her Canadian Context." *The Cambridge Companion to Margaret Atwood.* Ed. Coral Ann Howells. Cambridge: Cambridge University Press, 2006. 12–27.

Stein, Karen F. "Talking Back to Bluebeard: Atwood's Fictional Storytellers." *Margaret Atwood's Textual Assassinations: Recent Poetry and Fiction.* Ed. Sharon Rose Wilson. Columbus, OH: Ohio State University Press, 2003. 154–71.

Stickings, Michael. "The Audacity of Michael Ignatieff." *Guardian,* 23 Feb. 2009. Web. 6 Mar. 2009.

Sullivan, Rosemary. "What If? Writing *The Handmaid's Tale.*" *University of Toronto Quarterly* 75.3 (2006): 850–6.

Sutherland, Fraser. "Michael Ignatieff, Novelist." *Globe and Mail,* 28 Feb. 2009. Web. 10 Mar. 2009.

Taras, David. Introduction. *A Passion for Identity: An Introduction to Canadian Studies.* 2nd ed. Ed. Eli Mandel, David Taras, and Beverly Rasporich. Scarborough, ON: Nelson, 1993. 1–9.

Taylor, Charles. "Shared and Divergent Values." *A Passion for Identity: An Introduction to Canadian Studies.* 2nd ed. Ed. Eli Mandel, David Taras, and Beverly Rasporich. Scarborough, ON: Nelson, 1993. 218–38.

Taylor, Janelle. "On Recognition, Caring, and Dementia." *Medical Anthropology Quarterly* 22.4 (2008): 313–35.

Tensuan, Theresa M. "Comic Visions and Revisions in the Work of Lynda Barry and Marjane Satrapi." *Modern Fiction Studies* 52.4 (2006): 947–64.

Thacker, Robert. *Alice Munro: Writing Her Lives.* Toronto: McClelland and Stewart, 2005.

Thiem, Annika. *Unbecoming Subjects: Judith Butler, Moral Philosophy, and Critical Responsibility.* New York: Fordham University Press, 2008.

Toews, Miriam. *Swing Low: A Life.* Toronto: Stoddart, 2000.

– "'It Gets under the Skin and Settles In': A Conversation with Miriam Toews." Natasha G. Wiebe. *Conrad Grebel Review* 26.1 (2008): 103–24.

Tolan, Fiona. *Margaret Atwood: Feminism and Fiction.* Amsterdam: Rodopi, 2007.

"Tolerance." *OED.* 2013. Web. 5 Jan. 2013.

"Tolerate." *OED.* 2013. Web. 5 Jan. 2013.

Tronto, Joan. "An Ethic of Care." *Generations* 22.3 (1998): 15–20.

Turkle, Sherry. *Alone Together: Why We Expect More from Technology and Less from Each Other.* New York: Basic Books, 2011.

– "Authenticity in the Age of Digital Companions." *Machine Ethics*. Ed. Michael Anderson and Susan Leigh Anderson. Cambridge: Cambridge University Press, 2011. 62–78.

Ungerson, Clare. "Why Do Women Care?" *A Labour of Love: Women, Work and Caring*. Ed. Janet Finch and Dulcie Groves. London: Routledge and Kegan Paul, 1983. 31–49.

Valpy, Michael. "Being Michael Ignatieff." *Globe and Mail*, 26 Aug. 2006. Web. 6 Mar. 2009.

Van Hooft, Stan. *Caring: An Essay in the Philosophy of Ethics*. Niwot, CO: University Press of Colorado, 1995.

Vogler, Candace. "Much of Madness and More of Sin: Compassion, for Ligeia." *Compassion: The Culture and Politics of an Emotion*. Ed. Lauren Berlant. New York: Routledge, 2004. 29–58.

Waerness, Kari. "The Relationality of Caring." *Caregiving: Readings in Knowledge, Ethics, Practice and Politics*. Ed. Patricia Benner, Suzanne Gordon, and Nel Noddings. Philadelphia, PA: University of Philadelphia Press, 1996. 231–55.

Walker, Margaret. *Moral Contexts*. Lanham, MD: Rowman and Littlefield, 2003.

Ware, Tracy. "Tricks with 'A Sad Ring': The Endings of Alice Munro's 'The Ottawa Valley.'" *Studies in Canadian Literature* 31.2 (2006): 126–41.

– "'And They May Get It Wrong, after All': Reading Alice Munro's 'Meneseteung.'" *National Plots: Historical Fiction and Changing Ideas of Canada*. Ed. Andrea Cabajsky and Brett Josef Grubisic. Waterloo, ON: Wilfrid Laurier University Press, 2010. 67–79.

Watt, Lisa. "Media Review: A Critical Review of Ian Brown's *The Boy in the Moon*." *Journal on Developmental Disabilities* 17.2 (2011): 87–91.

West, Cornel. *Race Matters*. Boston: Beacon, 2001.

Williams, Bernard. *Ethics and the Limits of Philosophy*. 1985. London: Routledge, 2006.

Williams, Cara. Statistics Canada. "The Sandwich Generation." *Canadian Social Trends* 77 (Summer 2005): 16–21.

Williams, Patricia. *The Alchemy of Race and Rights*. Cambridge, MA: Harvard University Press, 1991.

Wiltshire, John. "Biography, Pathography, and the Recovery of Meaning." *Cambridge Quarterly* 29.4 (2000): 409–22.

Wolfe, Cary. *What Is Posthumanism?* Minneapolis, MN: University of Minnesota Press, 2009.

"World's First Robot That Can Lift Up a Human in Its Arms." RIKEN-TRI Collaboration Center for Human-Interactive Robot Research, n.d. Web. 1 Nov. 2012.

York, Lorraine. "'Over All I Place a Glass Bell': The Meta-Iconography of Margaret Atwood." *Various Atwoods*. Ed. Lorraine York. Concord, ON: Anansi, 1995. 229–52.

– *The Other Side of Dailiness: Photography in the Works of Alice Munro, Timothy Findley, Michael Ondaatje, and Margaret Laurence*. Toronto: ECW, 1998.

– *Rethinking Women's Collaborative Writing: Power, Difference, Property*. Toronto: University of Toronto Press, 2002.

Young, Iris Marion. *Throwing Like a Girl and Other Essays in Feminist Philosophy and Social Theory*. Bloomington, IN: Indiana University Press, 1990.

Index

www.ingramcontent.com/pod-product-compliance
Ingram Content Group UK Ltd.
Pitfield, Milton Keynes, MK11 3LW, UK
UKHW032121310125
454513UK00004B/166